Praise for *Loving a Depressed Man*

"While shelves teem with books on depression, focus on intimate, loving relationships with those suffering depression is sorely neglected. Doug Bey has written a very useful and important book for that confused and possibly desperate spouse.

Loving a Depressed Man is a hopeful and reliable guide to the facts and myths of male depression. The overall message of this book is clear and positive: you are not alone (though it may feel that way at times), you are deeply loved and appreciated (though your spouse may not always be able to express this well), and your marriage relationship can be strong, growing in affection and commitment (even when you might feel like throwing in the towel).

Doug Bey is a refreshing example of a psychiatrist who deeply understands that holistic treatment of depression extends far beyond the pill bottle."

—Daniel Liechty, PhD., DMin., ACSW, LCSW,
The School of Social Work, Illinois State University

This new book by Doug Bey is "just what the doctor ordered" for countless wives and girlfriends who are stymied by figuring out what their role should be when their menfolk get depressed. It is an incredibly helpful manual on the types of depression including all the latest facts from medical science, as well as how to cope with the various symptoms of depression.

Because Dr. Bey has had years of experience treating depression in his own psychiatric practice, his anecdotes are vital and vivid, so that almost everyone can find some real person to identify with in this book. I cannot imagine a better book to give to someone who loves a depressed man and wants to understand what he needs.

—Jacqueline Olds, MD, Associate Clinical
Professor of Psychiatry, Harvard Medical School;
author of "The Lonely American"

Loving a
Depressed Man

Loving a Depressed Man

Understand the Symptoms,
Find the Help He Needs,
and Maintain Your Morale

Douglas Bey, Jr., M.D.

LaChance publishing

LACHANCE PUBLISHING • NEW YORK
www.lachancepublishing.com

ISBN 978-1-934184-36-3

Edited by Richard Day Gore

Cover Design by Stewart A. Williams

Library of Congress Control Number: 2010927105

Publisher: LaChance Publishing
              120 Bond Street
              Brooklyn, NY 11217
              www.lachancepublishing.com

Distributor: Independent Publishers Group
              814 North Franklin Street
              Chicago, IL 60610
              www.ipgbook.com

This book is available at special discounts for bulk purchases for sales promotions or premiums. Special editions, including personalized covers, excerpts of existing books, and corporate imprints, can be created in large quantities for special needs. For information, email info@lachancepublishing.com.

The health information expressed in this book is based solely on the personal experience of the author and is not intended as a medical manual. The information should not be used for diagnosis or treatment, or as a substitute for professional medical care. The author and publisher urge you to consult with your health care provider prior to beginning any exercise program.

To Richard Doud Bey,
a brilliant neurologist,
a loyal and loving brother.

Contents

Contents

Contents

Contents

There Is Hope for Depression

Outside of a dog, a book is man's best friend.
Inside of a dog it's too dark to read.

—*Groucho Marx*

W hy a book directed at women trying to help the depressed men in their lives? At first glance, it seems counterintuitive; statistically, women suffer from depression twice as often as men. I've worked with depressed patients and their families in private practice for many years, and this has been my experience as well. Genetic and hormonal differences, as well as the differences in response to low serotonin levels between the sexes, are cited as factors influencing these figures. Low serotonin levels cause women to become sadder and introspective; men become more impulsive and irritable.

On closer examination, however, we realize that these figures are the result not so much of genetic or biological differences between the sexes as they are of the conditioning and socialization of males in our culture. These influences cause men to be reluctant to ask for help, to have difficulty recognizing their emotions, to find it harder to express their feelings, and to manifest their suffering in ways that are not easily recognized as depression. Men are, for example, more likely to self-medicate with drugs or alcohol. They are more likely to become irritable and aggressive. One study notes that, among the Amish, men and women are depressed in equal numbers. Amish men do not drink. There is a correlation between education and ability to recognize and express feelings. The rate of depression among college men approaches that among college-educated women, possibly because these men are more able to recognize depression and more willing to seek help.

Depressed men engage in compulsive drinking, risktaking, sexual acting out, aggression, working, somatizing (unfounded complaints of back pain, gastrointestinal difficulties, headaches, and so forth), withdrawal, and preoccupation with television or the internet. Eighty percent of all suicides are committed by men. Depression damages relationships and interferes with academic and vocational goals. At the very least, men suffering from depression experience a diminished quality of life.

Twenty million Americans experience depression during their lifetimes, and an estimated 60 to 80 percent never get help. Because of the difficulty recognizing depression in men and their resistance to seeking assistance, men are frequently undiagnosed and untreated.

Yet for each of the millions of men suffering from depression, there is probably a woman who loves him, recognizes his disease, and is affected by his illness as well. The fact that depression is a treatable illness makes these facts particularly troubling.

We are fortunate today to have treatments for depression that are usually successful in completely controlling the illness. There is a general acceptance that this malady has a genetic component and has its basis in an imbalance of brain chemistry. It is similar to medical illnesses such as thyroid disease, diabetes, and hypertension. Like most physical illnesses, the physician arrives at the best medication to control depression through a trial-and-error process. We know that the prognosis is generally better if the patient is also involved in particular types of psychotherapy in addition to medication.

Most men are resistant to seeing even a medical doctor, and it is especially difficult for them to seek psychological treatment. To do so, they must buck their tendency to deny the feminine aspects of their personality. They have to admit they are vulnerable, they must depend on the therapist, and they must learn to recognize and express their feelings. Men who are able to overcome these hurdles can benefit greatly from talking treatment. These days we have a better idea as to which types of psychological treatment are helpful and which are not.

> For each of the millions of men suffering from depression, there is probably a woman who loves him.

It is heartbreaking when a depressed man remains undiagnosed or untreated. Two examples from my experience illustrate the tragedy of failing to deal with this disorder. The first was a markedly depressed man who came to the hospital for treatment unwillingly. His spouse and his boss practically forced him in. He responded well, recovered from his depression, and became a "born again" depressed person who would identify and refer the depressed people he discovered to me for treatment. One of the individuals he spotted was his father, who refused to consider psychiatric consultation. Years later his father was in the hospital with terminal cancer. His family physician put him on an antidepressant to help with his pain. He recovered from his depression and told his son, "Now I understand what you were talking about—I must have been depressed my whole life." The son recounted sadly that his father passed away shortly after making this statement. "He was only able to experience freedom from depression for two weeks before he died."

Another distressing example was recounted by the daughter of a man in California. She and her husband were contacted by her father's physician to come at once because the father was close to death. When they arrived, the physician informed them that the father had Alzheimer's and was suffering from pneumonia. The doctor advised them not to aggressively treat the pulmonary infection because it would only prolong his existence as a terminally demented individual. They supported this recommendation but asked for an autopsy. The results showed that the father had died from pneumonia but did not, in fact, have Alzheimer's. He had a pseudo-dementia due to depression. The daughter was overwhelmed with guilt and anger when she realized that her father had died from two treatable conditions. Had the depression been recognized and treated, he likely would have enjoyed more years of independence.

> **It is heartbreaking when a depressed man remains undiagnosed or untreated.**

Diagnosis of a treatable dementia should lead to a positive outcome. One of my early patients was a businessman in his early seventies who had been hospitalized at another facility with a diagnosis of hardening of the arteries. The patient's internist had asked the social services department of the hospital to locate a nursing facility for him. The patient then tried to hang himself in his hospital room, resulting in his transfer to my psychiatric unit. I observed that he appeared clinically depressed and that his memory difficulties seemed to be due to impaired concentration. Because of his desperation and suicidal behavior, I began a series of electroconvulsive treatments. He responded with a complete remission of his symptoms and was able to return home to his family and manage his business.

As you are probably beginning to realize, this book is packed with stories from my years as a front-line psychiatrist. When you reach a certain age—some people refer to it as "anecdotage"—you have the urge to pass on stories and wisdom you think you have accumulated to the younger generation. I seem compelled to put what I have learned from my years in the psychiatric trenches on paper. I have included some of the changes in my field that I have observed over the years. *Loving a Depressed Man* is a product of my training, my peculiar brand of humor, and my lengthy professional experience diagnosing and treating depressed patients.

This book was specifically written to help women recognize depression in their male companions and provide practical advice as to how they can best support and help them. Over my nearly fifty years of practice, female caregivers have often asked me what they should say and do for their depressed men. Their requests have particular meaning to me. I have been in their shoes. Several of my family members have suffered from depression, and even though I am "in the business," I have known the frustration and helplessness that comes with trying to help a depressed relative. It is draining to coax loved ones to seek help, lessen their pain, instill hope, and worry about their safety on a day-to-day basis. You have to keep reminding yourself that this irritable, negative, unproductive fellow is the same man you respected and fell in love with in the past. I have encouraged women to take care of themselves and maintain their morale during the strenuous caregiving process. I did the same on the internet for Prodigy for a few years, answering hundreds of e-mails from depressed patients and their families.

This is a how-to book for women. It is not intended as a scientific treatise in which all sides of issues or all eventualities are presented in a fair and balanced manner. Rather, it is presented in the "Dutch uncle" style that I recommend the caregivers adopt when interacting with their depressed loved one: a positive, confident, unambivalent approach that will instill hope in the melancholic and in you as you support your depressed male.

Introduction

I have disguised the identities of the patients I mention, changing their names, occupations, ages, and even sex in order to preserve the anonymity of the individuals involved. All the examples that are provided and the suggested statements presented are intended for men. Men tend to think other men do not have depression and that they are weak or, heaven forbid, feminine for being depressed. By referring to male examples, you will be reassuring your man that real men do, in fact, get depressed.

It goes without saying that your depressed man must get to a physician for evaluation, medication, and counseling. This is not as easy as it sounds. The majority of depressed men do not receive professional attention. Men and their loved ones frequently fail to recognize that their problem is depression. They may attribute their pain and sadness to external factors and look for external solutions. They may fear that the diagnosis of depression might result in a negative response from their employer or an inability to obtain insurance. Some men equate a psychological disability with weakness. Some religious men may think that their inability to overcome depression is due to a lack of faith. To help your depressed man, it is important that you circumvent his resistance and help him receive the professional aid he needs.

> You have to keep reminding yourself that this irritable, negative, unproductive fellow is the same man you respected and fell in love with in the past.

To be prepared to provide support and counter the resistances to treatment presented by the depressed male, family and friends need to be fully informed about the illness. The introductory chapters to *Loving a Depressed Man* provide an overview of depression, its symptoms, and its treatment.

While psychiatrists are the best trained and most experienced professionals when it comes to evaluating and treating a depressed individual, it may be more difficult for your man to seek help initially from a mental health specialist. Most men find it easier to accept a physical problem than mental illness. For this reason, I advise families to convince their depressed male to see their family physician. The physical symptoms of depression (sleep disturbance, appetite disturbance, lack of pep, and constipation) provide reasons to consult with the family doctor.

Men frequently have an established, trusting relationship with their doctor. A significant percentage of a family physician's practice is made up of individuals who suffer from clinical depression. Generalists today are comfortable prescribing

> **Real men do, in fact, get depressed.**

antidepressant medications, and most of the newer drugs are capable of relieving the run-of-the-mill depressive illness quickly and with few side effects. The generalist will likely be the best person to make the referral to a psychiatrist if this is necessary. If your man does not have a trusting relationship with a primary-care doctor, then perhaps a relative, friend, minister, teacher, coach, boss, or other mentor in his life would be the best person to enlist for assistance.

Depression presents unique difficulties that make communication with the afflicted individual harder for loved ones and caregivers. The difficulty is increased and compounded when the depressed individual is male. This book will offer ways to bypass the obstacles presented by the distorted, negative perception of the depressed male patient. How-to statements are provided throughout. *Loving a Depressed Man* offers hope for most men currently suffering from depression and even greater hope for future treatment.

Acknowledgments

Thanking the many people who have helped directly or indirectly in the creation of this book is one of my greatest pleasures.

First of all, thanks to my wife Deborah, who tolerated my isolation while working on this book. She provided helpful female insights and examples from her work as a psychiatric nurse in our office. Debbie co-authored *Loving an Adult Child of an Alcoholic* with me and knows firsthand the time and energy required for a project of this kind.

My brother Dick provided input into the book as well. Dick graduated magnum cum laude from Yale Medical School before taking his neurological residency at the Mayo Clinic. His daughter Alex is getting straight A's at Duke medical school in their combined Ph.D. and M.D. program with a future goal of medical research.

I am proud of my wonderful children and grandchildren: Cathy and Dan Ward, Barbara and William White, Sarah Bey, Matt Bey and godson Alvis Martin. To my Ward and White grandchildren, Keslie and Kyle Douglas Ward; and Audrey, Andy and Rachel White: I hope that my writing will help keep me in your memories and perhaps give you additional insight into me as a person. I regret my father didn't have a

Acknowledgments

chance to record his experiences as a professor, but I'm thankful to him for encouraging me to write mine as a psychiatrist.

I've been fortunate to have a number of friends who have helped me produce this and my previous books. Bert Krages, my literary agent, has gone above and beyond the call of duty helping me get into print. Juris Jurjevics, former owner of the Soho Press and author of *The Trudeau Vector*, went out of his way to help place the manuscript for this book with LaChance Publishing. I want to thank Victor Starsia President of LaChance Publishing, Richard Day Gore, Senior Editor, Juliann Garey, Associate Editor, Maryann Palumbo, publicist, and all the members of the LaChance Publishing team for accepting this book and for their good work in shaping it.

Karen Zangerle is my kind, compassionate, genius friend who has corrected my grammar and given me helpful input into the content of my books over the years. I appreciate her taking time from her busy schedule to help me with my writing. Garold "Bud" Cole, an academic author, has given me many excellent suggestions. Professor Dan Liechty has been generous with his time and expertise and was kind enough to endorse the book as well. Gabriel Telot M.D., has been my friend and mentor since 1961. He is part of our family and provided valuable clinical input to the effort. Diane Wallace shared her experiences helping depressed men in her life. Retired English Professor and editor Stanley Renner and his nurse-instructor wife Charla helped with editing and made helpful suggestions. Our best friends Dave and Ruth Anne Klumb and my old college roommate Ron Naae and his wife Carole have cheered me on.

I gave rough copies of the manuscript to a number of women who were helping depressed male patients in my practice. I want to thank these anonymous contributors for their helpful and practical suggestions as well.

Our psychiatric office is in a French style cottage located in a pastoral setting. Glass display cases on the wall contain medical antiques that were thought to be the cutting edge of psychiatric treatment years ago. These curiosities remind us that the field of psychiatry is constantly evolving and inspire us to work with our patients to keep that cutting edge keen. My wife Deborah is the office nurse. Wendy Rosendale and Vicky Scott run our business office and provide special care to our patients and their families. Gabriel Telot M.D., Bruce Boeck M.A., LCPC, Dr. Karen Mark, Nancy Peterson LCSW, John Schultze LCPC, and Naomi Wilansky LCSW are independent practitioners working in our office providing excellent care to patients. I feel fortunate to be associated with these dedicated professionals. Both patients and professionals provided input for the book.

The development of effective treatments and modern mental health advocates have greatly reduced the stigma of mental illness in recent years, but chronically ill individuals who suffer from schizophrenia, bipolar disorder, chemical dependency, traumatic brain injuries, developmental disabilities, and severe personality disorders continue to be shunned and largely ignored. Many end up homeless or in the department of corrections, and there are few long term psychiatric facilities available to them. Since August of 2006 I have served as the psychiatric consultant to a successful program geared to care for this population at Sharon Healthcare in Peoria, IL, which cares for over 500 chronically ill residents. The owners, Stanley Aaron, John Schlofrock and Rick Duros, and the Medical Director, Dr. Phil Immesoete (who served with me in the 1st Division in Vietnam 1969–1970 when we were both army medical officers), have been encouraging and supportive, as have many members of the staff: Bobby Ford, Denise McGarvey (aka "Hot Lips" from her role in a production of MASH); Dan Santangelo; Beverly Lee R.N.; Lize Bare R.N.; Nadine Lee LPN; Randy Bauer; Louella Murray LPN; Tammy Rayner R.N.; Cindy Jones; Monica Zhou R.N; April Halverson R.N. and her husband, Chris Halverson.

Acknowledgments

I always like to acknowledge our good friends at our "pub," Jim's Steakhouse, because we clock a good deal of time with them and they have always supported my writing efforts. Our previous two books are framed and displayed there, and there is a space on the wall waiting for this one as well. Greg, Eddie, Mary Jo, Cyndi, Carl, Erin, Trish(es), Shannon(s), Iris, Kayla and Kiley, the future master chef, are all great people.

Finally, because of the mileage I've accumulated, I require considerable medical maintenance. I feel it prudent to acknowledge and thank those who keep me running. Dr. Mikell, cardiologist; Dr. Hanson, internist; Dr. Miller, rheumatologist; Dr. Lee opthalmologist; Dr. Dunkleberger, VA internist; Dr. Roszhardt, urologist; Dr. Shanahan, radiology-oncologist; Dr. Keller, dentist; Dr. Gerstein, periodontist; and Dr. Seehafer, dermatologist. In addition, both Dr. Yang, gastroenterologist, and Dr. Zander, my rectal-colon surgeon, can verify that I meet the necessary qualifications to be a story teller!

Loving a
Depressed Man

CHAPTER ONE

What Brings Men Down?

The bright silks and sparkling faces I had seen that day, in gala trim, swanlike sailing down the Mississippi of Broadway; and I contrasted them with the pallid copyist, and thought to myself, Ah, happiness courts the light, so we deem the world is gay; but misery hides aloof, so we deem that misery there is none.

— *Herman Melville, Bartelby the Scrivener*

Men are less likely than women to be diagnosed and treated for depression. They are reluctant to seek help, more likely to try to self-medicate, and often present with behaviors that are not immediately recognized as depression. Depression waxes and wanes, and the up-and-down nature of the illness tends to confound recognition and treatment. Clinical depression, which probably has a genetic predisposition, is caused by a chemical imbalance in the sufferer. It can come on for no apparent reason, and it can also be precipitated by stress or other external situations; i.e. loss of someone close, getting fired, receiving a Dear John letter. (This is not to be confused with "the blues," which we'll discuss later in the book.) Here's a story illustrating the difference between depression with an internal cause and situational depression, as well as how awful clinical depression can feel:

1

A man suffered from severe depressive episodes and received shock treatment until he finally got on lithium and his depressive episodes were controlled. One day he called me indicating he had to get in right away. Remembering his past history, I thought, "This is going to be bad." He reported his wife and son had been in an auto accident; the wife was killed and the son was paralyzed from the neck down. He went to his GP for a sedative and told him he was having double vision and tingling and the doc sent him to a neurologist who diagnosed him as having multiple sclerosis. I asked him how he was doing and he said he was not good, dealing with the loss of his wife, the paralysis of his son and his own MS…. "But it's not like those depressions." He had three events that would flatten most people, but he was handling them. Depression, however, was in a different league.

It is also possible to feel the crushing symptoms of depression without their being caused by one's body chemistry. Either way, the symptoms can be just as difficult to endure and need to be taken seriously, usually warranting treatment with medications and therapy.

Males are particularly sensitive to threats to their sense of adequacy, control, independence, and competitive natures. Aging and illness may exacerbate these fears. Military deployment may lead to depression as well. In this chapter, we will explore all the factors that are likely to precipitate depression in men.

Gender Differences

Differences between the sexes affect attitudes toward depression. Observations of young children demonstrate that boys are generally more aggressive and competitive while girls are more oriented toward relationships. Efforts to encourage gender-neutral play among children do not alter these differences. Boys use dolls as guns; girls cradle and nurture trucks. It has also been noted that boys' games last longer than girls' because they are able to negotiate differences when they arise, while girls tend to take their toys and go home rather than working out conflict. Girls identify with their mothers, while boys strive to be unlike their mothers. As a result, males eschew traits they perceive as feminine. Boys learn to be stoic, independent, strong, competitive, logical, problem-solving, and, as men, to be careful.

> Males are particularly sensitive to threats to their sense of adequacy, control, independence, and competitive natures.

The vast majority of healthcare consumption is under the control of women. Mothers go in for regular checkups, give birth, take the kids to the pediatrician, and make their husbands have a checkup now and then. Men account for a small portion of the healthcare dollar. Men are hunters and women are gatherers. Men know what they want when they shop. They go in to the store, buy the product, and leave. Women like to look through the racks and frequently, when they find exactly what they want, go to several more stores to see if they can find the same item for less money. Some men don't go to the standard sources of health care because they will be given tests and X-rays and referred to specialists; only after a long process of appointments and trips to various facilities do they receive diagnosis and finally treatment.

Today's men, supposedly, have moved beyond the "strong, silent" stereotype and are well into the generation where it is okay to share their feelings and cry. Approximately 160,000 men stay at home to care for the house and children while their wives work and provide the household income. Chris Ivany, M.D., a psychiatrist currently serving in Iraq, assures me that today's soldiers are "pretty open if you approach them in a way that makes sense to them." He also says we have pushed the idea that it is helpful to talk about trauma to the extent that both soldiers and spouses feel it is the right thing to do.

These changes might be seen as men getting in touch with their feminine selves and, from a psychiatric standpoint, men moving in the right direction. However, in my experience, men continue to have difficulty recognizing and expressing their feelings. They use language to express thoughts and ideas rather than emotions. Many of the men I see continue to feel they need to be strong and independent.

What He Thinks Caused His Depression May Not Have

A typical bout of depression lasts six to nine months. After this the individual gradually recovers but, if untreated, is at high risk for another episode.

Typically, the depressed man thinks whatever was going on at the time he developed depression caused the illness and whatever was going on when he came out of it was the cure. Since depression is a self-limiting and recurrent disease, it can mislead caregivers as well as patients. For example, back in the days when psychoanalysis was in vogue, we thought we were able to explain just about anything. If a man lost his job and then got depressed, he was reacting to loss. If the fellow was promoted, received a raise, and became depressed, he was suffering from a success neurosis. The dominant theory back then was that depression was caused by "anger turned on the self"; treatment programs featured activities and therapies designed to help patients express their anger without guilt. At the end of six to nine months they would recover, and the treatment staff would chalk up another success.

We now know that the typical bout of depression lasts six to nine months whether it's treated or not. Looking back, we could have permitted our patients to stay in bed or hang spaghetti on the walls for six to nine months and they would have gotten better, but we took credit for their recoveries. But that's not to say that treatment isn't vital. Some depressive episodes go immediately into another episode after six to nine months; some patients also have dysthymia, a smoldering, attenuated form of depression that is persistent and therefore the patient continues to be depressed after nine months. When I see a new depressed man in the office, I tell him he is going to get better no matter what we do and that we are just trying to speed up the process. From a practical standpoint we continue to treat patients after they have recovered because the proof of the effectiveness of our treatment lies in our ability to prevent further bouts of depression.

> A typical bout of depression lasts six to nine months.

This recurrent, up-and-down, self-limiting course of depression makes it difficult to understand at times. For example, a depressed patient goes to his doctor, says he does not feel well, and offers vague gastrointestinal complaints. The doctor orders an upper gastrointestinal (GI) X-ray, a lower GI X-ray, and some laboratory tests, then prescribes some stomach medicine, but the patient continues to return and to complain as his depression worsens. The doctor thinks, *Sometimes those gallstones don't show up on X-ray*. He takes out the patient's gallbladder. By this time, the patient's self-limiting illness is starting to improve, plus the surgery itself has an antidepressant effect, and the patient reports that he feels great. The doctor makes a mental note—and the next depressed patient with vague GI complaints gets his gallbladder out earlier!

Therapists are fooled as well. A depressed patient would see a counselor and continue to complain as his symptoms gradually worsened. He would tell the therapist, "I come in here and pay you each week and I feel worse." The therapist would nod and encourage him to express his negative feelings. Finally, after six to nine months, the patient would start feeling better, and the therapist would note that by helping the patient to vent his anger he was able to cure his depression.

pharmacologists are not immune to the self-deception that accompanies this self-limiting illness. A doctor might try the patient on one drug with no response, switch to another, and see the patient continue to worsen; then, after six to nine months of treatment, the patient begins to improve on a third drug, which both doctor and patient assume is effective. In reality, after six to nine months, the patient may simply have been coming out of that episode of depression; the drug may have had nothing to do with his recovery. The only way to be certain that a drug works is to follow the patient on the medicine and see if it prevents a recurrence.

Stresses That Appear to Bring on Depression in Men

Feelings of Inadequacy

Men react strongly to assaults on their sense of capability. Little boys get the message that they are supposed to be independent, tough, stoic, winners, nice to girls, and hardworking providers for their families. They must be role models for their children. They are the protectors of their spouses and may feel that they are responsible for the happiness of their wives and kids. Respect is very important to a man.

Women know that men are very concerned about anything that reflects on their feelings of adequacy. Inability to perform sexually, rejection by or an inability to satisfy their partner, financial reverses, demotion, job loss, aging, retirement, and illnesses that impose physical limitations are frequently associated with depression in men. Recent studies have suggested a correlation between economic fluctuations and suicide rates in men. Because of his sensitivity in this area, you will want to let your male know that you respect him, he excites you as a man, and his illness is separate from him as a person. You might say, "Hey, honey, I know you're under the weather, but you're my lover no matter what."

Feeling Defeated

Men are competitive, and defeat can be difficult. They tend to keep score as to how hard they work, how much they earn, the size of their automobile, their physical capabilities, and their sexual prowess. As their perceptions become increasingly negative with depression, they compare themselves unfavorably with others and see themselves as losers. Your man's feelings of shortfall and failure are likely to increase as his depression progresses. Being unable to function at his usual capacity, having to depend on his spouse rather than taking care of her, and failure to perform sexually are common events that reinforce the melancholic male's sense of inadequacy.

> You will want to let your male know that you respect him, he excites you as a man, and his illness is separate from him as a person.

Recently I saw a middle-aged business man who was experiencing financial stresses, which forced him to sell some real estate and which could have led to the bankruptcy of his business. His wife accompanied him to the appointment. As I asked him about his business reversals, he suddenly slumped back in his chair and started to convulse. We called 911 and he was rushed to the hospital where he was diagnosed with atrial fibrillation. He recovered and had a pacemaker and defibrillator implanted in his chest. His depression had caused him to magnify his negative perception of his circumstances. I mention this case because it illustrates how stressful business pressures can be for some men and how depression can exaggerate these worries.

Comments that might address and lessen these feelings are: "I know you're going through a rough illness right now—I'm just looking forward to having my old friend back when you recover." "I spoke with your boss and he says everyone is thinking of you and praying for your speedy recovery. They miss you." "I promised to love you in sickness and in health, and I meant it. I'll be with you until you recover. Don't worry, I'll give you plenty of chances to make it up to me when you're well!"

Loss

Loss is associated with depression in both sexes. Death of loved ones, the breakup of a relationship, loss of a job, failure to get a promotion, or loss of physical functioning can lead to depression in men. Men react to the losses of close friends and relatives, and sometimes the normal mourning brings about a depressive illness. The loss of a job is a major stressor for a man, because work is an important part of his identity and a source of his feeling of self-worth. In fact, one in seven unemployed men will experience depression in the first six months.

We know now that irrational guilt is a frequent symptom of clinical depression. Patients scour their lives for past sins and mistakes and, when they think they discover them, ruminate and beat themselves over the head for their supposed transgressions. If men lose someone close to them, they look for things they should have or could have done to prevent the death of their loved ones or made their lives more pleasant. This is the "shoulda-woulda-coulda" stinking thinking referred to in Alcoholic Anonymous that reflects the self-criticism so prevalent in depression. These ruminations are nearly always delusional and cannot be altered by logic.

Loss of control frequently adds to depression in men. During the early stages of the depression, the man finds he has to push himself to do things; he has lost his zest for life. He lacks energy, his tolerance for outside demands is lessened, and he finds it a struggle to focus and concentrate on his work. The fact that he cannot control these symptoms is in itself stressful. If you put a rat on a wire grid and shock it periodically, it will develop symptoms of tension. If you provide a lever for the rat to push that will stop the electrical shock, it will repeatedly push the lever and will not develop signs of stress. If you continue to randomly shock the rat whether it presses the lever or not, it will experience stress. This is felt to be a model for human stress: Symptoms develop when we have no ability to control pressure.

As we know, some women with hormonally-related depressions experience severe bouts of melancholy following childbirth. Less recognized is that one out of ten men has psychological problems after the birth of a child. The mother's preoccupation with the new baby, her lack of interest in sex, or her own depression may be experienced by the spouse as a loss of intimacy in the relationship and may precipitate a depression in a genetically vulnerable man.

> One out of ten men has psychological problems after the birth of a child.

Aging

Many men become depressed later in life. We like to be independent, and the older we get, the more we usually find we have to depend on others. We like to be tough, and as we age we become weak and frail. We like to be in control, and as the years pass, we begin to lose control over our bowels, our urine, our senses, our memory, and our sexual potency. The more rigidly we try to hang on to our manly ways, the more stressful aging becomes for us. In addition, many of our friends are ill or dying. When we retire, we lose the status that was associated with our jobs. Our income is reduced. The amount of medicine and medical attention we require increases. We worry about having a medical problem that will force us into dependency or a nursing home. Senior citizens frequently discuss their physical complaints, bodily functions and medical evaluations. These "organ recitals" tend to produce an anxious, negative pre-occupation that predisposes to depression.

Many senior males, once leaders in their vocations and families, find themselves overlooked and their opinions disregarded by the younger generation. One depressed octogenarian told me that, although he continued to provide financial support to his family, his advice and opinions were ignored by his offspring. The lack of respect shown to him by his children left him frustrated and angry. He said that he kept his irritation to himself rather than be seen as a curmudgeon. The kids continued to let him pick up the bills for vacations and restaurants, and let him chip in when they came up short financially, but disregarded his wishes and acted as though he were no longer in their presence. Anger turned on the self is no longer thought to be the cause of depression—but it may play a role in older men who, like this fellow, swallow their negative feelings.

It should not be surprising that among depressed men suicide increases with age. Old age is a time of loss. Sometimes it is loss of respect, as we've just seen. This is also the time of loss of friends and family through illness and death. Loss of income, loss of strength, loss of endurance, loss of sensation, loss of virility, loss of memory, loss of control all accompany aging. Adjustment to later life is even more difficult for men who feel the need to be in control. Suicide for some elderly men provides a means of taking matters into their own hands. Seniors respond to anti-depressant medications, though they must be given with some extra care. The axiom for medicating older patients is to start low on the dose and go slow when increasing it to avoid side effects, falls, and toxic reactions. In addition, possible interactions with other medications need to be considered.

> Old age is a time of loss.

Men can suffer from hormonally-related depression and respond when their antidepressant medications are augmented with testosterone.

Testosterone blood levels are easy to check. If they're low, the hormone is available in pill, intramuscular and patch form.

Time of Year

In the Northern Hemisphere, April and May are the peak months for depression and ulcers, with a second lesser peak in fall. The phenomenon is reversed in the Southern Hemisphere, with October being the peak and spring the smaller increase. No one knows exactly why this is. Perhaps it has to do with barometric pressure, change of seasons, light, or some other unknown factor. The farmers where I live attribute it to the stress of planting and harvesting, but it does not appear to be related to occupational stress and seems to be a worldwide phenomenon.

It is important to remember that clinical depression is an illness that may come on without any identifiable stress. Medication may appear to be controlling your man's depression and then, when April or October arrives, his symptoms may suddenly increase. He may need to have his drugs adjusted.

Holidays

The news media has the idea that people get depressed and suicidal during the holiday season. Our local paper publishes an annual article on this topic usually filled with quotes from local mental health providers, who note the many stresses of selecting gifts, preparing meals, sending cards, and paying the bills associated with holidays. They also note that getting together with family members, remembering family members who have passed away, unrealistic expectations of happiness associated with the holidays, and childhood memories that are sometimes unpleasant may also contribute to seasonal pressures.

There are indeed stresses associated with holidays, but, in my experience, most of the patients I see with depression over this season started to become depressed in the fall. They felt they should be happy but, because of their depressive illnesses they were unable to enjoy the holidays. Their depressions were probably further aggravated by the seasonal stresses noted above. In other words, the holidays added to a depression that was already present going into the season. The important fact to keep in mind is that the depression probably started in the fall or spring, due to some unknown seasonal influence, and was exaggerated when the sufferer was unable to experience joy during a subsequent holiday season.

Major Illnesses also Cause Stress

Most serious medical illnesses cause stress by limiting the individual's sense of control, increasing helplessness, confronting them with their mortality, and evoking a sense of loss.

Heart Attacks

Heart attacks are sudden, frightening events. Some studies indicate that as many as twenty percent of individuals suffering myocardial infarctions (MIs) suffer depression. Type A, workaholic men are especially vulnerable to myocardial infarction. These hard driving, aggressive go-getters suddenly find themselves on their backs wondering if they are going to survive. Their movements are restricted, and they worry that activity and aggression might lead to their deaths. The sympathy and concern their condition evokes in others makes them feel that they have forfeited their independence and masculinity. It is not unusual for some of these men to experience depression as a result of these stresses. Open heart surgery is also frequently followed by depression.

Stroke

Some estimates suggest that half of the patients suffering a cerebral vascular accident (CVA) experience depressive symptoms afterwards. This sudden insult to the brain often causes paralysis, speech problems, memory difficulties, sometimes visual problems, and marked fatigue. Again, an active man is suddenly thrust into a state of dependency and limitation. My neurologist brother tells me that depression is so common following stroke that many of his colleagues automatically start their stroke patients on antidepressants. The depression that frequently follows this event often responds to stimulants or Provigil, a new drug used for day time drowsiness, rather than antidepressant medication.

Diabetes

Depression accompanies diabetes nearly as often as it does heart attacks. Men with diabetes often have difficulty with impotency and this may be a stress that precipitates depression. Often the problem can be treated with one of the drugs for erectile dysfunction (ED) like Viagra or Cialis as long as the patient is not taking nitrates for his heart or has some other contraindication to their use.

Cancer

Cancer is a frightening word. Approximately 30 percent of cancer victims will develop depression. The treatments for cancer frequently cause fatigue, as well as hair loss, anemia, generalized malaise, and weakness. It is not unusual for men to develop depression precipitated by the stresses engendered by the illness and its treatment. Nearly all men will develop cancer of the prostate if they live long enough. In addition to the fear of death, it carries with it concerns about sexual potency that can lead to depression. Oncologists tell me that they follow patients who have cancer and depression more closely because the depression lowers the patient's immune response and this group is more likely to experience a reoccurrence.

Parkinson's Disease

Parkinson's disease is a fairly common illness in later years. Initially it can be mistaken for depression because of the slowing of movement and mask-like faces that are symptomatic of this malady. Depression can be and often is associated with Parkinsonism however and, if present, should be treated as well as the neurological condition.

Gastrointestinal Illness and Other Diseases

A study of hospitalized patients suggests that as many as sixty percent of individuals admitted to the hospital with gastrointestinal complaints suffer from depression. Many illnesses can produce loss of energy and fatigue which, at first glance, may be mistaken for depression. For example, anemia, vitamin deficiency, hypothyroidism, Addison's disease, mononucleosis, pneumonia, liver failure, renal disease, viral infections, sleep apnea, and other common ailments can cause tiredness. This is another reason to have a checkup. Most of these problems are correctable and none of them respond to an antidepressant.

>‹

As you've seen, threats to a man's adequacy, losses, illnesses, rejection, financial stresses, retirement, and aging are stresses that may precipitate depression. In the next chapter we'll focus on its symptoms.

CHAPTER TWO

Identifying the Symptoms of Depression in Men

"I know nothing, I can do nothing. I understand nothing. I know nothing. Nothing. And all this misery does not even make me particularly unhappy."

—Gerhard Richter quoted by Andrew Solomon in "The Noonday Demon"

Trust Your Woman's Intuition

You may be the first to recognize that something has happened to your man—even before he does. Because of your intimacy, you may sense subtle changes in his appearance and behavior. In the nineteenth century it was thought that "Veraguth's fold"—two vertical folds between the eyes—was a physical sign of depression. While this may not be true, depressed people do not look like themselves. Years ago there was a film called *Faces of Depression* in which depressed patients were filmed when they were first interviewed by a psychiatrist and later when they had recovered. Their before-and-after faces were put side by side on the screen. It was shocking to see the changes.

Women in general are blessed with the gift of intuition. Your gut feelings may be the best early signal that your man is becoming depressed. If you have become more concerned about him but cannot put your finger on the reason why, think of the possibility that he is becoming depressed. Has he seemed to pull away? Have his usual patterns of behavior altered? If you sense that your man is different, trust your intuition. The early, subtle nuances you sense may be the beginning of a depressive illness.

Given the up-and-down, but ultimately descending, course of depression, you may find it difficult to spot the illness initially. Men have a tendency to see the sources of their problems as external—and the solutions to them as external as well. They look outside themselves for the causes of their pain. In addition, men frequently do not display the classic symptoms of the disease. Nevertheless, it is important to make the diagnosis and get treatment as early as possible, because depression treated in its early stages responds more quickly and completely than depression that has festered.

> If you sense that your man is different, trust your intuition.

The Classic Symptoms of Depression

Mnemonics are memory aids. You may have used the mnemonic ROY G BIV to remember the colors of the rainbow (red, orange, yellow, green, blue, indigo, and violet). Medical students and psychiatric residents use mnemonics to help them remember anatomical structures and the symptoms and signs of various illnesses. The two used to remember the symptoms of depression are SIG E CAPS and C GASP DIE.

SIG E CAPS

Suicidal thoughts
Interests decreased
Guilt
Energy decreased
Concentration decreased
Appetite disturbance
Psychomotor changes
Sleep disturbance

C GASP DIE

Concentration decreased
Guilt
Appetite disturbance
Sleep disturbance
Psychomotor retardation (or agitation)
Death or suicidal thoughts
Interests decreased
Energy decreased

Sleep and Appetite Disturbances

One of the early symptoms of depression is sleep disturbance. There may be difficulties getting to sleep (initial insomnia), but the typical symptom is waking up in the early morning and being unable to return to sleep (terminal insomnia). Frequently men will self-medicate with alcohol or use over-the-counter sleep aids to try to treat themselves. Even if they are able to sleep, they won't feel rested during the daytime.

Lack of sleep contributes to other manifestations of the illness. Loss of energy, difficulty getting things done, impaired concentration, loss of pleasure, and increased irritability are aggravated by a lack of restful, restorative sleep.

The primitive part of the brain or limbic system controls sleep, appetite, and mood. The chemical imbalance associated with depression affects all three.

> One of the early symptoms of depression is sleep disturbance.

Classically, depressed patients lose their appetites and lose weight. However, some depressives overeat, resulting in weight gain. Others experience gastrointestinal problems; still others have no change in appetite. Disturbance of appetite is a less reliable symptom of depression, in my experience.

Loss of Pleasure

Depressed individuals typically appear sad and unable to experience joy. This symptom may be more difficult to recognize in men who more frequently show irritation and compulsive behaviors. Your guy may deny feeling depressed even when he seems to be in pain. Remember, these symptoms develop gradually over time; even when sadness and depression are visible to you, he may not recognize the changes in his appearance and behavior.

It should be noted that depressed men are not sad or blue but, instead, are unable to feel anything, like Gerhard Richter in the quote at the beginning of the chapter. One depressed man said he also felt fragile and less confident in his abilities. A man who held his son for the first time told me that he felt absolutely nothing and that this was frightening to him; he knew he should be feeling joy and a loving bond with his newborn son.

It's difficult for your depressed man to have fun. Activities that are ordinarily pleasurable are no longer a source of joy for him (anhedonia). Some studies indicate that men have sex just as often while depressed, but they do not feel as satisfied. This is a blow to his sense of manhood and, in some men, it may lead to sexual infidelity and risk-taking sexual behaviors. Some men sense that they are not themselves and try to relieve their unhappiness by going on vacation. A geographic cure usually ends up causing the man to feel worse. Friends and family are having fun while he stays in the hotel room feeling depressed. During the trip he sits apart from the others ruminating about the money he's spent and how badly he feels.

Diurnal Variation

Men with the classic form of depression will feel worse in the morning and better as the day goes on. As the illness progresses they continue to feel depressed throughout the day; eventually they're unable to see any difference between their feelings in the morning and at night. Depressed patients who fall asleep during the day frequently report feeling worse when they awaken. Later, as your man recovers, he will feel typically feel better later in the day. Eventually, when he recovers, he'll awaken feeling good.

Impaired Concentration

Depressed men have difficulty focusing and keeping their minds on their tasks. Your guy may pay little attention to what you're saying; later on he may fail to remember what you told him. He may mistake the issue for a memory problem. Many depressed patients initially think they are developing Alzheimer's disease. Concentration difficulties due to depression that are mistaken for dementia are known as pseudodementia. My neurologist brother sees depressed patients who try to con-

> Many depressed patients initially think they are developing Alzheimer's disease.

vince him they have Alzheimer's. I, on the other hand, see Alzheimer's patients who are brought by their families hoping that they are depressed.

This symptom will likely interfere with your man's ability to function on his job, which will be a source of stress for him. You can reassure him that he does not have dementia or a memory problem and that his problems with recall are the result of his impaired ability to concentrate. This is one of the last symptoms to improve during recovery.

Loss of Energy

A depressed man is convinced he doesn't have the energy to carry out his usual daily activities (anergia). He will complain that everything requires great effort. He has to push himself to do the simplest tasks (inertia). For a man who is used to being energetic and a hard worker, this symptom adds to his stress by supporting his assumption that he is weak. If you observe a deeply depressed man closely, you will note that even his thinking is painfully slow and requires effort. This is referred to as psychomotor retardation.

Social Withdrawal

At home, your depressed man will withdraw from social activities, friends, and family. He won't want to answer the phone. It will be an effort for him to smile and put on a happy front to others. Most depressed men feel like staying in bed, pulling the covers over their heads, and shutting out the world. He will not want any requirements placed on him and sees the most minor of social obligations as a demand. He may want you to make excuses for him to avoid interacting with others.

Impaired Judgment

Depressed men don't typically experience the markedly impaired judgment associated with manic episodes—the kind that causes men to drain their bank accounts or impulsively act in ways that get them into legal difficulties. Nevertheless, it's best to be wary in a depression, and not make major life decisions. Depressed men are hungry for affection and, because of their need for nurturance, may rush into relationships they later regret.

I once saw a young man whose father died while he was in college. He was so overcome with grief that he dropped out of school and stayed in bed for over a year. During this time a lonely, co-dependent girlfriend took care of him. She fed him, helped him bathe, did his laundry, and took care of his apartment. In the midst of his depression, he married her. Later, when he'd recovered, he could not believe what he had done. He told me that he made a lifelong commitment to a person he found unattractive and with whom he felt he had nothing in common. His only explanation was that in the depths of his depression, he felt worthless and unlovable. The girl had been kind to him, and given his low self-esteem, desperation, and hopelessness at the time, he had confused his gratitude with love. Needless to say, their marriage ended in divorce.

Indecision

Some men suffering from depression come into the hospital and stay in bed, unable to decide whether to shower or brush their teeth. Like most caregivers, you will have the tendency to try to give your depressed man as much control as possible. But it is important to recognize that he is challenged when it comes to

> Asking a depressed man to make a decision may be torture for him.

21

making decisions. Asking a depressed man to make a decision may be torture for him. Instead, take the lead and tell him when to shower, when to brush his teeth, when his next appointment with the doctor has been scheduled, what time to take his medicine, when to take a walk, and what to eat.

Crying Spells

Depressed men tear up easily and may break down and cry. This is particularly stressful for men who have been raised with the "boys don't cry" mentality. In my experience, most men will do everything they can to avoid crying in the presence of others and, when they do, experience embarrassment and shame at what they perceive to be weakness.

Negative Rumination

Cows bring up their cud and chew it again and again. *Obsessive rumination* is a bovine phrase used to describe one of the classic symptoms of depression. Depressed men get something negative stuck on their brains and then obsess over it, bringing it up continually—much the way a cow ruminates its cud. This phenomenon cannot be altered by logic. Distraction helps, but it can be difficult given the strength of a man's preoccupation with a particular topic.

I once treated a guy who had purchased a house at the time he was going into a depression. When he inspected his new home, he found some silverfish running around in the kitchen cupboard. He called in an exterminator but wasn't satisfied, convinced that there were still bugs in the house. He wouldn't let his children play in the kitchen or on the floor. He had the exterminator return several times. His wife thought they'd gotten them, but he was not convinced. He finally decided that the only way he was going to get rid of the insects once and for all was to burn his house down. Fortunately, he realized that this was an irrational conclusion and came in to see me for a consultation.

After taking his history, I pointed out that he had many symptoms of clinical depression and suggested he start on antidepressant medication. He said, "Okay, I can see how a pill might help my sleep and appetite—but what are you going to do about those silverfish?" I remember this patient vividly because he asked the same question every time I saw him until he'd recovered. Then the thought just faded away, and he could no longer understand why he had been so fixated. I've been diagnosing and treating patients with depression for many years and it still is difficult for me to accept that

> Depressed men get something negative stuck on their brains and then obsess over it, bringing it up continually.

a pill can change a thought—but it does. It is no wonder that patients who are new to depression doubt that their obsessive preoccupations can be helped with medicine.

Guilt

Irrational guilt is a common symptom of depression. You may observe that your man looks back over his past and dwells on acts he identifies as mistakes or sins on his part. His supposed transgressions are magnified out of proportion. I've seen patients ruminate about stealing a candy bar when they were children. Such trivial transgressions can be magnified into criminal acts and become lodged in the depressed man's mind.

One patient reported to me that he was depressed because he had embezzled funds from his employer and was going to prison. I had to take him at his word, but I cautioned him to wait until he recovered from his depression before drawing any conclusions. He disagreed, of course, but when he later recovered he saw the situation in a completely different light. Part of his job had been to deposit the week's receipts at a local bank Friday after work. One Friday, while depressed, he worked past the bank closing time and he was unable to deposit the money until the following morning. Because of his altered perception, he reasoned: "I cheated my employer out of twelve hours' of interest on his money. Cheating your employer is the same as embezzling. Embezzlers go to prison. Therefore, I am going to prison."

Some depressed patients feel that they are so evil, they're responsible for all the disasters in the world. When I began my residency, I took over a ward of patients at Topeka State Hospital. One patient on the unit—I'll call him Ted—was sure he was responsible for all the plane crashes, explosions, and mass deaths reported in the news. I told him that he was not that powerful and put him on a combination of antidepressant and antipsychotic medications. One day while I was leading a group discussion on the ward, the end of my cigarette fell off and onto my pants. I jumped up swatting my crotch in an effort to avoid a hole in one of my few suits. As I did, I glanced across the ward and spotted Ted smiling and giving me a knowing look, as if he had caused the event!

In severe forms of depression, patients may also experience auditory hallucinations telling them that they are bad, deserve punishment, or—in the case of command hallucinations—should take their own lives. Hallucinations are false perceptions without any stimuli in the environment. These symptoms are indicators that the illness has become severe (psychotic). Patients who act on command hallucinations may respond to their internal stimuli and harm themselves or others without warning. This is a dangerous situation; if you spot it, notify your physician. The patient must be closely observed, and hospitalization should definitely be considered. When in doubt, take your man to the emergency room and let the professionals decide the best course to keep him safe.

Negative Perception

The primary area of brain function impairment in depression is perception, and in this respect a depressed man is nearly delusional. It is as though he has negative filters. He tends to screen out anything positive, magnify anything he perceives as negative, and then ruminate about it. This will be frustrating for you in your efforts to cheer him up. He will ignore any positive information you give him, but dwell on and amplify anything even slightly negative in your conversation. This alteration in perception isn't usually considered a symptom of depression, but I believe it's an important aspect of the disease that should be kept in mind. Over the years I have seen men make self-destructive decisions because of the negative, altered perception that accompanies depression. Risky sexual behaviors, illegal activities that are totally out of character, poor financial decisions, and actions that disrupt and sometimes lead to the termination of significant relationships have all been the product of their distorted, negative perception.

Impulsivity and Irritability

The neurotransmitters serotonin and norepinephrine appear to be related to the symptoms of clinical depression. Low serotonin levels in women lead to sadness and introspection; in men reduced levels cause impulsiveness and irritability. The latter, in fact, is one of the most common symptoms seen in depressed men. Another root of the bad temper in depressed men is simply pain. The suffering they experience results in less energy available to deal with the demands of others. With that in mind, it is understandable that depressed men would be touchy when asked to take on emotional burdens. Another factor leading to petulance in de-

> Your depressed man is already extremely critical of himself. He may interpret neutral comments as disapproval.

pressed men is their sensitivity to criticism. Your depressed man is already extremely critical of himself. He may interpret neutral comments as disapproval. He will be less able to tolerate any perceived criticism and is apt to erupt in defensive anger.

Hopelessness and Helplessness

Depressed men build a case to support their feelings of hopelessness and helplessness. They paint themselves into a corner and convince themselves that there is no way out. Their inability to pull themselves out of their depression which makes them feel like helpless failures.

This marked pessimism is the natural result of their negative perception, which blocks positive input and magnifies the negative. Because he's depressed, his negative beliefs cannot be altered by logic — the definition of delusional thinking.

Suicidal Ideation

About one-third of depressed men experience suicidal thoughts as a symptom of their depression. Once a man convinces himself that there are no positive expectations for his future, he may think of taking his own life to remove himself from what he perceives is a hopeless situation. It is important to ask him about these thoughts and to develop a plan together about can be done if he feels unable to control these urges.

Other Types of Depression

Atypical Depression

The symptoms of classical depression are insomnia with early-morning awakening, loss of appetite with weight loss, and feeling worse in the morning and better as the day goes on. Another type of depression, known as atypical depression, is characterized by the opposite symptoms: oversleeping, overeating with weight gain, feeling worse at night, and, in addition, sensitivity to loss of relationships.

The symptoms of atypical depression tend not to respond as well to the typical antidepressants. They seem to do better with monoamine oxidase inhibitors (MAOIs). This is an older class of antidepressant medication that requires a special tyramine-free diet and extra precautions because MAOIs react, sometimes fatally, with many other drugs.

Bipolar Disorder

In the old days the term was "manic depression," because sufferers of bipolar disorder, in addition to enduring bouts of severe depression, experience mood swings in the opposite direction, to mania. About 2.1 percent of people will experience bipolar disorder during their lifetime. In classic cases, bipolar men have periods of depression lasting six to nine months and periods of mania lasting three months that occur with intervals of fifteen months in between. Some men with bipolar disorder are considered rapid cyclers with more frequent mood shifts. It is also possible to have mixed phases of both depressive and manic symptoms.

The mnemomic for mania's symptoms is DIG FAST.

DIG FAST

Distractibility
Indiscretion
Grandiosity
Flight of ideas
Activity increase
Sleep deficit
Talkativeness

Bipolar I, Bipolar II (Hypomania), and Cyclothymia

During periods of mania, men experience impaired sleep, pressured speech, pressured thought, overconfidence, inflated ideas, increased irritability, increased libido, and impaired judgment. Severe forms are diagnosed as bipolar I, less severe forms are bipolar II (hypomania), and the least severe mood swings are referred to as cyclothymic.

Recognizing the presence of bipolar illness is crucial, because these men do not usually do well with antidepressant medication. Antidepressants alone may push a bipolar depressed man into a manic episode; they can also convert a classical bipolar patient into a rapid cycler. Mood stabilizers and antipsychotic medications are better choices.

Bipolar men are more difficult to treat than those with unipolar depressive illness. Typically bipolar patients require several medications to stabilize their mood swings. The primary treatment problem with these men is their lack of compliance. It is not impossible to convince most depressed men to seek help and to take medication to relieve their painful condition. Men who are manic, on the other hand, are frequently euphoric and overconfident. They feel *better* than usual. If you suggest that they may be "high" or speeding, they will become angry and respond that you're just too slow. If they can be persuaded to take medication, they will likely complain that they feel like the brakes are on. Feeling slowed down, they may go off their medications.

Manic men are especially hard on their caregivers. They are hyperactive, up day and night, irritable, and likely to act out aggressively or sexually. Their uninhibited behavior usually causes embarrassment for loved ones and sometimes gets them into legal difficulties. Their impaired judgment and grandiosity may lead to their running up huge bills, even bankrupting the family.

The key to treating a manic man is to catch the symptoms early. This feat is largely up to you, his caregiver. You are living with him and are able to pick up the subtle signs that you have learned to recognize as the indicators that the he has begun to switch into mania. These precursors to the full-blown illness may include sleep disturbance, increased irritability, rapid speech, extravagant ideas, hypersexual behavior, over-confidence, increased spending, or other subtle changes. In my experience it is the gut feeling of the spouse or close friend that is often the earliest clue that the patient is about to switch into a manic episode.

> **The key to treating a manic man is to catch the symptoms early.**

In addition to early detection, it's critical that your man be able to trust and listen to you when you tell him he is starting to have symptoms. He must also follow your advice to contact his doctor about a medication adjustment. If the mania progresses beyond this point, it is difficult for anyone to reason with him or for him to accept his need for help.

All manic patients have tremendous energy. They are grandiose and overconfident in their thinking. They are fixed on irrational goals and don't change course if their goals do not work out. They are extremely impulsive and lack social restraint. Their judgment is impaired. They become irritable when confronted with their symptoms. They are reluctant to take medication or accept professional help. When a manic episode subsides, they have amnesia around the events of their mania and are embarrassed when told of their behavior. They are upset by the money they spent and their lack of social restraint.

Once you get professional help, the first task in treating a man with bipolar disorder is to prevent and control his manic mood swings. This involves minimizing the use of antidepressants, and the employment of mood stabilizers and possibly antipsychotic medication. A secondary task is to attempt to control the depression that frequently occurs when the manic episodes are dampened. A significant number of treated bipolar patients continue to have a smoldering residual depression (dysthymia) or continued major symptoms of depression.

The spouses of some bipolar men find themselves at their wit's end. Some obtain power of attorney over their husband's finances to prevent ruin. These wives live in fear of another manic episode because of the relational, legal, financial, professional, and social problems that inevitably result. They describe their exhaustion trying to keep up with manic men, who may be up day and night ranting about their grandiose ideas and plans, often with heightened irritability and impulsive aggressiveness. One wife reported that when she confronted her husband with his hyperactivity, he took a bayonet and punched holes in their family car while telling her that she could be next. It is difficult to help a depressed man accept assistance and to support him through his recovery, but it is even more trying to help a bipolar man through a period of mania.

Seasonal Affective Disorder (SAD)

A subcategory of bipolar disorder is known as seasonal affective disorder (SAD). This type of depression has its onset during winter months when the sky is overcast and daylight hours are limited; later, in the spring, those afflicted develop manic-like symptoms. Treatment includes using light therapy to extend the exposure to sunlight. It is important to obtain light sources specifically designed to treat SAD. These lights filter out harmful UV light and have a minimum of 10,000 lux of intensity. The website Mayo.com lists the characteristics to look for when purchasing a light source. Wellbutrin is the only FDA-approved antidepressant for the treatment of this disorder. I have observed that, on

> Sunlight appears to have a positive effect on nearly all patients suffering from depression.

gloomy and overcast days, my patients with classical depression seem to feel sluggish and down, while on sunny days these non-SAD patients tend to feel better. I have concluded that sunlight appears to have a positive effect on nearly all patients suffering from depression.

Dysthymia

Dysthymia is a milder, smoldering form of depression in which the sufferer is depressed most of the time for at least two years. He is never free of the depressed mood for more than two months. These men can continue to function at work but are in a constant funk and are unable to experience much pleasure in life. Some have recurrent episodes of classical depression, while between episodes they continue to experience a reduced intensity of depressive symptoms that are labeled dysthymia, or double depression. Men with this disorder begin to consider a state of partial depression as "normal."

I have treated a number of these men over the years; after they recover, they indicate that they had forgotten what it felt like to feel good. Indeed, they realize that they had been depressed for years rather than the few months they'd thought when they first came for help. Double depression is usually more resistant to treatment than other forms of depression.

The mnemonic for dysthymia is HE'S 2 SAD.

HE'S 2 SAD

Hopelessness
Energy loss or fatigue
Self-esteem is low
2 years minimum of depressed mood for most of the day, for more days than not

Sleep is increased or decreased
Appetite is increased or decreased
Decision making or concentration is impaired

Psychotic Depression

A proportion of depressed patients have delusional thinking in addition to their depressive symptoms. Their delusions may involve feelings of persecution, nihilism, guilt, or sinfulness. They may experience auditory hallucinations telling them they are worthless or command hallucinations telling them to commit suicide. This condition is known as psychotic depression or major affective disorder with psychosis. These men are more seriously ill and need to be observed closely for self-destructive behavior and potential hospitalization. Twenty percent respond to antidepressants, 20 percent to antipsychotic medication, and 85 percent to a combination of an antipsychotic and an antidepressant.

As we have seen, manic patients are frequently delusional. They have grandiose delusions, delusions of religiosity, and sometimes paranoid delusional thinking. They are, by definition, psychotic. Mood stabilizers and antipsychotic medications are used in the treatment of mania.

Adjustment Reaction with Depression

The terms *adjustment reaction, stress,* and *reactive depression* all refer to depressions that arise from a clear environmental stress. This is the type of depression most people think of when they think of depression. It is the psychological reaction to loss, helplessness, or some other stress that produces sadness, loss of confidence, and low self-esteem. As a caregiver to a depressed man, you are susceptible to developing this problem. It is the type of depression you can get from being in the vicinity of a clinically depressed individual for a period of time.

Sometimes what looks like an understandable reactive depression turns out to be a clinical depression that was precipitated by stress in a genetically predisposed individual. We used to classify depression as exogenous, meaning that it was caused by an outside stress, or endogenous if no outside stress could be detected. We treated exogenous depression with psychotherapy and the endogenous kind with medication. Now if patients with exogenous depression have the classic symptoms of depression, we treat them with medication as well, to good result.

The Confusing Course of Depression

As I've noted, depression follows an up-and-down course and is usually self-limiting, lasting six to nine months. If it isn't treated and controlled, however, the patient will most likely experience another episode. Given this roller-coaster course, depression often sneaks up on the sufferer. For example, he may wake up feeling down one morning, then feel a little better as the day goes on. He may think that he was just upset about some external stress he was dealing with at the time. The next day he feels okay in the morning, and he concludes that his self-diagnosis must have been correct. Then the following morning he is down again. In this way it is easy to progress to a severe state before he realizes something is wrong.

> Given its rollercoaster course, depression often sneaks up on the sufferer.

Typically there is first a disturbance of mood, which most men have difficulty recognizing and verbalizing. Then sleep is impaired—usually with the man waking up early in the morning and having difficulty getting back to sleep. He may notice a loss of energy. His appetite may become impaired. He becomes noticeably more irritable. He withdraws socially and reacts negatively to demands being put on him. He has difficulty focusing on tasks and concentrating and may think he is losing his memory. Nothing is enjoyable. He may experience a loss of libido. As the depression progresses he becomes increasingly irritable and withdrawn; ordinary activities become a painful effort, and he has to push himself to carry out the simplest tasks. His perception is selective. He screens out positive information and magnifies anything negative. He seems to be building a case that everything is hopeless and there is nothing to look forward to in the future.

As an outside observer of this process, you will see that he probably feels worse in the morning and a little better as the day progresses. You will also notice that while some days are better than others, there is a downward course overall; gradually the lows are becoming lower and the up times briefer.

Because of the recurrent and up-and-down course of depression, the patient and his outside observers may be fooled for a time as to the nature of his problems. He and they will likely blame outside events or other illnesses for the onset of his symptoms. Later, both he and they may attribute his recovery to an event, change in behavior, procedure, or medication that he undergoes or receives at around the time he seems to improve.

Why Men Are More Difficult to Diagnose

Men are less likely to seek help from caregivers and, because of their tendency to try to solve their own problems, males tend to self-medicate, hide their feelings, or rely on compulsive activities to relieve their depressive illnesses. They have difficulty recognizing or expressing their feelings. They tend to act out with irritability and anger rather than introspection and sadness when they become depressed. As a result, they present as having problems with alcohol, anger management, gambling, sexual indiscretion, or throwing themselves into work; some have physical complaints. They act out in self-destructive ways rather than expressing their feelings of hopelessness.

A number of sociological, psychological, and biological factors are behind these phenomena. John Gray in his popular book *Men Are from Mars, Women Are from Venus*, observes that men use language to express thoughts and ideas while women use words to convey emotions. John Lynch, Ph.D., and Christopher Kilmartin, authors of *The Pain Behind the Mask*, note that fathers are typically distant from a family; the primary caregiver is usually the mother. As a result, instead of identifying with the mother as do girls, young boys identify with what the mother is not. They imagine that the distant father is strong, rational, competitive, dominant, and restricted emotionally. They find models for masculinity in movie heroes like John Wayne, Clint East-wood, Charles Bronson, Chuck Norris, Steven Segal, Bruce Willis, and Vin Diesel. They want intimacy with their caregiver mothers but fear being engulfed or being labeled "mama's boys." They push away from their mothers but fear abandonment.

> Because of their tendency to try to solve their own problems, males tend to self-medicate, hide their feelings, or rely on compulsive activities to relieve their depressive illnesses.

Because of these influences, many men have difficulty admitting vulnerability—which they see as a sign of weakness. They struggle to recognize their feelings and, when asked how they feel, answer with their thoughts instead. Sometimes a male patient will ask me to tell him how he feels. I place my hands on both sides of my head, lean down, shut my eyes, and say, "There's a woman in the front row with a watch." The patient usually gets it—I am not a mind-reader.

Self-Medication

Men have difficulty expressing emotions other than anger. They think they have to be tough, competitive, independent, and unemotional—which means that the symptoms of their illness grow distorted in a number of ways. Frequently men drink, use drugs, or both to numb their painful feelings. Observers may note that their man is frequently intoxicated and miss the fact that he's depressed.

Some men get into dangerous relationships to relieve their melancholy. This may lead to rejection and embarrassment while the depression is undetected. Some men try to offset their depressed mood with the excitement of gambling, which leads to the stress of financial ruin. Others may work to the point of breakdown. All these self-destructive behaviors mask the underlying depression that is in fact behind the man's change in behavior. Most depressed men neglect their health, which can be seen as a passive form of suicidal behavior.

> Most depressed men neglect their health, which can be seen as a passive form of suicidal behavior.

Recent evidence suggests that biochemical factors may play a role in the ways men express depression as well. When serotonin levels are lowered in men, they become impulsive but not necessarily moody. When serotonin levels are lowered in women, they experience a depressed mood and increased cautiousness.

Irritability and Aggression

Men tend to become irritable and physically aggressive when they are depressed. This was demonstrated in the early 1970s shortly after lithium came on the scene in the United States. A study was done in which prison wardens were asked to identify prisoners who were periodically violent. Then these convicts were asked to voluntarily take lithium. To everyone's surprise, better than 80 percent of these men stopped their violent behavior. The investigators then interviewed the prisoners to ask them how they felt the lithium had affected them. One big, tattooed, rough-looking convict said, "It makes me philosophical." When asked to explain this statement, he said, "It used to be, when a guy bumped me with his tray in the lunch line, I would deck him — now I think about it."

A middle-aged businessman suddenly became so irritable and critical of his wife that she told him she was getting a divorce. This brought him up short. He apologized for his nasty behavior, adding that it was a symptom of Alzheimer's and that he had been hiding this from her. She forgave him and insisted that he see the doctor for evaluation and treatment. He complied. Neuropsychological testing, however, failed to reveal any memory problems. He was instead depressed. He thought he had Alzheimer's because of his difficulty concentrating, and his irritability was the product of his depression.

Physical Complaints

Because men give less verbal outlet to their feelings, they tend to develop physical symptoms that are expressions of their inner distress. I can attest to the validity of this observation. Years ago I took Tae Kwon Do classes; along with riding a motorcycle and marrying a younger woman, this was probably related to a middle-aged denial of my mortality. In any event, during the first two years of training my instructors would continually tell me to relax my upper body. I did not know what they were talking about. I thought my upper body was relaxed. Then, while working out on the heavy bag one day, my upper body became loose and I was able to hit with several times the force I had previously been able to generate. So *this* was what my masters had been referring to!

Following this breakthough in training, I found that even when I was at work in the hospital, I was able to identify the moment when my neck and shoulders began to tighten as I walked down the hall toward the psychiatric unit. I was anticipating that nurses and patients would be asking me questions, the phone would be ringing for me, and I would suddenly be overwhelmed by numerous demands for my attention. I found that if I took a deep breath and focused on one request at a time, I was able to keep my upper body relaxed.

Many men are not aware of the stress they are experiencing, storing it in their muscles and only registering aches and pains. Others may have hyperacidity and gastrointestinal complaints. Still others have hypertension and cardiovascular problems resulting from their suppressed feelings of distress.

One case of depression masking as a physical problem stands out in my mind. A middle-aged man went to his internist with complaints of stomach pain. The doctor took a history, did a physical examination, performed routine laboratory tests, and then ordered upper and lower gastrointestinal X-ray studies. All were negative. The patient continued to complain, and additional studies were performed. After a few weeks the man called his physician and said, "I'm sitting here with a loaded shotgun—either you do something about my stomach or I will." The internist referred the patient to my office as an emergency, and I admitted him to the psychiatric unit. He had all the classic symptoms of depression, but remained unconvinced of this diagnosis. He told me, "All I know is my stomach hurts." Because of the severity of his depression, his suicidal threats, and his desperation for relief, we gave him a series of electroconvulsive treatments. His symptoms, including his stomach pain, resolved quickly. "Now do you believe you were depressed?" I asked him.

"Well, you call it depression—I call it stomach pain," he answered.

One study suggested that up to 60 percent of individuals admitted to the hospital for gastrointestinal complaints had an underlying clinical depression. One year at the American Psychiatric Association's annual meeting, a panel of psychiatrists and gastroenterologists discussed this relationship and whether or not to tell patients they were receiving antidepressants.

The psychiatrists all said, "Just give them the antidepressants and tell them it's for their stomach." The gastroenterologists disagreed and felt the patients should be convinced they had depression: "Otherwise they'll go home and read their Physicians' Desk Reference and wonder why we're giving them antidepressants for their stomachs."

If you suspect depression and he is complaining of backaches, ulcers, headaches, tiredness, constipation, sleep problems, or appetite disturbance, chances are he's not in touch with his feelings of distress and is experiencing the physical manifestations of his suppressed emotions. This provides you with a means to help him receive professional help. You can say: "I know that you aren't feeling well, so I made an appointment for you with Dr. Jones. It's high time you got some relief from all the pain you've been bearing."Note that you didn't ask him about making the appointment. Depressed men have difficulty making decisions, and men have difficulty asking for help. You can bypass both problems by going ahead and scheduling

> Many men are not aware of the stress they are experiencing, storing it in their muscles and only registering aches and pains.

the date with the doctor's office. In addition, you should speak to the doctor's nurse with your concerns about depression. Of course you want your doctor to arrive at his or her own diagnosis, but you want the doctor to have the advantage of your observations as well—your depressed male will likely minimize his complaints during the appointment.

Alon Gratch, Ph.D., author of *If Men Could Talk*, notes that among depressed men, the communication of distress becomes distorted and difficult to recognize. Gordon Schulz, M.D., one of our local orthopedic surgeons, once asked me if pain could mask depression. I asked him what he meant and he said, "I saw a fellow recently with chronic, severe back pain. I operated on him, did a beautiful job, and completely relieved his pain. Then he became depressed. I was wondering if by relieving his pain I had uncovered his underlying depression."

I said, "I don't know, Gordon — did he become depressed before or after he got your bill?"

Women are better equipped to adjust to the death of a spouse than men. Widowers have difficulty getting along on their own. They are lonely but do not want to impose on their children or permit others to care for them. Some of these men develop psychosomatic illnesses or unconsciously aggravate existing physical problems to solicit attention from their doctors and family. They consciously deny any wish or need for attention and protest when their children offer assistance, but reluctantly accept both because they are physically ill. These men deny their depressive illnesses and their dependency needs. They focus on their physical complaints. The family physician may spot their depressive illness and the secondary gain of support and attention that accompanies their physical complaints.

> Depressed men have difficulty making decisions, and men have difficulty asking for help.

Compulsive Behaviors

Prior to the introduction of medications in 1970, patients who were depressed or bipolar frequently developed compulsive behaviors to cope with their illnesses. By scheduling themselves, they could push themselves to get going when they were depressed and keep themselves under better control when they were manic. This did not solve their problems or cure their illnesses, but the compulsive schedule helped them function better and decreased the negative effects of their illnesses on their lives. Men have the need to deny their vulnerability, deny what they perceive as feminine qualities in themselves, maintain their independence, appear strong, and be in control. It is not difficult to see how men self-medicate with alcohol and drugs as a way to take charge of their own problems when they begin to experience the pain of depression. Some employ less obvious behaviors to cope with their suffering. The compulsive behaviors listed below are some common ways that men attempt to control their depressive and bipolar illnesses today.

Chemical Dependency

Men think they are supposed to be tough, independent, and unfeeling. They solve their own problems and consider themselves to be weak if they complain or ask others for help. If they have a vague sense of discomfort, they take matters into their own hands and have a few drinks or take some pills to solve the problem. (It always seemed ironic to me that among men, sucking on a bottle is generally perceived as a masculine image.) There is a saying that captures the preference for self-medication over professional psychiatric treatment: *I'd rather have a bottle in front of me than a frontal lobotomy.*

Stinkin' Thinkin'

As with any irrational, compulsive activity, men attempt to rationalize their compulsive behavior using addictive logic. It is like the fellow sitting at the bar drinking. The bartender asks him why he spends so much time at taverns getting drunk. The man responds, "Because my wife doesn't understand me." The bartender asks what she fails to understand and the man explains, "Why I spend so much time at bars drinking." Anyone who has been around alcoholics for any length of time has seen this "stinkin' thinkin,'" as it is referred to in Alcoholics Anonymous.

I have seen a number of men over the years who have told me that they drink because they are anxious or depressed and, if I could treat their anxiety or depression, they would be able to stop drinking. I do not accept this premise. If I did, it would be up to me to make them feel comfortable enough to give up alcohol—which will never happen. I tell them that first they must abstain; then we will work on the anxiety and depression. When men abstain from pain medicine, they don't say "I am craving drugs." They say, "I have pain." When men are addicted to sleep medicine, they don't say, "I am hooked on sleeping pills." They say, "I can't sleep. I've got to get some sleep." The same goes for other drugs and alcohol. "You have to give me something to calm my nerves" is a frequent request from this group.

The tendency to self-medicate, of course, leaves your depressed man with two problems—depression and dependence on drugs or alcohol. Usually the chemicals selected have depressant effects themselves, which only increases the depth of his dysphoria; studies have shown that chemical dependency along with depression increases the risk of suicide by five times. Scolding him about his chemical abuse will likely elicit an angry, defensive response. Instead, schedule an appointment with your family physician for an evaluation of his sleep problems, his appetite problems, constipation, or any other physical complaint he has that would justify a visit. Tell the doctor's nurse in advance that you suspect he might be depressed and self-medicating. When the doctor prescribes an antidepressant for him, he or she will likely tell him not to drink or use drugs with it. The prescription bottle will also indicate that he is not to drink with the medication.

Mnemonics for substance dependency are ADDICTeD and WILD.

ADDICTeD

Activities are given up or reduced

Dependence, physical tolerance

Dependence, physical withdrawal

Intrapersonal (internal) consequences, physical or psychological

Can't cut down or control use

Time-consuming

Duration or amount of use is greater than intended

WILD

Work, school, or home role obligation failures

Interpersonal or social consequences

Legal problems

Dangerous use

If your man is unable to abstain, it may be necessary to explore detoxification in a hospital setting and a 12-step program. You might want to tell him, "I can tell that you haven't been feeling well lately. You don't seem to be getting restful sleep, and you seem to have to drink on a regular basis before bed. I made an appointment for you with Dr. Jones to see if he can help you."

If he denies problems with alcohol when he sees his doctor, the physician may point out that his laboratory biomarkers for alcoholism are elevated. Liver function tests (LFTs) and mean corpuscular volume (MCV) can suggest a heavy intake of alcohol. Discussing such results can lead to a discussion of his compulsive drinking habits.

Is He Addicted?

If you're worried that your man has a problem—he probably does. Here are a few of the criteria used by the National Institute on Alcohol Abuse and Alcoholism to determine if he is addicted as well as depressed:

- A man should have no more than four drinks a day and no more than fourteen drinks a week.

- Does he put himself at risk while drinking? Does he drink and drive?

- Has drinking caused problems in his relationships?

- Has it caused problems at work, academically, or with the family?

- Are there legal problems related to drinking?

- Has he been unable to stop?

- Has he been unable to limit his drinking?

- Has he developed a tolerance to alcohol, requiring more of it to achieve the same effects?

- Has he shown signs of withdrawal such as tremors, sweating, nausea, irritability, and insomnia when not drinking?

- Has he continued to drink despite having problems as a result of drinking?

- Is he spending lots of time drinking, thinking about drinking, or recovering from drinking?

- Has he spent less time on other matters because of drinking?

Compulsive Work

Compulsive work is a less obvious manifestation of depression in men. A recent public example of the differences in attitude toward men and women when it comes to work was demonstrated by the reaction to Sarah Palin's selection as the Republican candidate for Vice President. The media questioned her ability to parent five children and take on the work of Vice President. No man has ever been questioned in this regard. In our society hard work is valued, and the man who is a good provider is outwardly seen as doing his duty as a husband and a father.

The family living with the Type-A workaholic knows otherwise. Workaholics rationalize that they have to work hard to give their families what they want in life, but the families will tell you that they didn't ask for all the material rewards and they would rather have more time with the workaholic if they had the choice. Families whose workaholic men are in the helping professions sometimes feel their husbands and fathers devote more of their time and attention to their patients, parishioners and clients than they do to their loved ones at home. They are reluctant to complain because the professionals are doing good work.

Compulsive workers tell themselves they are able to enjoy the finer things in life because of their extra effort on the job, but they don't have time to enjoy much outside of their work. One executive who proudly described the expensive, crewed yacht he was able to maintain in Florida admitted that he hadn't used it in more than a year. "I've been too busy at work." When it was suggested that he might want to see a therapist to help him achieve more balance in his life, as to be expected the executive couldn't fit therapy into his busy schedule.

These men feel they can work their way out of any problem. When there is emotional stress, they take on more work. When there are demands for intimacy, they throw themselves into a project. When they start to become depressed, they increase their time and effort on the job. If you observe that your man is showing some symptoms of depression and has also increased his time at work, it may mean that he is attempting to cope with his suffering by increasing his compulsion. Addiction counselors have long noted that work is usually the last activity to become impaired by chemical dependency. When taking a history from an alcoholic, the addict will often say, "I go to work every day." In the same way, the depressed man will hang on to his job, which represents a good part of his identity and purpose in his life. When he finds it impossible to go to work, you know his depression has reached an advanced stage.

> These men feel they can work their way out of any problem.

Type-A workaholics seen in private practice tend to be counter-dependent, counter-phobic men who eschew psychiatric consultation. When they do arrive for help, they are usually in a state of total collapse. Surprisingly, many later report that they were thankful for their breakdowns, which led to changes that greatly improved the quality of their lives and relationships. I've treated Type-A patients who told me they were relieved when they had heart attacks—it permitted them to slow down and let others take care of them, and relieved them of their perceived roles as family caretaker.

As you likely know, it is difficult to intervene in these cases. Rather than confronting your man with the compulsiveness of his behavior, you might try to support his hard work by saying, "You've had to work very hard lately. I scheduled a checkup for you with Dr. Jones just to make sure everything's in good working order." Again, you know your man and how to approach him. Use your intuition to get him to the doctor.

I am not certain that Type As can be converted to Bs. After I had two open heart operations and several near-death experiences, I stopped doing hospital work, cut back my hours in the office, and stopped trying to micromanage the staff. I was bragging about how I had turned myself into a B when one of my patients pointed out, "You may have become a Type-B psychiatrist but you turned into a Type-A writer." I think he is probably correct.

Gambling

Gambling is another compulsive activity adopted by some men to avoid their depressive feelings and to seek the "high" that comes from winning. Of course, the stakes increase as it takes more and more winnings to achieve the same degree of euphoria as the first win. And as we all know, the odds are in favor of the house. Compulsive gamblers rationalize that they are having fun, that they might win and pay off their debts, and that it's just a way to relax. Their reasoning follows the irrational pattern of any addictive individual. Abraham J. Twerski, a psychiatrist and a rabbi who works with addicted individuals, wrote *Addictive Thinking: Understanding Self-Deception*. It describes the convoluted logic used by addicted individuals, which has its basis in perpetuating the compulsive activity.

One gambler in our area, in an effort to control his compulsion, had himself voluntarily restricted from all Illinois gambling boats. Then one evening, while intoxicated, he decided to go to Iowa to gamble. He did and won $40,000. When they did a background check on him before awarding the money, they found that he had restricted himself from gambling. He had, by mistake, gotten on an Illinois gambling boat thinking he was in Iowa! Naturally he was depressed. However, when we went over his history, he had been depressed for a considerable time; his gambling had been his way of trying to cope with his dysphoria. The inevitable financial losses explain and justify the painful feelings the depressed man is experiencing; of course he is depressed, he just lost a fortune gambling.

Sexual Indiscretion

Dangerous sexual behavior is a tough issue for the woman caregiver to accept. Nonetheless, it must be included because some men who become depressed cope with their pain by seeking intimacy with women (or men) other than their wives. Some studies indicate that men have sex just as often when they're depressed as when they're not, but find it less satisfying.

They may attempt to solve this problem by seeking a relationship outside of the marriage. They are hungry for affection and may seek to bolster their flagging self-esteem and self-confidence in impulsive, inappropriate ways. Think of Jack Nicholson in *About Schmidt*. Warren Schmidt is a lonely, recently widowed man who is befriended by a nice couple he meets. When the husband leaves the room, Warren exposes his vulnerability to the woman and then starts kissing her passionately. She is shocked and outraged by his behavior and throws him out of her trailer home. It is obvious that Schmidt doesn't realize how lonely and depressed he is. His neediness causes him to mistake kindness and friendliness for sexual attraction. Passionately kissing a married woman he just met is completely inappropriate. This is an accurate portrayal of the behavior of some depressed men.

> Some studies indicate that men have sex just as often while depressed, but find it less satisfying.

Depressed men may have unprotected sex with prostitutes or other individuals who are at risk for sexually transmitted diseases. This is another example of risky, potentially self-destructive behavior that is the product of their depressive illness.

Men who become involved in impulsive affairs are frequently self-medicating with sex. They are attempting to offset their feelings of weakness, vulnerability, and dysphoria by taking control of the situation,

Self-Destructive Sexual Behavior

A prominent married man in our community consulted with me years ago. He was fearful that someone might recognize him in our office and asked for an after-hours appointment. I complied. When he finally did come in to see me, he revealed that he had been frequenting the men's restrooms in public places and paying young male prostitutes to hug him. He felt guilty for what he saw as a bizarre compulsion that was repugnant to him. "If my wife and children find out what I'm doing," he said, "I would kill myself."

He had the symptoms of clinical depression and responded to antidepressant medication. Once he recovered, he had no urge to continue this dangerous behavior. His compulsion to seek out young men for affection appeared to be behavior that justified his suicidal thoughts and would have justified his taking his own life had he been discovered.

Another equally well-known man revealed that he had started to seek out and pay female prostitutes for sexual favors. He was embarrassed and guilt-ridden about his actions, which were totally contrary to his religious beliefs and lifestyle. He told me that he had a good marriage and that his wife and children would be devastated if they found out, adding that he could not understand his recent dangerous behavior, which he described as a compulsion. Like the fellow above, he was depressed, and after recovering from his depression, his compulsion to act out sexually stopped.

"solving" their problems by reinforcing their masculinity and offsetting their feelings of failure. Because of the loss of pleasure that accompanies depression, they are joyless, and they seek a remedy in sexual dalliance.

Just as the gambling losses above serve to justify depressive feelings, the guilt that accompanies unfaithfulness serves to justify the underlying dysphoria. There is a self-destructive aspect to this behavior as well. These depressed men may feel that they are no longer deserving of their family's love and respect and are unconsciously acting in a way that is likely to result in rejection and loss of favor by their family and loved ones.

In addition to the risks noted above, impulsive sexual acting out can put the man into a dilemma. Over the years I have seen male patients who got involved outside their marriages and then found themselves going back and forth between their wives and paramours. At home they are dissatisfied and long to be with their lovers. With their mistresses they feel guilty and want to return to their wives. Most of us have consciences that will not permit us to be in love with two people at the same time. There is a saying about golf being like a mistress: *If you don't take it seriously, it isn't any fun, and if you do it will break your heart.*

Passive Self-Destructive Behaviors

Other behaviors can put a man at risk of damaging his health, finances, and relationships. I have treated men who have been scrupulously honest and law abiding throughout their lives only to impulsively, in a lapse of judgment, break the law while depressed. You may also observe that your man has begun to engage in dangerous activities with little regard to his personal safety. He may take up sky diving, scuba diving, mountain climbing, motorcycle riding, or other chancy behaviors that are

> He may take up risky behaviors that are out of character for him.

out of character for him. At a more passive level, the depressed man may disregard his health. He may take up smoking or drink to excess. He may eat unhealthy foods. He may neglect looking after his diabetes, hypertension, or other chronic medical condition. In various ways the depressed man is playing Russian roulette with his life.

It has been noted that survivors of the Holocaust and prisoner-of-war camps frequently committed suicide or engaged in risky, life-threatening behaviors after they were released. It seems odd that someone who has survived the horrors of torture and imprisonment would put himself in danger after gaining freedom, but it is often the case. The suicides by combat soldiers in Vietnam appeared at first glance bizarre, because most of these men had been so long preoccupied with the wish to stay alive—when a unit was under fire, just standing up could result in death. In 2007 128 army soldiers took their own lives. For the first time since Vietnam, the army suicides surpassed the civilian rate (20.2/100,000 in the army versus 19.2/100,000 civilian). The Department of Defense reports that this alarming trend has continued with 140 active duty suicides in 2008 and 160 in 2009. After returning home, many of the individuals who made it through suffered from survival guilt—those close to them died while they lived. Many of these survivors were clinically depressed.

Your depressed man may be having self-destructive thoughts, and his risky behavior may be an unconscious, passive means of self-destruction. It is important to identify and obtain treatment for the underlying illness that is driving his self-destructive behaviors.

His Depression Will Be Hard on You and Your Relationship

One goal of this book is to help you recognize and understand depression. A second is to provide you with suggestions as to how you can best help and support your man while he recovers from his illness. Hopefully, this knowledge and guidance will reduce some of the stresses you are facing, but I realize that you are confronted with a very difficult task and I don't mean to minimize the problems you will be encountering. A third objective is to help you preserve your relationship and marriage. Men who are depressed are like the Hyde of Jekyll and Hyde. The fun-loving, kind, thoughtful, compassionate, energetic, loving man you married has gradually become a different person. You may be faced with a man you do not know. He may have become withdrawn, self-centered, irritable, negative, recalcitrant, and self-destructive. He may have adopted or increased his compulsive activities to the exclusion of everything and everyone else in his life. It will take considerable strength on your part to stay with him, to separate the illness from the man you married, and to take care of yourself through this ordeal.

> The fun-loving, kind, thoughtful, compassionate, energetic, loving man you married has gradually become a different person.

If his depressive illness drags on, it is likely that the two of you will require some counseling together after he recovers. At that time you can share with him how frustrating and difficult your caretaker role has been. Depression can tear a relationship apart or it can, in the long run, pull you together. A good deal depends on your taking care of yourself and not getting caught up in the bleak, hopeless vortex that accompanies this painful malady. It is important that you separate the illness from the man. In the next chapter we will discuss strategies for communicating with your depressed man.

CHAPTER THREE

What to Say and Not Say to a Depressed Man

How weary, stale, flat, and unprofitable seem to me all the uses of this world!
—*William Shakespeare*, Hamlet

Now that you have recognized that your loved one is suffering from depression, I'll discuss what you can say to him to help him get the professional care he needs and to support him through his recovery. I have organized the chapter around the symptoms of depression because this is, in the words of Winston Churchill—himself a depressed man—the "black dog" you are dealing with when you communicate with him.

Your Internal Conviction Is Extremely Important

Before you think about what is best to say to your depressed man, it is important to focus on your own thoughts and feelings about him and his illness. The information in the introduction to this book is meant to help you convince yourself that he has an extremely painful condition that will respond to medication and therapy. It is important that you believe this in your heart because, no matter what you say, he will detect your empathetic, positive attitude about his recovery. If you start to feel discouraged, take steps to look after your own morale and then read again the introduction of this book to recharge your motivation and optimism. Your certainty is important to your efforts to help your depressed man. You must be convinced that he has a treatable illness that is chemically based, most likely genetically determined, and from which he will recover. While you cannot fully appreciate the degree of torture he is suffering, you must realize that he is going through one of the most painful illnesses in existence. You must also be convinced that therapy will be good for him in many ways and that he will greatly benefit from admitting his vulnerabilities, learning to depend on others, and being able to identify and express his emotions. That you know and believe these things in your heart is more important than what you actually say to him. He will respond to your unspoken confidence.

> You must be convinced that he has a treatable illness that is chemically based, most likely genetically determined, and from which he will recover.

As a woman, you already know how to communicate with men. You are aware that men have fragile egos and are challenged when it comes to feelings. Throughout this book I give you examples of things to say to your depressed man. These are just suggestions that may stimulate your own thinking as to what would be best to tell him. It is more important that your statements consistently convey the main themes below. So don't think I have all the answers. I'll just try to point you in the right direction, and you take it from there.

No matter what specific words you use, you want to convey the following:

- You know he is suffering.
- He has a treatable medical condition from which he will recover.
- You love him.
- You will stick with him throughout his treatment and recovery.

It is also important for you to remember:

- The illness is an entity separate from him that causes him to think and behave differently.
- Men are insecure. Your respect is of great importance to your guy.
- He is the same person with whom you fell in love. He now has an illness. Try to keep the illness and the man separate in your mind.

Using Your Feminine Talents to Help Your Man

Most women are skilled at getting their message across to men in a non-threatening way. You know how to make men think they are making a decision that you have made for them. My wife, Deborah, is a nurse who works in our office. Part of her job is to accompany patients into the consulting room, check their blood pressure, weigh them, and write down their medicines. Next, she sits and asks them how the medicines are working, if they are having side effects, and how they are doing in general. Sometimes I catch up with her and am able to listen to her talking with a patient. It always surprises me how open patients are with her. They are able to express their feelings freely in her presence and then seem to pull themselves together and become more formal when they are communicating with me. We have discussed this over the years. She likes to point out that nurses catch all the flak and then, when the doctor comes in, the patients and family are all hunky-dory. There appears to be some truth to this. Of course many patients cry, express frustration and anger, and show their emotions talking with me, but it seems to be easier for them when they are with Deborah. She is an empathetic listener, but I think there's more to it than that.

Most children turn to their mothers for support when they have problems or are injured. A boy will cry on his mother's shoulder but pull himself together around his father. It is my impression that men find it easier to open up to a woman and to express their feelings to a woman than they do with another man. On the other hand, studies of young children have shown that boys will ignore directions from girls but listen to their male peers. It may be easier for him to accept direction from a male friend, relative, or physician.

Women are natural nurturers. You, and your sisters, are experienced at venting your feelings and not expecting or even wanting a solution for your problems. Listening nonjudgmentally is one of your vital skills. Men, on the other hand, tend to be goal-driven and think they have to jump in and try to solve the other person's problems. Make use of your ability to listen quietly, offering encouragement and support to your guy.

Men are taught to be stoic. It is unlikely that your depressed man will be able to easily vent his feelings, but he will listen. Your deliberate pace will make your comments more significant. Men with depression frequently have psychomotor retardation. You can almost see them straining to think and answer questions as they listen and then, with painful slowness, attempt to answer your questions. It is more effective for you to be patient and not jump in and finish their sentences for them. Active listening is difficult, but it tells the speaker that you find his words and thoughts important, and it can boost his self-esteem and self-confidence.

> It is unlikely that your depressed man will be able to easily vent his feelings, but he will listen.

You know that the only person you can really change is yourself. You did not get involved in the relationship with the idea you were going to remake him. On the other hand, borrowing a technique from behavioral therapy, it is possible to shape his responses and his behavior. Jeff Foxwor-thy describes how he discovered he was being trained when his wife said she was hot and he jumped up to adjust the temperature and then thought, *I'm not hot.* He goes on to relate how his wife called her mother to tell her of his trained response; the mother said she would pass the good news on to her husband, but she had mentioned to him that she was hungry and he went out to get her a sandwich. This is funny but true. You women do have the ability to train the men in your lives. It is unlikely that you are going to make much of a dent in your depressed man's negative thinking, but you can reinforce any move-ment he makes toward:

- Accepting help.
- Recognizing his illness.
- Being able to verbalize feelings.
- Being compliant with his medications and with treatment recom-mendations.

Anytime you observe him doing what he is supposed to be doing in treat-ment, tell him how proud you are of him, how much strength it takes to let others help him, how having the courage to do what the doctor says will lead to his recovery, and how some men don't have the courage to see a therapist, look at themselves, or seek help.

General Tips

Include the Following Elements in Your Statements

You love him. Love is powerful, and telling him you love him is never wrong. When he thinks he is worthless and when you, who know every-thing about him, still assure him you love him, this helps him believe that perhaps he is of value. Men are more likely to accept unsolicited direction from their spouses when they know it is given out of love. One recovering melancholic male patient told me, "I hated to force myself out of bed in the morning but I knew my wife had my best interests at heart and I tried to do as she asked."

You will be with him to love and support him for the duration of his illness. No matter how crabby and negative he may seem, he is afraid that you will leave him. He probably feels like a failure and a burden. You can tell him about your frustrations with his illness, but assure him that you will be loyal and supportive to him.

Use statements that separate him from his illness. You may choose to name the illness and speak of it as a separate entity.

He has a common, treatable condition and he will get over it.

You know that, unless you have suffered depression yourself, you cannot fully comprehend the depth of his suffering, but **you do realize that he is in great pain.**

His illness has a genetic component and is similar to most other medical conditions like hypothyroidism or hypertension.

You will assist him in getting the treatment he needs.

If it comes naturally to you, use humor to lighten things up and make your point.

You have probably been in the relationship for a period of time and know each other well. You have developed a style of interacting. It is best if you continue what is natural for the two of you when you attempt to help him with his depressive illness. If you normally tease each other, you can continue to kid him about his illness and recovery. If you ordinarily play jokes on each other, you can squirt him with a water pistol in the morning to get him out of bed. If you are typically a straight shooter, you may want to intervene at times with "tough love."

I have seen several depressed men whose wives were nurses. They reported that their spouses would kick them out of bed in the morning and insist that they get dressed and exercise. These women demanded that their spouses comply with their medications and the instructions from their doctors. All these men felt that their wives' actions were key factors in their recovery from depression. They knew their wives had their best interests at heart and saw their interventions as loving behaviors. As one fellow said, "I didn't like hearing what she had to say, but I knew she loved me and that she was telling me these things for my own good."

If you're a more passive and subtle type, hint at how attractive he is when he shows progress. Do whatever you can to help your guy understand that, for you, being a macho man means being able to admit his vulnerabilities, asking for help, letting others assist him, and learning to identify and express his feelings. He has grown up with the "boys don't cry" mentality. Help him understand that you are impressed by men who are strong enough to get in touch with their feminine side and flexible enough to change their behaviors. The point is, be yourself when you communicate with your guy.

> When he thinks he is worthless and when you, who know everything about him, still assure him you love him, this helps him believe that perhaps he is of value.

Accentuate the Positive

It is always better to begin any discussion with recognition of the other person's strengths. When a man is reminded that you love and respect him, he is more likely to see your suggestions as attempts to help him. Norman Vincent Peale talked about the sandwich technique in communication. You compliment your man, then make suggestions as to how he could make a change, and finish up with another positive statement about him.

In my practice, I know that if I lead off with what the patient perceives as a negative statement, it is unlikely that he will open up and tell me much. For example, if I'm seeing a new patient, I don't begin with "I understand you've been staying in bed much of the day." Instead I say that I've heard he's a successful farmer and a highly respected member of his church. I tell him that Dr. Jones thought a lot of him and called me personally to make sure that I was going to see him right away. I add that Dr. Jones wants me to give him a report and to keep in close contact with him throughout his treatment.

As a woman who is used to talking to men, you probably know these things, but it is important to let him know that you appreciate his many talents and abilities. It never hurts to bolster a man's masculinity. Reassure him that you know he is a strong, potent, capable man who is currently suffering from a painful but treatable illness.

Be a Good Listener

Try to remain calm and nonjudgmental in making your interventions. Remember, most depressed men are very critical of themselves and feel guilty for their inability to overcome their illnesses through willpower and determination. As a result, they are very sensitive to perceived criticism from others. Most men dislike being in a dependent situation and hate to feel babied. Therefore, try to keep your tone neutral, uncritical, and nonsolicitous. Women are better than men at being able to listen empathetically without trying to offer solutions.

One reason men avoid emotionally charged topics is that it takes them a long time to settle down when they become stirred up emotionally. Women have learned to soothe themselves quickly; some authors think this may stem from breast-feeding and staying calm with one's baby. If he does talk, do not overreact to his statements or he will likely avoid these topics in the future.

For example, if he says he sometimes gets chest pains, stay calm and make a mental note to tell the doctor's nurse and to get him to the doctor—but don't get excited or you won't hear about his chest pains in the future. If he says your parents or the children tick him off, just listen and remember that you're trying to find out what's going on in his head; you won't learn anything further if you react. If he feels that he is supporting everyone else in his life and no one respects him or cares about his feelings, don't tell him that no one asked him to do this—just listen and make it easy for him to keep telling you what frustrates him. If he gets into a tizzy over the mortgage payment or taxes,

> Most men dislike being in a dependent situation and hate to feel babied.

remain calm and listen. Remember, your goal is to encourage him to express his thoughts, concerns, and frustrations to you. Interrupting, reacting, changing the topic, or anything that stops the flow of his verbalizations will likely impede future communication between you.

"Tell me how you feel" is a sure way to shut off whatever topic he is trying to communicate. Think of it as an emotional stiff arm. This is something that new therapists have to learn. When patients bring up a topic that is uncomfortable for novice therapists, they frequently will say, "Tell me how you feel"—which causes the patient to move on to something else. So, just listen quietly and empathetically to whatever your guy chooses to tell you.

Feel Your Way

You may have to feel your way as you intervene to help your man. Martial arts teaches its practitioners not to meet force with force but to guide the opponent's energy where you want it. Your guy is not your opponent, but this is what I mean when I say feel your way. Do not argue or get into a struggle for control with him. Women's intuition is the female ability to pay attention to unconscious, right-brain hunches. Use this gift when interacting with your depressed man.

If you feel your man reacting negatively to your comments, back off and take another tack. You know him well and can use your judgment in this regard. For example, if you begin by saying, "You don't seem yourself recently. You aren't sleeping, you don't seem to have much appetite, and everything seems to be an effort" — and you sense that your man is withdrawing and building up resistance as you speak — drop this approach and adopt another. You may want to wait a bit before attempting to intervene once more. If he declines your suggestion to socialize or to go for a walk, tell him that you understand and you can see that he has not been feeling up to par. Then tell him you have made an appointment with the family physician to evaluate his loss of appetite and decreased energy. Try to tie your goal of getting him into the doctor to his apparent needs.

> If you feel your man reacting negatively to your comments, back off and take another tack.

Even if you do everything right, you are likely to become a target for his frustration and anger. Chances are he'll let you have it when you encourage him to exercise, eat healthy foods, get out with others, see the doctor, take his medicines — anything that forces him out of his state of withdrawal. If you have to say something he might find objectionable, blame the pros — it's why we get the big bucks. You are with your guy 24/7. You will probably see the professionals less than one hour a week. If your guy has to be ticked with someone, let him be irritated with doctors and not you. You might say, for example, "Dr. Jones said it was important for you to take your medicines at the same time each day. I'll put your medicines in a pillbox and remind you." Or, "I read in Dr. Bey's book that it helps to go for a daily walk—I'll go with you." (If he has a sense of humor, you can add, "Dr. Bey said to hit you with the book if you didn't follow his advice.") Or, "Dr. Jones's nurse said it is good for you to shower every day." Or, "Dr. Jones and his nurse both told me that it was my job to see that you were up, dressed, with your teeth brushed by 8:00 a.m."

> If you have to say something he might find objectionable, blame the pros—it's why we get the big bucks.

Remind him that you love him and are on his side. You chose him and are on his team. Studies reveal an increased divorce rate in couples where one partner is depressed. The stress of depression can tear a relationship apart or bring you closer together. Make sure it is the latter in your relationship. Emphasize that you are going to work together to get the right treatment and to help him recover from his illness. You might say, "I know it is difficult for you to do everything the doctors recommend, but we're a team. I'll do everything I can to support you and help you follow their suggestions."

Depression affects concentration. Your depressed man isn't capable of much abstract or philosophical thinking, so keep your interventions simple and concrete. A severely depressed man cannot follow the instruction to clean the kitchen, for example, so you have to break the task down into steps. "Empty the garbage and then put a clean sack in the pail. Wash out the sink. Pick up the dishes and silverware, rinse them and then put them into the washer. Put soap in the dishwasher and then turn it on."

> The stress of depression can tear a relationship apart or bring you closer together.

Touch him when you speak. He may pull back, but a loving touch is healing. Think of yourself as a conduit of affection. He may think he is undeserving of your attention, but he wants it just the same.

Separate the Illness from the Man

For your own mental health and for the sake of your relationship, try to keep the illness separate from him as a person. We will discuss this further in Chapter 12, but you need to separate the illness from the man in your own mind. You can be frustrated and angry with the illness, but not with the man.

Having said this, you do need to tell him your boundaries and let him know which behaviors you will tolerate and which you will not. If he says, "You don't understand what it is like to be depressed," you can respond, "From what I've read, depression is one of the most painful illnesses in existence. I admit I can't possibly comprehend what you're experiencing, but I love you and it hurts me to see you suffer. Is there anything I can do to help?" If he says (because he feels unlovable), "I don't think you really love me," you might respond with, "Your depression may make you think you're unlovable, but I assure you this is not the case and I do love you." As I've mentioned, Winston Churchill referred to his own depression as "the black dog." You might mention this and use it to personify the disease afflicting your guy: "Winston Churchill called his depression a black dog. It looks like the same dog has you. That hound always growls at me when I try to get you up in the morning."

Try to keep the ball in his court. When men are frustrated, they tend to blame and react with irritation toward those closest to them. You may recall reading how men in the Middle Ages burned "witches"—women they accused of putting sexual thoughts into their minds. Kings blamed their wives for not giving them sons. I read a newspaper clipping some years ago about an elderly man who shot and killed his wife for making him impotent. It is likely that your man will be sensitive about the limitations imposed by his illness and his inability to overcome the symptoms of depression. Instead of defensively reacting to his anger, try to empathize with his situation. Remember that it is the illness and not your guy talking most of the time. Talk about how badly he must feel, how frustrating it must be for him—rather than what a jerk he's being toward you.

> For your own mental health and for the sake of your relationship, try to keep the illness separate from him as a person.

Use "I" Statements

It is okay for you to let him know how his behavior affects you, but you want to communicate this information in a way that will not cause him to become self-protective. The well-known family therapist Virginia Satir developed the technique of using "I" statements to reduce defensiveness in communication. You are the only one who knows how you feel, and you are never wrong when you begin a statement with *I feel*. More important, you are sharing your feelings but not accusing him. For example: "When you go to your room and pull the covers over your head, I feel rejected—that you don't want to be near me. But I do understand that you're doing this because of your depression, and that I shouldn't take it personally." Or, in the case of a public display of rude behavior, "When you criticized me in front of our friends last night, I felt hurt and embarrassed. Intellectually, I realize that you are depressed and frustrated, but it was painful for me nevertheless." Or to express your frustration when he defeats your efforts to help him, you might say, "When you ignore my requests that you get up and out of bed, I feel helpless and defeated. In my head, I know you're not rejecting my help; you're overwhelmed by your depression, and everything is a huge effort for you. It still makes me feel a little down, as though my efforts are for nothing." Remember to be yourself and use your own words. If it feels more natural to say, "I know it is your illness that makes you come across as a butt"—then do so.

> Point out and reward any positive behavior. At the same time, ignore any negative statements or actions.

You can be therapeutic in your interaction with him without becoming his therapist. Depressed men have negative filters. Cognitive-behavioral therapy (CBT) tries to change the negative thoughts into positive ones. You can conduct a type of CBT at home. Point out and reward any positive behavior. At the same time, ignore any negative statements or actions. "I enjoyed being with you on our walk this morning. I could see that you were making an effort to be more positive in your thinking." "You thanked me when I got your coffee this morning. It may seem like a little thing, but I appreciated the fact that you recognized my effort on your behalf." Your goal is to reinforce his positive behaviors and shape his overall behavior in an affirmative direction.

You want to reward any efforts in which he demonstrates he is trying to change the independent, stiff-upper-lip, John Wayne role that most men adopt. If he admits he is vulnerable in any way; if he makes an effort to recognize and express his feelings; if he is compliant with treatment; if he allows you and the professionals to help him—these are all positive changes that you want to recognize and reinforce. Praise him for his hard work. "I am so proud of you for having the strength to share your feelings with me. I know that it's difficult for you to do this, but it's important to me because it tells me that you trust and care for me. It also shows me that you're man enough to let others help you when you need it."

Depression is an illness that has plagued humankind since the beginning of recorded history. The current view is that it is a genetically determined, chemical imbalance that can best be controlled with medication and cognitive-behavioral therapy. In my opinion, this is the most acceptable explanation to convey to your loved one, because it describes depression as an inherited disease that is out of his control. It is similar to most medical illnesses—a problem that can be treated with medication. To a self-critical man who is suffering, unable to make a decision, and concerned with the stigma of mental illness this is, pardon the pun, the easiest pill to swallow. Because of this, I have not included a balanced discussion of the scientific evidence to justify or deny this assertion. I want you to have one single-minded message you can repeat to your melancholic male that will encourage him and help restore hope for his eventual recovery.

Organize a Team of Helpers

A key step to your depressed man's well-being—and your own— is to organize a group of helpers to share the burden of supporting him throughout his recovery. Think of a tree with one root. If something happens to that source of nurturance, the tree is in trouble. Now think of yourself as that tree. The more sources of support you have available, the stronger you will be, and the more stress you will be able to weather.

From the beginning you need to involve others in the task of helping and supporting your depressed man through his recovery. Who are the family members, fellow workers, church members, and friends you can enlist to assist you with this task? What professionals (family physician, minister, psychiatrist, therapist, and so on) can you count on to help? You will need others for backup to spell you and give you support as you help him recover from his depressive illness.

Responding to the Specific Symptoms of Depression

In the previous chapter we reviewed the classic symptoms of depression to help you identify them in your depressed man and to help you organize the observations you share with professional caregivers. I will again present these symptoms but with the focus on how they may impact on your relationship with your depressed man and some suggestions as to how you might respond to him.

Negative Perception

A depressed man thinks his brain isn't functioning properly, but if you gave him an intelligence test, he'd do fairly well. His concentration and speed of performance are impaired, but his cognitive functioning is pretty much intact. What *is* off is his perception. Depressed men have a distorted view of the world that borders on delusional. This is frustrating for caregivers attempting to cheer them up. If you say: "You're a great person and you have a bright future," he thinks—and may respond: "You're just trying to baby me."

An example of this alteration in perception was demonstrated by a professional who was also a friend and a depressed patient of mine. He asked to see me on an urgent basis and then reported that he'd ruined his family financially. He felt his only option was to commit suicide and leave them the life insurance money. I pointed out that he had most of the symptoms of clinical depression and suggested that he wait until he recovered before drawing conclusions about his finances. He responded, "You don't know anything about business." I conceded that this was no doubt true, but insisted I did know something about depression. My friend acquiesced, but refused to consider

> Depressed men have a distorted view of the world that borders on delusional.

psychotherapy. He did agree to a prescription. Within weeks he'd recovered from his depressive illness. When he felt better, he was able to see that the financial stress he'd reported as disastrous was, in fact, nothing more than his yearly property tax bills for some rental properties he owned. The bill had been essentially the same in previous years, but he wasn't depressed then. This year he'd convinced himself that he was ruined and that his family would be better off without him.

Later, I was able to convince him to see a clinical psychologist for therapy. I ran into him as he was leaving his counselor's office and asked him how treatment was going. "I think I'm helping him," he responded. Being the true counter-dependent individual that he was, he thought he was giving his therapist helpful advice!

You may want to encourage your man by saying, "I cannot imagine what you are going through with this illness, but I think you can do a little more than what you are doing." This doesn't sound like a positive intervention, but it is. You are conveying that you feel your man is capable of performing at a higher level than he is currently, and that you are confident he'll do better.

When your man seems to be withdrawing into a couch potato, you might say, "I read that exercise helps speed recovery and distracts from the pain of depression—let's take a walk together." In this way you will be encouraging activity and reminding your guy that you will be there to love and support him until he recovers from his illness. You might note, "I read where one psychological approach to depression involves having the patient try to change negative thoughts into positive ones. As an experiment, how about trying to do this—just to see what happens? It can't hurt, and it might help."

Some depressions reach psychotic proportions and are accompanied by delusions and hallucinations. The former are false beliefs that are not altered by logic; the latter are sensory misperceptions with no outside stimulus. If he has delusions that he is causing bad things to happen, you can tell your man that these are symptoms and that he's not powerful enough to produce disasters. Ask him to tell you when he is hearing voices, and ask him what the voices are saying. If they are command hallucinations, you need to be more alert and warn him not to do what the voices tell him to do. Of course, if psychotic symptoms are present you need to immediately tell professional caregivers.

Do not try to confront your depressed man with reality. Instead distract him and encourage healthy activity in another area. For example, "I know that because of your depression you can only see the negative and that you're extremely critical of yourself, but I do think you could be doing a little more than you are doing. Put on your jacket and come for a walk with me—there's plenty of time to beat yourself up later." You also might say, "I read that depressed patients have irrational guilt and tend to blame themselves for everything. Just remember that you are ill and that what you are thinking and feeling right now is a symptom of your depressive illness. When you recover you won't know how you could think these things."

Social Withdrawal

Depressed men withdraw socially. They do not want to answer the phone, answer letters, respond to e-mails, or visit with family and friends; they lack the energy required to meet the demands of social interaction. One benefit of talking with others is that it forces the depressed man to get his thoughts off himself and distracts him from his pain. For this reason, it is generally a good idea to encourage him to interact with other people. You might say something like, "I know you don't have much energy right now and it's an effort to smile and be social, but it will help you to get your mind off the negative thoughts and self-criticism that make you feel bad. Besides, everyone misses you."

Extroversion versus Introversion

Social withdrawal is a symptom of depression because it requires energy to smile and interact with others. If your man is by nature introverted, however, he may have always had to withdraw to build up his energy for social interaction. Extroverted men, on the other hand, get their energy from others and may benefit more from encouragement to join with others in groups and collective relations.

Irritability

Your depressed man is probably self-centered and irritable. Although these are annoying symptoms for you to deal with as a caregiver, it is best to bite your tongue to keep from responding in kind. These symptoms should not be surprising. When we are ill, we have little patience or energy to deal with the demands of others. He is preoccupied with his pain and suffering. He magnifies the negative and screens out the positive. He's critical of himself and frustrated by the limitations imposed by his illness. As a result, he may react angrily to any perceived demand or criticism. If you are able to use humor in your relationship and you have named the depressive illness, you might want to remove yourself from his presence for a while. For example, "That black dog depression of yours just bit me again—I'm going to go out for a walk until he settles down a bit."

> He magnifies the negative and screens out the positive.

Obsessive Rumination

Some behavioral psychologists use a technique called thought stopping. They encourage the patient to ruminate with his eyes closed; the therapist then shouts, "STOP!" The patient is usually surprised. The therapist then has the patient put a rubber band on his wrist and snap it while telling himself "stop" to interrupt his ruminating thoughts at home. You may try this technique to interrupt your man's obsessive thinking.

One wife of a depressed man said that she found it helpful to have her husband listen to and repeat positive affirmations. They did this together in the morning. She had him watch comedies on DVDs and listen to comedians on tapes and on the radio—and to avoid news broadcasts. She also encouraged him to do positive self-talk. Another wife said she suggested her husband limit the time of his negative rumination. When he complained he couldn't get out of bed in the morning, she responded, "Okay, you have until 10 a.m. to lie there and think negative thoughts, then we are going out for a walk and try to think positively."

Sleep Disturbance

Sleep disturbance is an early symptom of depression. You can use it in your efforts to get your loved one to help. You may suggest that you consult with your family physician to see about something to help him sleep. You might say, "You need your rest. I'm going to make an appointment for you with Dr. Jones to ask him for something to help you sleep." Some depressed men sleep too much. I once had a man suffering from atypical depression tell me, "I sleep pretty good at night and in the afternoon, but mornings I just toss and turn."

One wife told me that she encouraged her husband to write down all the things he felt thankful for each evening before going to bed. She helped him with this task. She said he had a tendency to be thankful for things he did, such as helping a neighbor remove a tree from his yard. She reminded him that there was more to be grateful for than actions. He could be thankful for being healthy enough to be of help to someone else, he could be grateful for having a tractor to facilitate the task, he could be appreciative that he was allowed to make life easier for another person. She reported that, after thinking of his blessings each day, he was able to get to sleep without the negative rumination that kept him awake in the past.

Appetite Disturbance

Another vegetative symptom—meaning one controlled by the primitive limbic system of the brain—is appetite. Typically depressed men experience anorexia and weight loss. Atypical patients may overeat and gain weight. Again, this symptom provides an opportunity to get your loved one to the family physician for help. For example, "You've lost ten pounds over the last two weeks. I've made an appointment for you with Dr. Jones to ask him to give you a good checkup." Or, in the case of weight gain, "You've been tired and put on some weight in a short time. I got you in with Dr. Jones to check your thyroid and your heart."

Indecision

As the depression deepens, you will observe your man's inability to make a decision. Depressed individuals cannot make choices. This is an important symptom to recognize because the natural tendency on the part of the caregiver is to give the patient choices. In this illness, instead of giving the individual a sense of control, it causes distress because he is unable to make up his mind. For example, it would not be a good idea to say to your loved one, "Would you prefer to see Dr. Jones or do you want me to set up an appointment with a psychiatrist?" A better option is, "I spoke with Dr. Jones's nurse today about your weight loss and problems sleeping. She can get you in at 3 p.m. I'll go along because I want to talk to the doctor and see if there's anything I can do to be of help to you."

> **Depressed individuals cannot make choices.**

Loss of Pleasure

The Greeks identified *anhedonia* as a symptom of depression. Depressed patients find that they are unable to have fun. Things that were ordinarily pleasurable are no longer sources of joy for them. This includes sex. While it's easy to feel that your irritable, withdrawn, unaffectionate mate has lost his love for you, it's important not to take these changes personally. They are symptoms of his devastating, but treatable, illness. You might say something like "I hate to see my sexy guy suffering so much. I realize that nothing gives you pleasure right now—but you will be able to enjoy yourself again once you recover. We can look forward to having fun together when that happens."

> **Depressed patients find that they are unable to have fun.**

Crying Spells

Most men have been taught early in life that crying is a feminine trait and that boys don't cry. It is not uncommon for depressed patients to tear up and cry with little or no provocation. This is particularly disturbing for males—especially men raised to be stoic and unemotional. Because of their negative perception, self-criticism, and guilt, they see this as further evidence of their inadequacy and weakness. You might say, "Naturally you are tearful—you are suffering from depression." If teasing fits your personality and is natural in your relationship, you might say, "Now you are getting to know what PMS is like—irritability and tears."

Hopelessness and Helplessness

As the depression continues, your depressed man may become increasingly discouraged until he reaches a point of feeling hopeless and helpless. His inability to pull himself up from the depths of depression causes him to feel powerless. Depressed patients paint themselves in a corner and convince themselves that there is no hope for the future. As we have seen, they magnify the negative, screen out the positive and build a case to justify their overwhelming

> Depressed patients convince themselves that there is no hope for the future.

despair. You can comment that this is a symptom of his illness that will fade away as he recovers. You can also maintain a positive, optimistic, hopeful outlook in your interaction with your loved one. Do not pull back; this will confirm to your partner that he's a burden to you and that you would be better off without him in the future.

Inertia

You have seen elderly men who appear unkempt, with poor personal hygiene and food stains on their clothing. Some may be suffering from dementia, but frequently these men are depressed. You may observe that your depressed man no longer seems to care about his appearance or hygiene. Encourage him to take care of the way he looks. You might say, "I know that everything is an effort for you right now because of your illness, but you'll feel better with a nice hot shower, a haircut, and clean clothes. Alcoholics Anonymous has a saying: *Fake it until you make it.* If you appear and act like you feel better, it may make you feel a little better."

Suicidal Thoughts

If your man loses hope, he may think about ending his life. It is common for depressed individuals to think of suicide. To paraphrase Nietzsche, the thought of suicide has saved many individuals. It reduces their immediate stress by reassuring them that they can get relief from their suffering. Suicidal thoughts are more serious among depressed males who tend not to talk about their plans and to act in a lethal manner when they decide to kill themselves. Family and professionals tend to avoid the topic because they fear they will be putting ideas into the patient's heads. If he says he's feeling suicidal, the caregivers aren't sure what to do next. I'll go into more detail on this topic in Chapter 10, but it is helpful to inquire about suicidal thoughts and plans. "When you get down, how bad is it? Do you ever think of giving up? Do you think of suicide? How would you do it?" Of course you would want to pass on any suicidal ideation to the treating physicians and get your loved one in to see them or to the emergency room if you feel the risk of self-harm is present.

If he has been through an episode of depression in the past, it will be helpful for you to remind him. Previous experience with depression and its successful alleviation can help you inspire hope and optimism in him. You might remind him of how different his thinking was before, during, and after his depressive episode. Help him recall how he had difficulty understanding how pessimistic and negative his thoughts were while he was depressed. Assure him that he recovered from his previous episode and he will from this bout as well. You might say, "Hey, you're a veteran. You've been through this before. Remember how you thought everything was hopeless and that everyone would be better off without you? When you came out of it you couldn't believe you'd been thinking that way. You recovered from it then and you will now. Just hang in there, it won't be long."

A Few Things *Not* to Say to Your Depressed Man

He is probably angry with himself for being depressed. He thinks he's weak for not being able to overcome his symptoms and snap out of it. If he is religious, he wonders what he has done or failed to do to deserve this suffering. He is frustrated by not being able to discover a reason for his condition. If you make a comment that reinforces any of these thoughts, you will add to his suffering and make him angry.

A man once bought a new Cadillac. He felt a little self-conscious, wondering if others might think he was trying to show off with this expensive car. As he was driving one day, a tire blew out. He opened the trunk to prepare to change the tire and saw that he had no jack. He had passed a gas station a few blocks back and decided to walk to the station and borrow a jack. As he walked he thought, *I'm going to walk in there an they're going to ask me what kind of car I have. I'll say "a new Cadillac" and they're going to wonder what sort of dumb guy buys an expensive car like that and doesn't check to see if there's a jack. They're going to look at me and say, "Who does that guy think he is buying a Cadillac?"* By this time he reached the station and the attendant looked up and said, "Can I help you?"

"You can keep your damn jack" the man replied and stormed out of the station!

Similarly, you may recall being late for class as a child. All the way there you were thinking how everyone was going to turn and look at you and how the teacher was going to scold you for being tardy. When you walked into the classroom with your head down, one of the kids said, "You're late." It is likely that you blew up in response, or at least inwardly fumed, because he was telling you what your conscience had been saying to you all the way to school.

Don't Try to Talk Him Out of His Misperceptions

Irrational guilt in depression qualifies as delusional thinking. That is, it's a false belief that is not altered by logic. Telling your loved one he's not guilty won't get through and will likely convince him you just don't understand his situation. "You have a nice house, a nice family, a good job

> Irrational guilt in depression qualifies as delusional thinking. That is, it's a false belief that is not altered by logic.

and a nice car—what do you have to get depressed about?" "If you would just get right with the Lord, you'd be fine." "Whenever I'm depressed I just whistle a happy tune." "You need to pick yourself up by your bootstraps and get going." "Every cloud has a silver lining." "When I was depressed I just made myself do things." All such comments will only add to his stress and probably elicit an angry response.

Remember: He's Ill and in Pain

Depressed men have little energy. They have to push themselves to get up and get dressed in the morning, and even simple decisions require painful effort. This is referred to as the inertia of depression. Every activity is a huge endeavor for a depressed man. In some cases even his thinking is slowed; when you ask him a question, his responses may be labored and delayed. This is known as psychomotor retardation. Because of their lack of energy, many depressed men curl up in bed and pull the covers over their heads. Their recovery time probably won't be shortened much by activity, but their suffering will be reduced. Think of depression as being similar to pain. If you can get your mind off pain, it doesn't hurt as much. If your man lies in bed ruminating on negative topics, beating himself over his head with irrational guilt, he will feel worse. At the end of the day, if all he has accomplished is to stay in bed, he will begin to convince himself that he is useless and a burden to his loved ones.

You do not want to tell him he is lazy or a wimp because of his inactivity. It's not helpful to point out how little he accomplished during the day. Telling him he isn't trying is counterproductive as well. It does little good and considerable harm to scold. Yelling at him to get out of bed and get going is not likely to achieve positive results. He is lying there thinking that he is weak, and this reinforces that notion. Similarly, telling him that he needs a "kick in the butt" is not motivational and may make him feel that he deserves punishment.

The important thing for you to remember is that loss of energy and inertia are symptoms of his illness. Don't take his angry comments personally. You might be tempted to say, "You ungrateful jerk! Here I am cooking, cleaning, taking over all the responsibilities while you curl up in bed, and then you have the audacity to criticize me or complain!" This would not be helpful. Later, when he has recovered, you will be able to vent some of your frustrations. (I

> It's not helpful to point out how little he accomplished during the day.

always tell depressed patients that they will know when they are fully recovered: Their loved ones will stop tiptoeing around them and will let them have it with all the frustration and anger they bottled up throughout the illness.)

Do Not Pull Away from Him

Because of his illness, your man is likely to be withdrawn, negativistic, and irritable. In fact, he's likely a pain to be around, and it would be odd if you *didn't* become fed up with him at times. Still, if you're tempted to blow up at him and point out how ungrateful and selfish he has been acting, this would only add to his feelings of guilt and worthlessness. Focus on the illness as an entity that is separate from him and that has him in its control. Be angry with it and not with him.

Much of his behavior seems aimed at driving you away. The worst thing you could do is withdraw from him, tell him how miserable he makes

> No matter what he says or does, he is in desperate need of your love and support.

you, or announce that you're leaving. No matter what he says or does, he is in desperate need of your love and support. Frequently when men appear the most unlovable, they have the most need for affection. If he picks up that he is hurting you, he may conclude that you would be better off without him; this could lead to his taking his own life. Again, recognize that it is the illness that's responsible for the hurtful remarks and frustrating behavior with which you are dealing, not your man.

You Are Walking a Tightrope

Never berate him for not being able to perform. Men are very sensitive to perceived failure. Caregivers often ask me how much they should push their depressed men. I tell them there is no simple answer. Every step toward more independence will elicit increased anxiety, while regression and withdrawal result in increased depression. You are always walking a tightrope. On the one hand, you want him to be as active as possible and to be distracted from his negative rumination. On the other, when you ask him to do something he is not capable of doing, he will see it as evidence that he is useless and a failure.

> Laughing at him will cause him great pain and suffering.

Humor can be helpful or harmful depending on your relationship and how you employ it. Never use humor in a way that can be seen as belittling his condition. Laughing at him will cause him great pain and suffering. Laughing at yourself or with him may be good for both of you.

→←

Now you have an idea as to the messages of love and hope you need to convey to your depressed man. Don't lie to him, but it's important that your interventions be empathetic, positive, and loving. In the next chapter I will turn to ways you can help your depressed man get to a professional for evaluation and treatment.

CHAPTER FOUR

How to Get Him the Help He Needs

It is well known that panic, despair, depression, hate, rage, exasperation, frustration all produce negative biochemical changes in the body.

—*Norman Cousins*

Men who are clinically depressed need to be evaluated and treated by a medical professional. You do not want his treatment to be delayed by his resistance to seeking professional help. Like most illnesses, depression responds more quickly and completely when discovered and treated in its early stages.

It's important for you to get your melancholic male to a medical professional as quickly as possible. To do so you will have to overcome or bypass his resistances to treatment. You may need to call on your team of other relatives, friends, church members, coworkers, and treatment professionals to assist you in your effort to get your male to a doctor.

Responses Your Man May Give You

Here are some of the resistances I have encountered over the years:

"There is nothing wrong with me."

Depressed men sometimes convince themselves that, if they drag themselves around every day, no one (including you) recognizes that they are depressed. When confronted with their depression, they respond, "There is nothing wrong with me." There are a number of reasons for this denial.

> Rather than pointing out that everyone else around him can see that he's depressed, focus on the symptoms that cannot be denied.

The man is usually unable to identify what is wrong. He may know that he isn't resting, his appetite is down, he is more tired, things bother him more than usual, and he does not seem to be able to find much joy in life. His solution may be to push himself harder at work, have more to drink, and try to avoid as many demands as possible. If the thought of depression does enter his mind, he probably thinks it's something that happens to women or to weak men. He probably doesn't believe that his problems can be helped by medication or seeing a doctor. Talking to a therapist would likely be perceived as useless and another demand on his time and energy.

Rather than pointing out that everyone else around him can see that he's depressed, focus on the symptoms that cannot be denied. "You haven't been sleeping and you've lost weight. I love you and I hate to see you in pain. I've spoken to Dr. Jones's nurse, and he will see you at 3 p.m. today to check you over and help you with your sleep and appetite."

"I'm not ill—I'm just depressed."

Many men fail to recognize that depression is an illness. He may tell you, "I'm not ill—I'm just depressed." Armed with your knowledge of depression, you can educate your partner about his having a chemical imbalance and the need for medication to correct the problem. You can tell him that depression is a malady similar to low thyroid, diabetes, or hypertension. The predisposition for it runs in families, and it is chemically based. Its symptoms can be controlled with medication, but it cannot be relieved by willpower or trying harder. It is similar to his entering a footrace with anemia. He will do better if he pushes himself, but he isn't going to win. You might add, "The bad news is that you are ill, but the good news is that it's treatable and it's not your fault."

"Do you think I'm nuts?"

If he asks you, "Do you think I'm nuts?" you may respond, "No, but I can see you aren't sleeping and that you're not rested in the morning. You've been losing weight, you appear to be in pain. I'm concerned because I love you." Rather than listing all the other depressive symptoms you observe, it is probably better to pick two physical symptoms that he can't deny—sleep and appetite. You can also assure him that no one thinks people with depression are "crazy" these days. It is an accepted medical illness that is controllable with medication. "There may be questions about the sanity of people who have a treatable illness but continue to suffer while resisting help, but I know you're not one of those people."

"I'm not a wimp."

Some men are particularly counter-dependent and counter-phobic. These tough guys are society's warriors. Included in this group are the elite troops of the military who fight at the tip of the spear. Many police officers, firemen, ironworkers, rodeo workers, and other strong, masculine individuals find it difficult to admit fear or a need to lean on someone else. If your man is the macho type, he may ask you, "Do you think I'm a wimp?" Even though we are in the "it's okay to show your feelings" era, there's still enough cowboy in most men's minds to make them think they're less than manly if they show their emotions or require help.

Macho men deal with fear with counter-phobic defenses. That is, if they are afraid of heights, they take up mountain climbing. The problem with this, from the standpoint of your efforts to help him, is that he may deny and resist acknowledging his depressive illness until he reaches the point where he is overwhelmed—and then completely collapse. We used to call this "the 101st Airborne syndrome" when I was an army psychiatrist. It appeared to us that many of the airborne troops were little guys who had a Napoleon complex. They were counter-phobic and counter-dependent. If you said, "Better watch it, this is a hot area and it might be dangerous"—they would charge right in. They would not seek medical assistance and certainly not psychiatric help until they were in such bad shape that they had to be carried in on a stretcher (or, in our case, strapped between two stretchers).

Recognizing that this macho factor is likely present in your loved one, you will want to emphasize the medical aspects of the depression and emphasize the lack of control he has over his symptoms. "The symptoms you have are like hypothyroidism or diabetes. You can't pull yourself out of this any more than you can make your thyroid hormones go up or your blood sugar go down. That's why we're seeing a physician. It's the doctor's job to give you something to treat this disease."

"Just leave me alone."

Your man may respond to your efforts to help him by telling you, "Just leave me alone." You may want to respond, "No, I can't do that, because I love you and you need help with your illness. I've spoken with Dr. Jones's nurse and you're scheduled to see him this afternoon at three. I'm going with you to hear the doctor's recommendations and to take notes so I can remind you what he said as you recover from your depression." In this way you are making the decision for him, as well as indicating that you love him and will be with him throughout his recovery.

Richard Pryor described how his friend Jim Brown came to help him when he was addicted to drugs. Jim just repeated the question, "What are you going to do?" while Richard answered with his irrational, drug-addicted logic that he was going to be alone with his pipe doing the same thing he had been doing. Jim repeated his question, "What are you going to do?" Eventually it began to dawn on Richard that if his behavior did not change, nothing else was going to change in his life.

"No one can help me."

Your loved one may feel hopeless and may tell you, "Nothing can help." Your response to his nihilism might be, "That's your depression talking. I know you're suffering and, because of your depression, you feel hopeless, but this is a symptom of your illness and it'll fade away as you recover. Dr. Jones has treated many patients with similar symptoms, and he'll be able to help you as well. You know you aren't sleeping well and your appetite is off. Let's get you checked out and ask him for something to help you feel better."

"People will see me at the psychiatrist's office and gossip about me."

Another common response to depression is embarrassment and concern about confidentiality. He may say, "What if someone sees me in the psychiatrist's waiting room?" If this is his resistance, tell him that mental health professionals do all they can to protect their patient's confidentiality. People seeking help are preoccupied with their own problems and are not worrying about who else is there. You might also say: "They're in the waiting room because they're seeing the same counselor. They're probably worrying that you're going to gossip about *them*."

Picking the Professional

The best-trained medical professional to evaluate and treat your guy is a psychiatrist. Evaluating and treating individuals with depression is their bread and butter. However, the majority of men these days are first seen and usually treated by their family physicians. Only one-third of patients treated for depression are treated by psychiatrists. Why?

- Men usually know their family physicians and trust them to help them with their medical problems.
- Family physicians evaluate and treat two-thirds of patients with depression. They are familiar with the illness and are used to taking care of patients who suffer from it.
- Some physical problems may have symptoms resembling depression. It's prudent to have a good physical evaluation at the onset of treatment to rule out these infrequent causes of melancholia. (Occult cancers, anemia, hypothyroidism, Addison's disease, mononucleosis, and others fall into this category.)
- Current antidepressants are effective, have few side effects, and are able to control depressive symptoms within a few weeks in most cases. I joke with my male patients that I try to make the illness complicated because I'm a specialist and want to justify my exorbitant fees, but the typical patient goes to the family doctor who hands him the last drug sample left by a drug rep and he gets better. For most depressed men, it is as simple as that.
- Mental illness, including depression, carries a stigma. Patients are often denied insurance benefits when they report they have seen a psychiatrist. Most male patients are comfortable going to their family physicians for evaluation and treatment but uncomfortable and resistant to seeing a psychiatrist they do not know. If family physicians later refer an individual to a psychiatrist, they must be careful to let the patient know that they intend to continue to follow him and are merely enlisting the assistance of a specialist in order to provide the best care (otherwise your guy may feel that the family doctor has given up on him or does not wish to see him because he's "crazy").

Having said this, it is a judgment call for the caregiver whether you take him to his family doctor or go directly to a psychiatrist. You know what would be more acceptable to your loved one. Some individuals do not have a relationship with a primary care physician, and some feel more confident going to a specialist. Go with whichever you feel would be easier for your guy, but you make the decision.

If you decide on a psychiatrist for the initial contact, check with your physician, your clergyman, and people you know who have had treatment to try to determine the best psychiatrist for him. Accompany him to the appointment and introduce yourself to the doctor. Have your loved one sign a release so that you can keep in touch with the psychiatrist throughout his treatment. Ask if you can participate when the psychiatrist makes recommendations for treatment, and take notes so you can support these suggestions with your man in the future.

If you decide that it would be easier for your partner to first see his family physician, call the physician's nurse prior to the visit to discuss the purpose of the consultation. It will be easier if the doctor is forewarned

Take Advantage of Television Advertisements

Physicians are divided as to whether drug companies should advertise their products directly to consumers. In the case of depression, it might be helpful. Ads for sleeping medications, for example, might be pointed out to your depressed man and utilized to get him in to the family doctor. You might say, "Look, dear, they have a new sedative that's supposed to be safe. Let's ask Dr. Jones if he could prescribe some for you so that you can get a full night's sleep." Antidepressants are advertised as well, and you can note how his symptoms resemble those described in the ads: "Did you see that? Insomnia, appetite problems, tiredness, and pain—all symptoms you've been having—are helped by that drug. Let's check with Dr. Jones and see if he thinks it would help you."

that while your loved one is coming in for help with sleep problems and weight loss, for example, the main concern is depression—which he is unlikely to bring up. Tell the nurse if your guy is feeling embarrassed or self-critical about needing help with depression. It won't hurt to have the physician reassure him as to how many depressed patients he or she treats daily. Go with him to the appointment and, again, ask if you can be present and take notes when the doctor gives recommendations for treatment. Again, have your guy sign a release so you can communicate with the doctor throughout his treatment and recovery.

> It is a judgment call for the caregiver whether you take him to his family doctor or go directly to a psychiatrist.

In either case, you will need to take the initiative when it comes to making appointments. He is probably in no shape to make decisions, make appointments, describe his symptoms, or ask for help. In addition, he is resistant to the idea of having a problem that requires professional help. You will need to step in and take over these tasks.

Take Notes at Home and at the Doctor's

A written record of your observations at home will be helpful to the professionals—and to you as well. You will be able to document and point out progress to your man. In addition, you will have a summary of your observations and his reports over a period of time, which will be useful to the treating professionals. Bring to the doctor's office your observations of the changes you've noticed in him and a list of his current medications. Note any alterations in his sleep, appetite, concentration, energy level, irritability, moods, energy level, daily routine, and thought processes, and especially any evidence of self-destructive behavior. If he has a family history of depression, be sure to include any medicines that may have been helpful to other family members; this is the best indicator of what medicines will work for him. Depression is a genetically determined illness, and response to medication appears to be genetically determined as well. In other words, if his aunt Tillie did well on Effexor, it is likely he will as well. Bring notes of any medicines he is taking and his past history of medical illnesses and surgeries.

During his appointment take notes of the professional's recommendations. This will be helpful to remind him and you later on—and also to let you off the hook when you're pushing him to be more active, eat his food, take his medicines, or keep his appointments. One of the primary reasons for failure in the treatment of depression is noncompliance. Antidepressant medications are usually effective and have few side effects. The problem is that if the patient is feeling bad, he thinks the medicine isn't helping and stops taking it. He may not want to feel "dependent" on medication. If he feels good, he may think he doesn't need the medicine.

> Bring notes of any medicines he is taking and his past history of medical illnesses and surgeries.

Another difficulty for depressed individuals is they are not able to concentrate and may forget to take their medicines or might take them incorrectly. You may need to step in and supervise the medicines. You might say, "The doctor gave me a pillbox and instructions for your medicines. I'll set them up for you a week at a time. Even though you may doubt your need for the medicine, it'll make me feel better if you take it. I want you to feel well again." If you are using humor you might say, "Preventive medicine doesn't mean preventing me from giving you the medicine." A weekly pillbox is helpful in keeping track. If he is having difficulty remembering whether he took a pill or not, a glance at the container will let you both know. Do not have a large quantity of medication available if there is any chance of the patient taking an impulsive overdose. Putting the medicine out a week at a time will lessen this risk.

Medicine and Therapy Are Best for Depression

Doctors are less likely to recommend therapy to men than they are to women. You and the doctor's nurse may need to conspire to encourage the physician to refer him to a counselor. Therapy, coaching, and lifestyle change are good for everyone. While the therapy will be directed at his depression, there are many side benefits for him from talking treatment. I have often thought about the patient who goes to his doctor with an ulcer, hypertension, headaches, irritable bowel syndrome, neurodermatitis, or any other common ailment and receives a pill to alleviate his symptom. To me this is a Band-Aid approach. Of course doctors will explain that they're limited to so many minutes per examination and don't have the time to explore the factors that may have led to these stress-related illnesses. They will also likely say that many patients would be upset to be directed to a therapist.

Nonetheless, I think we do our patients a disservice by not talking about why they happened to develop these physical ailments at this particular time in their lives. What are the stresses that may have led to these symptoms, and what changes might they make to reduce or cope with these pressures? Psychological therapy is expected with psychiatric treatment, but I believe it should be an adjunct to all medical treatment as well. You might want to quote me as part of your efforts to convince your man that therapy is a good thing. While most people want a pill to cure their problems, most also realize that it makes sense to understand the influences that caused them to develop the problem and the changes they can make to prevent a recurrence in the future. Therapy continues to be helpful after his recovery to mend the damage that the illness has done to your communication and relationship.

Your family physician or the psychiatrist will know the local therapists who would be most compatible, best trained, and most experienced in working with your loved one. As part of your general morale-boosting support for your guy, as well as facilitating his getting in to see the therapist the first time, talk about the many positive traits of the counselor. "The therapist you're about to see is experienced and has an excellent reputation. Dr. Jones said he referred many men to this counselor. I spoke with two people at church and one at the beauty shop who recommended this therapist." If you know others, especially male patients, who have benefited from psychotherapy, mention it. "I talked to Officer Murphy, the policeman who spoke in the neighborhood. He told me that he saw the therapist Dr. Jones recommended and it changed his life for the better."

I have had a few male patients who seemed to get into competition with the therapist. They were intent on putting down the therapist's intelligence, religion, sex, size, or some other factor as a reason for not seeing the counselor. "He told me to change my negative thoughts into positive—if I could do that I wouldn't be depressed." "She just gave me trite advice that I already knew." "I can get that sort of advice from my neighbor talking over the fence." Men who seek a therapist of a particular size, sex, religion, or orientation are frequently resistant to therapy and are attributing their reluctance to the particular therapist. In this situation you might want to say, "From what I've read men generally feel they should solve their own problems, have difficulty recognizing and expressing their feelings, and are hesitant about seeing a therapist. On the other hand, men who overcome these resistances seem to benefit in many ways. Why don't you give the therapist a try?"

Hospitalization

In some cases you may be asked to assist the doctor in convincing your man to go into the hospital. The primary reason for this step is to reduce the risk of suicide. Depressed men often paint themselves into a corner and convince themselves that they have no future. This negative perception will change when he recovers; he will then wonder how he ever could have thought this way. The job of hospitalization is to put him under close observation in a safer environment where higher doses of medicines, more frequent therapy visits, or electroconvulsive therapy can be administered.

A second factor might be the presence of psychosis. There is a danger that individuals who are delusional or experiencing auditory hallucinations might act on these irrational thoughts and perceptions in a way that would be harmful to themselves or to others.

Failure to recognize his illness will likely result in noncompliance. If he does not accept his illness, he won't see any reason to see a doctor or to take medication. Under these circumstances the illness will worsen and may eventually result in the need for hospitalization. If your guy is experiencing psychotic symptoms but realizes that he is ill and that his misperceptions are a product of his illness, you and your informal treatment team members may be able to persuade him to come to the hospital voluntarily. If he lacks insight, you may have to go through the legal process to have him admitted on an involuntary basis. He may feel you have betrayed his trust by doing this; it's important that you explain to him why you found it necessary to go through this process.

Physically getting him to the hospital may be difficult. You may have to call on your treatment team for assistance. As a last resort you can call your local mental health crisis team and/or the police to transport him. You may be reluctant to do this, but if it is a question of possible self-injury then you must do all you can to keep him safe.

Being forced into treatment is not always a bad thing. This is generally the case with addiction. Most chemically dependent patients have to hit bottom and be forced by circumstances or be pressured by families or employers to accept help. Later, they are thankful that they were required to do what they needed to do. When I was in charge of the in-patient psychiatric unit at Ireland Army Hospital at Fort Knox, I instituted a chemical dependency treatment program that required compliance or discharge from the army. Many of the regular army participants complained that this was not a voluntary program. I told them it was "sort of voluntary." However, all of the participants who remained in the program and established their sobriety later thanked me for helping them get on the right track.

Answers to Questions Depressed Men Ask

"How long does it take the medicine to work?"

One of the first questions men have is, "How long will it take the medicine to work?" I usually tell patients that, assuming we hit the right drug the first time, they should start noticing improvement in two to three weeks. Actually many patients report feeling better earlier than this, but if you give them an earlier date and no improvement is noted, they may become discouraged. I tell them that if everything goes perfectly—and it seldom does—they should be over most of their symptoms in six weeks. If they do not respond to the first antidepressant we try, I tell them stories about the old days, before medication, when patients were hospitalized routinely for months. Sometimes the first medication doesn't work, I continue, but we'll keep trying until we discover the right one. I remind them that it isn't their fault and that it's our job to find the medication or combination of drugs that will control their symptoms.

"Do I have to take these drugs forever?"

If the patient asks this when the medicines are first prescribed, I tell him that this is a topic we can discuss after he has recovered. I do not want him worrying about this when he's still depressed. Because of negative thinking, he'll begin conjuring up visions of a lifetime of invalidism as part of his efforts to convince himself that the future is bleak and all is hopeless. This can become a point of resistance to taking the medication at all. Once he has recovered he is likely to have a more positive attitude about the medicines.

The facts are that if an individual has one depressive episode, he has a 50 to 70 percent chance of a recurrence. With two episodes, the likelihood increases to 80 percent, and with three episodes we can be 100 percent sure that he will have another episode. A recurrence is even more likely without medicine. On the other hand, there are no long-term harmful effects from taking antidepressant medication as directed. In addition, some antidepressants, particularly the serotonin reuptake inhibitors (SSRIs), are not as effective when they are stopped and restarted. I always leave it to the patient to decide, but most patients do not want to go through another depressive episode. And since there is no harm from continuing the medicines, they opt to take antidepressants to prevent this.

Psychotropic Medications

I have been writing prescriptions for psychotropic medicines for decades. The following is a nontechnical discussion of my experience with the various drugs on the market. This is information based on my own observations. You will not find it in any other book. I am including it as a resource to help you understand your man's treatment—the drugs he is taking and the rationale for their use. I hope it will help you reassure your man that there are many treatment options when it comes to medication and combinations of medicines.

Some form of somatic treatment has been prescribed since 500 B.C. The Greeks prescribed cathartics for depression. Drilling holes in the skull (trepanning) was a treatment for some patients with mental illness during the Middle Ages. Tranquilizing chairs, rocking beds, hydrotherapy, hot sheets, cold sheets, various restraints, insulin coma, and lobotomies were treatments used up until the 1950s. Electroshock therapy (ECT) continues to be used today.

Chloral hydrate (the "knock-out drops" once used for Mickey Finn), barbiturates, and paraldehyde were the pre-1950s drugs that were used for sedation.

To give you an idea of the prevalence of depression and its treatment with medication, the number of prescriptions for antidepressant medications increased from 154 million to 170 million between 2002 and 2005. About 29 percent of these prescriptions were written by psychiatrists.

The Monoamine Oxidase Inhibitors (MAOIs)

Nardil (phenelzine), Marplan (isocarboxazid), and Parnate (tranylcypromine) were three early MAOIs. They slowed down the activity of monoamine oxidase, which is the enzyme that breaks down norepinephrine and serotonin. As a result, the levels of these neurotransmitters were increased in the brain.

These were effective drugs. Nardil was later found to be especially helpful in the treatment of panic disorders. Early in their use, however, several patients taking MAOIs in Italy had strokes. Investigation revealed that the afflicted patients had been eating aged cheese and drinking Chianti wine. (It should be noted that some individuals who ate aged cheese and drank Chianti did not have strokes.) Both contain tyramine. It was then observed that some patients taking MAOIs experienced a rise in blood pressure when they ingested foods

> Despite the problems associated with the drugs, we used them because they were so effective.

containing tyramine. Many medicines also interacted with MAOIs, causing a rise in blood pressure or other severe reactions. Because of this, patients taking MAOIs had to be on a tyramine-free diet and avoid many medicines because of the potentially fatal reactions that could occur. In addition, the MAOIs had a number of side effects, including blurred vision, dry mouth, constipation, drop in blood pressure, difficulty urinating, loss of libido, and difficulty maintaining an erection.

In addition, MAOIs took five to six weeks to show any antidepressant effects. Patients objected to the diet and side effects, and their doctors objected because many drugs had to be avoided while taking MAOIs. In England psychiatrists told their patients to avoid Chianti wine, aged cheese, and liver. In the United States, which has many more lawyers and lawsuits than Great Britain, psychiatrists gave their patients a laundry list of foods to avoid, including aged cheese, colored liquors, beer, bananas, bean curd, fava beans, liver, ginseng, sausage, bologna, pepperoni, salami, sauerkraut, shrimp paste, miso, yeast, Marmite, overripe avocados, caffeine, and smoked, fermented, or pickled fish. Also to be avoided are large amounts of chocolate, cream, sour cream, yogurt, peanuts, coconuts, Brazil nuts, raspberries, soy sauce, and spinach.

Despite the problems associated with the drugs, we used them because they were so effective. One famous psychopharmacologist at Harvard remarked that if he had to go to an island and practice psychiatry and could only take one drug with him, it would be Nardil. It helps a wide range of problems including depression, atypical depression, panic disorder, and anxiety. Another MAOI, selegiline, has recently been produced in the form of a patch (Emsam) that permits higher blood levels with fewer side effects. At the lowest dose (6mg patch), there are no dietary precautions. In my experience this drug is frequently helpful for symptoms of atypical depression, but is not as effective as the oral Nardil for anxiety symptoms.

First-Generation Tricyclic Antidepressants

Two tricyclic antidepressants were developed in the 1950s: Tofranil (imipramine) and Elavil (amitriptyline). These drugs were as effective as today's dual-acting antidepressants but had many anticholinergic side effects such as dry mouth, blurred vision, constipation, delay in cardiac conduction, hypotension, sweating, and difficulty starting the urinary stream. Patients were happy to put up with the side effects in exchange for relief from their symptoms. In addition to helping with depression, Tofranil was useful for panic disorder, obsessive-compulsive disorder (OCD), and, because of the anticholinergic side effects, bed-wetting in children. In addition to depression, Elavil is used for pain and sleep disturbance.

Second-Generation Tricyclics

In an attempt to lessen the side effects of Tofranil and Elavil, a second generation of antidepressants was developed utilizing the active ingredients of these drugs. Tofranil became desipramine in the body and was isolated and marketed as Norpramin. Similarly, Elavil became nortriptyline and this was isolated and marketed as Pamelor and Aventyl. Vivactil (protriptyline) was also developed during this era. It should be noted that the tricyclic antidepressants and second-generation antidepressants as well as the monoamine oxidase inhibitors continue to be effective drugs that work for severe depression and sometimes are effective where the newer antidepressants fail. It is possible to measure the blood levels of the first- and second-generation antidepressants (not the MAOIs), which can be useful in making sure of the proper dose for the patient. I will discuss this advantage in Chapter 8.

Novel Antidepressants

Following the development of the second-generation antidepressants, some unusual antidepressants were marketed. Merital (nomifensine) seemed effective but was taken off the market in 1986 because it caused blood dyscrasias in Europe. Ludiomil (maprotiline) was no more effective than the other available antidepressants and caused seizures. I used it occasionally to pre-medicate patients with high seizure thresholds who were having electroconvulsive therapy. As a result I was able to give them a lower treatment dose of electricity. Serzone (nefazodone) was effective for some patients but caused sedation and later was found to create serious liver problems in some patients. Asendin (amoxapine) initially acted quickly as an effective antidepressant but, over time, behaved like a major tranquilizer with less antidepressant effect and the potential for serious neurological side effects. Desyrel (trazodone) caused sedation at the treatment dosage range of 200 to 600mg per day and couldn't be tolerated by most patients. Desyrel is the only one that is still used to any degree. It's prescribed not for depression but for night-time sedation typically at doses from 50 to 150mg two hours before bedtime. It is not addicting and is sedative—but leaves some patients feeling "hung over" in the morning.

Wellbutrin (bupropion HCL) was introduced to the market in 1985 and taken off the market in 1986 because some patients developed seizures. It was found that if an individual dose of the original SR form was 150mg or less and the daily dose spread out morning, noon, and night was limited to 450mg or less, and if patients with eating disorders and seizure disorders were excluded, the incidence of seizures was no higher than that of any other antidepressant. Later a long-acting form of Wellbutrin (XL) was developed that could be given in a single 450mg dose but was released slowly and did not exceed the 150mg limitation at any time during the day. Wellbutrin tends to be a little stimulating and doesn't help with panic disorder (PD), generalized anxiety disorder (GAD), or obsessive compulsive disorder (OCD). It is effective for some depressions and it has few side effects—most notably no weight gain and no sexual side effects. It was noted that some patients being treated for depression observed that they lost their craving for cigarettes. Marketed under the name Zyban, it is used for smoking cessation. It can cause hypertension if used in conjunction with nicotine patches.

Prozac and the SSRIs

The SSRIs (selective serotonin reuptake inhibitors) were an improvement over the earlier antidepressants. In 1986 Prozac (fluoxetine) was introduced to the market by Eli Lilly. The first of the SSRIs, it quickly became the leading antidepressant medication. It did not have the bothersome side effects that were associated with the older antidepressants and it was hard to underdose patients, which had been a problem with earlier medications. Prozac's success spawned a number of imitators in the same class of drugs. Paxil (paroxetine), Zoloft (sertraline), Celexa (citalopram), Lexapro (escitalopram), and Luvox (fluvoxamine) followed and were easy to use, well tolerated, and effective; they helped depression as well as anxiety disorders. Prozac and Zoloft tend to be stimulating, so we prescribe these to be taken in the morning. The others are, if anything, a little sedating. These medicines can upset the stomach, produce headaches, and cause diarrhea. They frequently cause delayed ejaculation in men and anorgasmia in women. The latter is the most objectionable side effect and usually results in requests to change medicines. As one of my young patients explained, "I have to have my cheery-Os."

The sexual side effects of the SSRIs were first brought to my attention shortly after the introduction of Prozac. One of my patients noticed that she was unable to have an orgasm and asked if it could be the drug. I looked it up and, according to the literature at that time, the incidence of sexual side effects was about 0.5 percent. I told her it was unlikely, but possible, and to stop the drug and see if the problem resolved. She did, and it did. I then started asking all my patients on Prozac if they were noticing any sexual side effects. To my surprise most were but hadn't associated the problem with the drug or were too embarrassed to bring it up with me. Usually men are not as upset by delayed ejaculation. They are concerned about erectile dysfunction and loss of libido, but frequently these are symptoms of the depressive illness itself and improve as the man recovers from the melancholic episode.

Any of the SSRIs can cause flu-like symptoms if they are stopped abruptly. In my experience, Paxil is the worst offender of the group. The SSRIs are antidepressants but also help with panic disorder (PD), obsessive-compulsive disorder (OCD), generalized anxiety disorder (GAD), posttraumatic stress disorder (PTSD), and bulimia. In some instances, when the SSRIs are stopped and then restarted they do not work as well the second time. Also, in about 20 percent of patients, the positive effects of the SSRIs seem to "fade" in time; we have to increase the dose or try another type of antidepressant. Fibromyalgia patients usually benefit initially but end up changing medicines periodically.

New Dual-Acting Antidepressants

Recent dual-action antidepressants, also referred to as serotonin, norepinepherine reuptake inhibitors (SNRIs), include Effexor (venlafaxine), Remeron (mirtazapine), Cymbalta (duloxetine), and, the latest on the market, Pristiq (desvenlafaxine succinate). These block the reuptake of both serotonin and norepinephrine. They sometimes work when the others don't. The theory is that some patients are low on norepinepherine as well as serotonin. Effexor, Cymbalta, and Pristiq tend to be stimulating while Remeron is sedating. The dosage range for Effexor XR is 150 to 450mg a day. It goes out of the system quickly and, if stopped abruptly, may cause dizziness and flu-like symptoms that can be very uncomfortable. Pristiq is a new dual-acting antidepressant that is the active ingredient of Effexor. I have prescribed it for a number of patients, and it seems to be effective with few side effects. The starting dose of 50mg appears to be adequate for most patients. Remeron is less sedating at 30 mg or 45 mg than it is at 15 mg because the norepinephrine-blocking action kicks in at 30 mg, which offsets the sedative side effects at the lower dose. Effexor acts like an SSRI until the dose is increased beyond 150mg/day. At that point it begins blocking the reuptake of norepinephrine. The higher the dose of Effexor, the more effective it seems to be. It can be increased to a dose of 450mg per day. Remeron stimulates the appetite as well as causing sedation. This is an advantage in older depressed patients who have symptoms of anorexia and insomnia.

Antidepressants and Antipsychotic Medications for Psychotic Depression

Twenty percent of patients with psychotic depressions respond to antidepressants, and another 20 percent respond to antipsychotic medications, but better than 80 percent respond to a combination of an antidepressant plus an antipsychotic. Triavil was a combination of Trilafon and Elavil in the same tablet. More recently, Symbyax is a combination of Zyprexa and Prozac.

Antipsychotic Medications (Major Tranquilizers)

In 1954 Thorazine was introduced to the US market. Tested as an antihistamine, it was discovered to be a major tranquilizer — and a miracle drug for state hospitals, which housed over 600,000 patients at the time. It became possible to furnish wards, to institute treatment programs, to consider unlocking the doors of some units, and to contemplate discharge for many patients. It wasn't until years after the introduction of Thorazine (chlorpromazine) and Mellaril (thioridazine) that we began to discover some of the side effects caused by these medications. The neuroleptic malignant syndrome (NMS) and sudden death are two rare horrific events that can be caused by major tranquilizers.

Despite the negatives associated with the antipsychotic drugs, the good far outweighed the bad in terms of a more optimistic attitude toward severe mental illness. With the advent of medication, it was possible to decorate and furnish psychiatric hospital wards. Efforts were made to develop individual treatment programs for patients. Discharge planning replaced lifetime custodial care.

Lower-Dose, High-Potency Antipsychotic Medications

The next generation of antipsychotic medications were lower-dose, higher-potency drugs like Prolixin (fluphenazine), Stelazine (trifluoperazine), Haldol (haloperidol), and Trilafon (perphenazine). These had the advantage a lower dose but actually had more neurological side effects.

Young male patients were especially susceptible to neurological side effects like akathisia. This is a restlessness that feels as though you have a motor inside you. Patients with this side effect would often appear to be agitated, causing the caregivers to prescribe higher doses of the medication, which produced more restlessness. Some patients committed suicide because of the extreme discomfort they experienced from this side effect. Dystonia or a painful twisting of the neck muscles or bridging of the neck was another side effect. Movements of the tongue (fly catcher's tongue), involuntary wormlike movements (coreiform movements) of the extremities, rocking of the torso, and a dancelike gait were all neurological side effects that could become permanent results of these medicines (tardive dyskinesia). Two of these drugs, Prolixin and Haldol, were manufactured in injectable forms, which could be given every two to four weeks. Patients who were noncompliant or who cheeked their pills could be given shots to make sure they received their medication. This was helpful for controlling the psychotic symptoms of noncompliant patients who lacked insight into their illnesses, but, should the patient experience an adverse side effect from the drug, he would have that side effect for the entire two to four weeks the drug remained in his system. Malpractice attorneys referred to these drugs as "highly invasive medications."

Atypical Antipsychotic Medications

After the accidental discovery of Thorazine, pharmaceutical companies thought that, in order for drugs to have an antipsychotic effect, they had to block the D-2 dopamine receptor. For several years the watchword in research was "D-2, me too." However, the highly effective antipsychotic Clozaril (clozapine) did not block the D-2 receptors, and this ushered in a new line of investigation and the development of new atypical antipsychotic medications that were less likely to produce the neurological side effects characteristic of the older drugs.

The newer antipsychotic medications have their own disadvantages, however. They may cause weight gain and diabetes 2, prolongation of cardiac conduction, and premature death in the elderly. The so-called atypical antipsychotics are Abilify (aripiprazole), Seroquel (quetiapine), Geodon (ziprasidone), Zyprexa (olanzapine), Risperdal (risperidone), Invega, (paliperidone), Saphris (asenapine sublingual tablets), Fanapt (iloperidone tablets), and Clozaril. All are used to treat schizophrenia, to control bipolar disorder, and to augment the antidepressants for treatment of resistant depression; they're combined with antidepressant medication for the treatment of psychotic depression. Clozaril is usually reserved for the treatment of schizophrenia. It is one of the most effective drugs for this disorder but has the disadvantage of causing aplastic anemia. A strict schedule of blood testing must be followed with this medication. Like all medicines, some patients do better on one than another, and it is pretty much a trial-and-error proposition. Risperdal Consta is a long-acting, injectable form of Risperdal that is given intramuscularly every fourteen days. Its use is generally reserved for noncompliant, psychotic patients who refuse to take their medicines by mouth. A long-acting injectable form of Invega has recently been introduced.

Tobacco and Antipsychotic Medications

When hospitals went smoke-free, I saw a number of newly admitted patients who were sedated, uncoordinated, disoriented and had slurred speech caused by their antipsychotic medications. I soon learned that these individuals were heavy smokers; outside the hospital, their smoking lowered the blood levels of their drugs. On the same doses in the hospital, their blood levels went up and they appeared overmedicated.

In the same vein, I saw a farmer who told me his wife noticed that his symptoms of irritability and depression appeared to be associated with

Antidepressants and the Placebo Effect

A frequent criticism of antidepressants is that they are not much better than placebos. As a psychiatrist who has treated depressed patients before and after the advent of antidepressant medication, I can say that this is not true—antidepressants are definitely more effective than placebos. However, to get an antidepressant on the market, a drug company must demonstrate that it is more effective than a placebo—and this is difficult, because there is a strong placebo effect among depressed individuals in drug trials. Patients participating in these investigations are frequently paid by the universities conducting the trials. The researchers want these patients to return and take part in future studies, so they treat them very well. It has been demonstrated that paying attention to individuals and treating them kindly and with respect has a positive effect on them; hence a placebo response occurs.

This so-called Hawthorne effect was demonstrated in a study of the effect of lighting on worker productivity in the Western Electric Company. They wanted to see what level of light would result in the greatest worker productivity. They interviewed workers in each section of the company and, to the researchers' surprise, all areas of the plant showed increased output regardless of the level of light. The deciding influence was that researchers paid attention to the individual workers and talked to them.

his use of chewing tobacco. He thought that the increase might be related to the increased stress associated with planting and harvest, but had to agree that, even in less stressful periods, he did seem to feel worse while chewing tobacco. We discussed the situation and surmised that there might be a relationship between nicotine and the blood levels of his medicines similar to what has been observed in patients who smoke.

The Mood Stabilizers

Lithium

Up until lithium appeared on the scene, the analysts said that antipsychotics (major tranquilizers) were "chemical strait jackets" and antidepressants were "mood elevators;" in other words, these drugs weren't treating the unconscious roots of the illness but were masking symptoms or artificially elevating a patient's mood. Lithium, a naturally occurring salt that is excreted by the kidney and not metabolized in the liver like the other drugs, actually controlled a major psychiatric illness (bipolar I disorder) and therefore had to be acting on the root of the problem. This discovery caused the pendulum of psychiatric thinking to swing toward biology and away from psychological causes and treatment.

When visiting Australia with a Roy Emerson–led tennis group in the early 1970s, I met with Peter Marriott, M.D., an Australian psychiatrist in Melbourne who had written to me asking for copies of some of my papers on military psychiatry. Dr. Marriott showed me around his psychiatric facility and introduced me to the head of the hospital, Dr. John Cade. Dr. Cade was the psychiatrist who wrote the original paper in 1948 describing lithium's ability to control mood swings. He was curious about our use of lithium in the United States and shared some interesting anecdotes with me during this memorable meeting. Lithium is one of the best-studied treatments available today. It continues to be an effective mood stabilizer; it has been shown that the risk of suicide among bipolar patients who stop taking their lithium is sixteen times higher than among those who do not.

Lithium's side effects include an intention tremor, which increases as you try to do things. For example, if you pick up a cup to drink, the shaking increases as the cup approaches your mouth. It causes a problem with writing; attorneys, for example, do not like it because it makes them look nervous when signing contracts. The same type of tremor occurs in some families in the absence of lithium. It is then referred to as a "familial tremor." Usually this problem can be alleviated by taking 10 to 20mg of Inderal (propranolol hydrochloride). In the past, patients learned that alcohol would relieve intention tremor, and some patients became addicted to alcohol through their efforts to self-medicate their familial tremors.

Lithium tends to raise the white blood cell count and can lead to an excess of white cells (leukocytosis). This characteristic can be useful when patients develop a low white count (leucopenia) with other medications like Tegretol (carbamazepine) or Clozaril. Simply adding a low dose of lithium may increase the white count to the normal range. Another common side effect of lithium is diarrhea. This can be eliminated by using the liquid form (lithium citrate), which is absorbed in the stomach instead of the colon. Diabetes insipidus is a fairly common side effect of lithium. Patients drink excessive amounts of fluid and urinate copiously. They may be kept on lithium despite this problem if they can be convinced to limit their fluid intake.

The primary disadvantage of lithium was the cognitive dullness that some patients experienced. I saw a farmer who had been on lithium for a number of years. He indicated that he had stopped his lithium twice during his initial treatment and had ended up in the hospital on both occasions. He said he learned his lesson and was careful to take it as directed and to stay on it despite the fact that he had constant diarrhea. I switched him to the liquid form. He found it a bother but still preferred this inconvenience to having loose stools. We discussed his switching to Depakote (divalproex sodium), but he was fearful because of his past hospitalizations when he went off the lithium. I told him we would keep him on the lithium until he was established on an adequate dose of Depakote and then gradually reduce the lithium. He agreed to this plan and, over a period of several months, we switched him from lithium to Depakote.

Shortly after making this change, he bought two farms. He said that both he and his family were initially apprehensive at his seemingly impulsive purchases, but on reviewing the expenditure carefully he discovered that the transactions were both prudent and wise. The price for the land was reasonable, and the expansion of his enterprise was good from a business standpoint. He said, "In retrospect, I was not hypomanic—I was just thinking more clearly than I had in years once I got off the lithium." He has continued to do well on Depakote.

> The primary disadvantage of lithium was the cognitive dullness that some patients experienced with this medication.

In my experience the few patients who have developed lithium toxicity over the years were those who, inadvertently, were put on or took nonsteroidal analgesics (Ibuprofen, Celebrex, Advil and the like) or diuretics. The former drugs can interfere with the excretion of lithium, causing a buildup to toxic blood levels. The diuretics produce fluid loss and elevated lithium blood levels. Patients on these drugs or who are losing fluid from vomiting, excessive perspiration, or diarrhea need to have their lithium levels monitored closely. Elderly patients and those with impaired renal functioning are also at risk for elevated lithium levels and need to have this level monitored closely. One of my elderly bipolar patients, for insurance reasons, had his internist take over his care.

His daughters came to me indicating that he had been hospitalized for delirium and was being transferred to a nursing home. I ordered a lithium level, which came back in the toxic range. We reduced his lithium dose, his delirium cleared, and he returned home. Lithium can lower thyroid function, and it is important to periodically check the thyroid profile of anyone on lithium for an extended period of time. Lithium may cause kidney damage in some patients and renal function studies must be done periodically to avoid this problem.

The Anticonvulsant Mood Stabilizers

The next mood stabilizer after lithium and the first anticonvulsant to be used as a mood stabilizer was Tegretol. Investigators were looking for medicines that controlled periodic illnesses. Tegretol helped temporal lobe epilepsy and was found to control mood swings for some bipolar patients. After observing that it helped bipolar disorder, researchers theorized that since it controlled epilepsy by limiting the spread of the seizure (kindling), perhaps its method of action was to stop kindling in the primitive areas of the brain (the limbic area) that controls sleep, appetite, and mood.

One practical problem using Tegretol is that it interacts with some medications to produce toxic levels. For example, I had a bipolar patient who was stabilized on Tegretol and who came in for infrequent, brief follow-up visits. He called in between scheduled appointments to report that he was having episodes of confusion, lack of coordination, trouble walking, loss of balance, and daytime sedation. I had him get a Tegretol blood level, which was found to be in the toxic range. His dose of Tegretol had not been changed, but he then recalled that his family physician had started him on Erythromycin for an upper-respiratory infection. Erythromycin is one of the drugs that can cause Tegretol to reach toxic levels. We held his Tegretol and asked his doctor to use a different antibiotic.

Another treatment difficulty that arises in some patients on Tegretol is a reduction in the white blood cell count. When I used to start a hospitalized patient on Tegretol, the internist on the case would frequently get nervous about the low white count and start checking blood counts and talking about getting a bone marrow. Rather than put the patient through an elaborate work-up, I would add lithium, which raised the white blood count.

Depakote was another anticonvulsant that was tried and found to be effective in controlling bipolar disorder. It is effective for patients who have rapid-cycling mood swings. Weight gain, sedation, brittleness of the hair, and fluid retention are some of the common side effects. It can sometimes cause ovarian cysts in women. It may also cause Lamictal levels to increase.

Lamictal (lamotrigine) is an anticonvulsant that is helpful in treatment-resistant depression and acts as a mood stabilizer in bipolar disorder. The main difficulty with this medication is the possibility of severe rash, which is more likely if the dose is increased too rapidly. If a patient misses the medication for a day or so, he has to start all over with a gradual dosing schedule. I have patients start low and go slow with Lamictal. I start with 25mg every other day for two weeks, then 25mg daily for two weeks, and continue gradually increasing the daily dose until they reach a dose of 200mg per day the ninth week. By following this slow schedule of dosage increase, the patient may be assured that there is little or no chance of developing the rash. The advantages of Lamictal are its effectiveness in relieving depression and its lack of sedation; in addition, for some patients it causes weight loss instead of weight gain.

Most patients with bipolar disorder are on a combination of drugs. During depressive episodes antidepressant medication may be added to their mood stabilizers.

> **Most patients with bipolar disorder are on a combination of drugs.**

Wellbutrin and trazodone are preferred antidepressants to add because they are less likely to cause rapid cycling. Antipsychotic medication may be added to a mood stabilizer for increased control of the mood swings. In some instances combinations of mood stabilizers are prescribed. When anticonvulsant medications are discontinued, they must be tapered to prevent the patient from experiencing a seizure.

Minor Tranquilizers

The benzodiazapines—Xanax (alprazolam), Ativan (lorazepam), and Klonopin (clonazepam)—are the most commonly prescribed tranquilizers used today. In the past, Valium (diazepam), Serax (oxazepam), Centrax (prazepam), Librium (chlordiazepoxide), Vistaril and Atarax (hydroxyzine), and Tranxene (clorazepate dipotassium) were prescribed as well.

The minor tranquilizers are used as Band-Aids to treat anticipatory anxiety in panic disorder, to help with generalized anxiety disorder, and to decrease anxiety in acute psychotic conditions. It is, for example, better to give a low dose of antipsychotic medication along with intramuscular Ativan rather than a higher dose of the antipsychotic because the latter puts the patient at greater risk for long-term neurological side effects including neuroleptic malignant syndrome (NMS).

Ativan and Xanax typically take thirty to sixty minutes to start to work and last three to four hours. Klonopin takes one to two hours and lasts five to six hours. The main problem with the minor tranquilizers is the development of tolerance and the development of psychological and physical tolerance at doses of 2mg of Xanax or more per day for an extended period of time. Some patients will reach a point where they are sedated from the minor tranquilizer but still anxious; this is a problem because it means gradually weaning the patient off the tranquilizer. Another problem is caused by suddenly stopping the benzodiazapines, which can result in severe withdrawal symptoms including seizures. Finally, these drugs act on the cortex of the brain in a manner similar to alcohol. As a result, use of the benzodiazapines can produce craving in individuals predisposed to alcohol addiction. In addition, they potentiate alcohol. Patients have died accidentally from depressing their respiratory center or from aspiration from depressing their gag reflex due to the combination of alcohol and benzodiazapines.

In private practice individuals who call on the weekend for medication refills are frequently the ones who are psychologically and physiologically dependent on drugs. It is never lithium or the major tranquilizers that are inadvertently flushed down the toilet or eaten by the dog. Only the benzodiazapines and pain medications seemed to disappear in peculiar ways and require weekend refills. I presented a man who was addicted to sleeping medications to a group of medical students. "Where does he get the sleeping pills?" one of the students asked. "From doctors and pharmacists," I answered. "Why do they give them to him?" the student asked. I whispered to the patient to see if he could get some drugs from the student and then had the student interview the patient. The exchange went as follows:

> **Patient:** I can't sleep.
> **Medical student:** Have you tried methods of sleep hygiene?
> **Patient:** Yes, I've done all those things and I still can't sleep. I've got to get some sleep.
> **Medical student:** Well, we can't give you medication because you'll get dependent on it.
> **Patient:** I haven't slept in two days. I can't take it. I'm exhausted. I've got to get some sleep.
> **Medical student:** (becoming restless) Well, the sleeping pills aren't good for you.
> **Patient:** I have to sleep, I can't stand it. I need rest. I've got to have relief. I need help. I'm desperate! Can't you do something?
> **Medical student:** (Jumps up and leaves the room).

We then discussed how the patient transmitted his anxiety to the student and how uncomfortable the student became. I asked the students to imagine the same scenario talking to the patient on the phone at two in the morning on the weekend. Most doctors would give the patient whatever he wanted just to shut him up so they could get back to sleep themselves. One weekend caller reported he was out of his Librium and requested a refill. I asked him the dose and he excused himself from the phone to go to the medicine cabinet and check. He returned and said: "I think it is 10 roaches." He misread the label which said 10 mg and the manufacturer was the Roche drug company—but I had an idea of his recreational habits from his response.

Medication Side Effects

It has been said that if the airlines had to disclose all the things that could go wrong in a flight in the same manner that the pharmaceutical companies are required to with their products, no one would fly. Virtually anything that could happen while a patient is taking a particular drug is included in the package warnings. When I was a resident in psychiatric training, a young man in his late twenties arrived at the psychiatric hospital for admission. He had traveled a considerable distance and it was close to noon, so I told him to go to the cafeteria and have lunch; I would take a history and examine him after he ate. He went to the lunchroom, promptly fell face-first into his plate, and died. Efforts to resuscitate him were unsuccessful. I attended the autopsy, which was conducted by a neuropathologist. He concluded that the cause of death was "Sudden death due to phenothiazines." I said, "There's just one problem with that diagnosis, Doctor. This patient has not taken any medication." The pathologist stammered, "Okay then, sudden death."

This event stuck in my mind because of not only my shock at a young man's unexpected death, but the fact that had he been taking a drug, it would have been blamed for his demise; whatever drug he was on would then have had "sudden death" listed as a possible consequence. The fact is that sudden death, and many other medical and neurological phenomena, can occur in the absence of medication. Tardive dyskinesia is a permanent neurological condition that is caused by some antipsychotic medications, but it can occur in the absence of medication as well. People have strokes all the time, but if they happen to have one while receiving elec-

> Virtually anything that happens while a patient is taking a particular drug is included in the package warnings.

troconvulsive therapy you can bet that this procedure will be blamed for the cerebral vascular accident and the treating physician will be sued.

Therapy

Cognitive-behavioral therapy is the psychological treatment recommended for depression. If other problems, in addition to depression, are present, psychodynamic psychotherapy, gestalt therapy, or others might be indicated. I trained in a psychoanalytically oriented program and still believe that Freud gave us the best theoretical framework for understanding human behavior. However, I would like to add a few comments about therapy that you will not find in any other book.

Over the years I have hired many therapists for our office. I have reviewed their training, experience, and recommendations. I have found that the best indicator of their later success with patients has been whether I liked talking with them. I realize that this is akin to Harry Stack Sullivan's selection of aides to work with his schizophrenic patients. He said he found the ones he liked were the best, and most of them were a bit odd. However, the ones I liked to talk to were intelligent, interesting, and listened attentively to me. You might keep this in mind when you are evaluating therapists for your man.

Electroconvulsive Therapy (ECT)

Ugo Cerletti and Lucio Bini in 1937 used electrical stimulation to induce convulsions. They found that the treatment was not generally effective in schizophrenia—but dramatic results were achieved for many patients with depression. This was the birth of ECT. Initially it was given without anesthetic or muscle-blocking drugs. Patients were unconscious as soon as they received the stimulus. One drawback to this method was that some patients had bone fractures from the convulsions. Memory difficulties were noted among the patients who received ECT treatments as well.

To prevent fractures, succinyl choline (Anectine) was given prior to the treatment. This drug is a derivative of curare, the poison used by South American Indians on their blowgun darts to paralyze their prey. It blocks the nerves to the muscles so that the animal is alert but completely paralyzed. As a result, patients were unable to speak or to breathe prior to treatment. This was a very frightening experience, and patients understandably associated this anxiety with ECT. In essence we were conditioning patients to fear the treatment.

Later, to prevent this terror, a quick-acting anesthetic (Brevital) was given prior to the administration of succinyl choline. This relieved the panic associated with the muscle-blocking agent, but patients continued to have memory difficulties following the treatment. It was then discovered that much of the memory loss was due to anoxia, a problem greatly reduced if patients were oxygenated prior to treatment. Giving the electrical stimulation unilaterally on the nondominant hemisphere further reduced confusion and memory problems.

ECT continues to be used for some treatment-resistant depressed patients, patients who cannot tolerate medication, agitated elderly patients, and acutely suicidal patients who cannot wait for the medications to alleviate their depressive symptoms. It is a very humane and often lifesaving procedure if used judiciously and properly.

What actually goes on in therapy that makes people better? I have struggled with this question since I was a resident in psychiatry years ago. At that time there were a number of books written by analysts who used widely diverse techniques but claimed to have helped the small population of patients they worked with intensely for an extended period of time. One kept a schizophrenic girl in her house, sat her on her lap, and fed her ice cream, saying, "This is your good mother's milk." Another did dance therapy to help his patients with their ego boundaries. Patients receiving treatment from one famous analyst had to sign releases permitting him to curse and hit them. I observed a psychodramatist, Adelaide Starr, working with a ward of state

> I have found that the best indicator of a therapist's success with patients has been whether I liked talking with them.

hospital patients and thought at the time that just being in her presence made people feel better—it was not her technique as much as it was her personality that was therapeutic. She exuded an aura of kindness and warmth. I concluded that among these successful approaches the common elements were:

- In each case the doctors were energetic and motivated to prove their theory.

117

Freud's View of Depression

Sigmund Freud thought that melancholia, or depression, was a type of pathological mourning. The melancholic had both positive and unconscious negative feelings for the lost object and suffered guilt as a result of this. Freud's treatment for depression involved helping individuals develop insight into the presence of their angry feelings and then facilitating the expression of these negative feelings.

- They gave their patients a great deal of individual attention for an extended period of time.
- They required little of the patients.
- They were nonjudgmental.

Over the years following my residency, I have worked closely with many well-trained, experienced, and skilled therapists. I asked them what they thought made their patients better. Initially they all answered in terms of the theoretical structure they used. For example, the Freudians would talk about unconscious conflicts that were resolved. Gestalt therapists brought up the inner child issues of their patients. However, as I continued to ask them for what actually went on in the sessions that led to their patients' improvement, most said they did not know. We concluded together that the theoretical structure of the therapist was primarily for the therapist's benefit. It permitted the therapist to sit and listen carefully to the patient one or two hours a week over an extended period of time. The therapist was accepting and nonjudgmental. In addition, it appeared to me that the therapist provided compassion and a kind of love for the patient that was curative.

> Trust your intuition when you evaluate and select a therapist for your man.

These are just subjective observations and thoughts on my part about therapy, but I mention them because I hope that you will trust your intuition when you evaluate and select a therapist for your man. Your feelings are probably as good an indicator as are diplomas, experience, or recommendations from others.

➤◄

Hopefully you have been able to overcome your man's resistances to receiving help and have found the information in this chapter to be useful in helping him find the right medicine and therapist. In the next chapter I will provide suggestions as to how you can support your doctors' suggestions.

CHAPTER FIVE

How to Support the Professionals' Recommendations at Home

While those with the illness are abysmally poor givers of love, and are adept at killing it in those who offer it to them, they respond to its presence and are acutely aware of its absence.

—*Anne Sheffield*

Educate Yourself

By reading this book, you are educating yourself about depression. This is the first step toward helping the professionals. You may want to reread the introduction in order to reinforce your positive attitude toward treatment and recovery. At the end of the book, you'll find a resource section that gives many sources of additional information. In addition, there are support groups for caregivers online and probably in your community. As you strive to aid and support the melancholic through this painful illness, it is important to understand the illness and learn how to protect and sustain your own well-being.

Accompany Your Man to His Appointments

Over the years I have come to the realization that it is vital for female caregivers to be closely involved in their men's treatment. As we have seen, men have difficulty identifying their feelings and even more problems expressing them. They feel they should solve their own problems and have difficulty seeking help or depending on others. If you send him to see the doctor on his own, he will likely minimize his symptoms, fail to ask questions, and later have difficulty recalling the recommendations that were made to him.

You have succeeded in having him seen by the medical professionals who have diagnosed his depression and prescribed treatment for his recovery. The next step is to go with him to provide information to the professionals and help him benefit from their recommendations.

> You may meet with mild resistance from the doctors when you voice your desire to be a part of your man's treatment.

You may meet with mild resistance from the doctors when you voice your desire to be a part of your man's treatment. It may come in the form of concern for his privacy and the professional's reluctance to talk with anyone other than him because of confidentiality issues. The Health Insurance Portability and Accountability Act (HIPAA) requires all health care providers to protect the confidentiality of their patients' medical information. However, these concerns can be answered by having your guy sign forms authorizing the release of his medical information to you by the professionals.

Knock-knock.
Who's there?
HIPAA.

HIPAA who?

Can't tell you.

Probably more important than the voiced concern about HIPAA regulations is the busy doctor's reluctance to spend more time with the two of you. Your depressed man is not going to ask questions; nor will he question the suggestions of the doctor. He will likely answer the doctor's questions briefly and tell the physician that his medications are working in order to get out of the office as quickly as possible. The doctor has a waiting room full of patients and is under time pressure to move on to the next client.

In contrast, you will be coming along armed with your list of observations and questions and, because of your presence, the professional is going to be required to spend considerably more time with the two of you than he or she would have with your man alone. You can diminish the professional's opposition to your being there by acknowledging the additional burden your presence is creating. To lessen resistance, let the doctor know you realize you will be taking more of his or her time and that you want to pay for extended visits. Explain that your depressed man's concentration is impaired by his illness. Inform the professional that you want to share your observations and take notes when the doctor makes suggestions. Again, a release can be signed permitting the doctor to freely exchange information with you.

Another source of resistance to your presence in the psychiatrist's office may be the lingering influence of psychoanalysis. Traditional analytic treatment was one-to-one. An illustration of orthodox analysis occurred when Anna Freud attended the first international meeting of child psychoanalysts held in Topeka, Kansas. I was privileged to attend this historic gathering and to witness the following interaction between Miss Freud and an analyst from Cincinnati. The analyst presented the case of a nine year-old child afflicted by a dog phobia. The therapist had involved the child's parents in the treatment and encouraged them to work with the child at home by using some of the insights discovered in the child's analysis. This was a departure from orthodox psychoanalysis—and a sin to Miss Freud's way of thinking. She responded as follows: "We would like to thank our esteemed colleague from Cincinnati for this interesting paper of the analysis of a child with a dog phobia, but we wonder—does this paper belong in a meeting of psychoanalysts? Or, rather, as I think it should, in a meeting of sociologists." The analytic tradition of one-to-one treatment does indeed run deep. Nevertheless, do insist that you be involved in your man's treatment. If a professional forbids your involvement, find another doctor who will allow it.

> A release can be signed permitting the doctor to freely exchange information with you.

There are several reasons why I believe it is crucial for you to accompany your melancholic male to his medical appointments.

- Physicians and counselors need your observations and input to have an accurate picture of your man's symptoms and functioning at home. Your loved one will have difficulty conveying an accurate assessment of his illness. He will likely want to get out of the doctor's office as quickly as possible, return home, get under the covers, and shut out the world. He will minimize the extent of his suffering. You are with him twenty-four hours a day. You are more objective. The doctor sees him for brief periods of time at infrequent intervals when he is cleaned up, dressed, and trying to put on a good front.
- Because of his impaired concentration, you should be there to hear what the doctors have to say about him and what they recommend.
- His perception is altered by his depression as well, so that he will tend to screen out positive information and magnify the negative.

- You need to be acquainted with the medical doctors and nurses on his case and have the necessary releases signed so that you can communicate freely with them.
- It is an opportunity for you to acquire a face-to-face acquaintance with the therapist and have releases signed so that you can communicate with each other even though it is unlikely that you will accompany your man to most of his therapy sessions.

Work with the Doctor's Nurse

Because doctors are so limited in the time they can spend with patients, most employ nurses and nurse practitioners in their office as "physician extenders." Chances are you won't be able to talk directly to Dr. Jones when you call his office. Speaking to the office nurse on the phone to share your observations and concerns has some advantages. She, or he, will have more time to listen to you.

- It is likely that the nurse will be female, and you may have an easier time sharing your feelings about the situation and commiserating about men's difficulties asking for help, admitting vulnerabilities, and recognizing and expressing emotions. She may agree with you that they are pains at times.
- The nurse has no doubt dealt with similar cases in which depressed male patients resisted treatment, were reluctant to engage in psychological therapies, and failed to recognize that they were depressed.
- You can tell the nurse that you will be coming with your man to his appointment; that you are aware of the HIPAA restrictions; and that you'll have him sign authorizations allowing you to exchange information with the doctor and the nurse in the future.
- Tell her you know accompanying him to his appointments will take more of the doctor's time and you want to compensate their office fully.

- You can ask her, or him, to help you out by giving you instructions in his presence. For example, "It is important that you see that he takes his medication each day. Make sure he is up, showered and dressed by 8:00 a.m. Accompany him on a walk daily." Explain that this will make your job easier at home because you can blame her when he gripes at you.
- Tell the nurse that you are likely to need someone to give you a boost from time to time and ask her if you can call her to vent your frustrations. Add that you don't intend to take up her time without compensation, and ask if you could work out an arrangement in which you pay for the extra time she spends with you on the phone or in person.

Manage His Medications

It bears repeating that the number one reason for treatment failure in the management of depression is noncompliance with medication. It is vital that you take an active role in administering your man's medicines. He cannot concentrate. He needs you to keep track and make sure he takes them daily as directed. Taking medicine reminds him that he is ill, which is difficult for him to accept. Most men like to be independent and solve their own problems. Think about it: Will he even ask for directions when he's lost in the car? Relying on medicines and professionals goes against his desire to be self-sufficient.

When patients skip doses of medicine, they often feel better initially because the blood level of the drug drops, resulting in fewer side effects. Still, despite the lower level in the blood, antidepressants remain at effective levels in the brain for a time. It is only after missing the medicine for two or three weeks that the full force of the illness returns. If left to his own devices, after missing a dose or two, your man may conclude that he's better off without the drugs and stop them.

Another situation that may lead to noncompliance has to do with mis-understanding how the medicines work. Antidepressant medicines typ-ically take two to three weeks to take effect and, meanwhile, the depressive illness is continuing to worsen. Your man may observe that he feels worse during the first two weeks on medication and decide that he'd be better off without it. In the same vein, once he has recov-ered from the depressive episode, he may conclude that he no longer needs the medicine, stop it, and then find himself at high risk for relapse. Your job is to make sure he takes his medicine each day. If you observe that complaints of side effects are justified, contact the doctor to make changes. Do not let him give up on a medication until he has taken an adequate dose for several weeks. The current thinking is that an adequate trial on the maximum dose of a drug is twelve weeks. Antidepressants take time to begin to work. If you switch medicines too soon, you may miss the one that would work best for him.

> Do not let him give up on a medication until he has taken an adequate dose for several weeks.

Tell Him You'll Be Involved in His Treatment

Do not ask him if it's okay that you're involved in his treatment. Tell your melancholic that you *will* be involved. You may want to say some-thing like, "I want to learn all I can about depression because I love you and I want to be able to help you through this painful illness. I need to go with you to your appointments so I can ask the doctors questions and learn what I can do to speed your recovery. It will make me feel better to talk with them." You might add that you know he is having problems with concentration due to his illness, and you will take over the job of scheduling appointments, looking after his medications, and carrying out the doctor's directions at home. If you think it will help, quote this book. "Dr. Bey says it's my job to see to it that you get the most from your medicine and your doctor's appointments. He says to accomplish this I need to educate myself about depression and play an active role in your treatment and recovery."

Take Notes at Home and at the Doctor's Office

Jotting down your daily observations at home will help the professionals assess his condition and progress in treatment. Taking notes at the doctor's office will help you when you get back home and will be useful in your efforts to help him comply with treatment recommendations. Take notes during your meetings with the doctors. Your companion's concentration is impaired, and he will have difficulty recalling the details of the sessions. Hang on to your notes as a treatment record you can refer to in the future and show your depressed man how he has improved since the initial sessions. You will also have a record of the medicines, doses prescribed, side effects, and what responses occurred.

> Do not ask him if it's okay that you're involved in his treatment. Tell your melancholic that you will be involved in his treatment.

Bring your record of your daily observations to appointments. This will help the doctor with his or her assessment of your man's response to medication. As I've noted, depression is generally at its worst in the morning, getting better as the day goes on. (In atypical depression, the pattern is the opposite, and in some cases there is little variation in the intensity of the symptoms.) If your melancholic's symptoms are typical, it will be helpful to make observations twice a day and note any improvement later on.

Although this is infrequently done, you can plot a more objective record of symptoms and progress in treatment using some of the self-report depression inventories that are currently available online. To locate these tests, use your search engine to look up "self-report test depression." The Beck Depression Inventory (BDI) is a self-rated scale in which individuals rate themselves from 0 to 3 on a twenty-one-item scale, with a range of final scores from 0 to 63. The primary value of this self-rating scale is to provide the professionals with an objective record of your man's response to treatment and to provide him with concrete evidence of his improvement. The Cornell Dysthymia Rating Scale (CDRS) is another less frequently used self-reporting test that examines twenty symptoms of depression and has the patient rate each one on a spectrum of 1 to 4. Finally, the Zung Self-Rating Depression Scale (Zung SDS) is a twenty-item self-report test rated on a 1 through 4 spectrum that's frequently used to follow the course of a depressive illness. None of these tests is difficult or time consuming. There are scales for bipolar disorder as well, but most are completed by an observing clinician rather than self-report.

Record your observations in the morning and in the evening. The daily variations in symptoms and the up and down course of the illness can be confusing; twice-daily observations will provide a more accurate picture for the professional caregivers.

Quote the Professionals

It is hard to care for a depressed man. He becomes irritated when you encourage him to engage in more activity, take his medicines, eat good foods, and think positively. You can enlist support and deflect his irritation by quoting the professionals. Write down any positive, encouraging statements made by the doctors. The physician, of course, has to be in control and make the final decision; but you can set him or her up to say what you hope to hear. Encourage the statements you want the doctor to make by your questions. For example, "Doctor, Joe is beating himself up for being depressed. He thinks he's weak because he can't pull himself out of it. What do you think?" Or "Joe feels ashamed of his depression. He thinks that people who find out about it will call him crazy. What should I tell him, Doctor?" Questions like this will elicit positive statements from the professionals that you can repeat to Joe later. The doctor will likely explain to Joe that he has a common, treatable illness and that he will soon recover. The physician will reassure Joe that he or she sees many depressed patients every day from all walks of life, and that it's an illness like thyroid disease, diabetes, or any other medical condition.

> Write down any positive, encouraging statements made by the doctors.

Another helpful technique is to ask the professionals about medicines and activities in such a way that you can use their directions to encourage him later on. For example: "Joe says he feels everything is hopeless and there is no need to take walks or do anything other than stay in bed and pull the covers over his head." "Joe says that medicine can't help a problem like his. He doesn't want to take the medicines because they're for 'crazy people.'" This type of questioning will produce instructions from the professionals that you can refer to later when you are attempting to motivate your Joe at home. For example, "Remember, Joe, Dr. Jones said it was better for you to get up and take a walk rather than staying in bed. He said depression was like pain and, if you could distract yourself, it would feel better to be active rather than lying there and thinking negative thoughts."

Let the Professionals Help You

The professionals can lift some of your burden at home. In the army, the commanding officer will frequently ream out the first sergeant in front of the troops. He is not doing this to lord it over the noncommissioned officer (NCO), but to make the NCO's job easier. The men can see that their sergeant is not giving them orders simply to be bossy—he is just passing on instructions given to him by his own commander. You can use this technique by talking to your doctor's nurse about the problems you are having with your depressed man. She, or he, and the doctor can then instruct you in your man's presence during your next visit. For example, if you are having a problem getting him up and moving in the morning, the nurse and the doctor can tell you, in front of him, "You must see to it that he is showered and his teeth are brushed by 8:00 a.m." As you are attempting to pry him out of bed the next day, you can remind your man that you were given this assignment.

Give Your Man Positive Feedback

Emphasize the positive observations and comments by the doctors. Reinforce the professionals' recommendations and point out positive changes you observe as a result of the medication and the psychotherapy. "You're starting to get your sparkle back." "You seemed to sleep more peacefully last night." "You're eating more, and the nurse told me you're starting to regain the weight you lost." "I noticed that you made an effort to change your negative thoughts into positive ones yesterday the way your therapist suggested." "The doctor said you look more alert and energetic." Of course you cannot be upbeat at all times. When you are feeling particularly optimistic and positive, you can slip into your cheerleader mode and try to boost his morale. When you start feeling drained, other members of your informal treatment team may be able to step in to cheer him on and to provide you with some relief.

Distract Him with Activities at Home

Various nonmedical approaches are employed by caregivers in the treatment of depressed men at home. In my opinion, the primary value of these activities is to distract the patient until the medications and conventional therapies work. These activities lessen his suffering and keep him occupied until he regains hope. They are things that you can do with him at home. In the next chapter I will describe some of the alternative therapies that you might consider as well. Because of his inertia, it is likely that you will have to accompany him to many of these activities. The main idea is to get his mind off the suffering from his depression just as you would if he had chronic pain.

Socialize with Strangers

While not a therapy per se, it's helpful to involve depressed men in social activities with healthy individuals. Depressed men withdraw from social contacts because it takes energy to smile and pay attention to others. They do not want to run into friends and family who tell them how they've changed or ask them what's wrong. Therefore, take him to social situations with people who do not know him. He will be forced to pay attention to others and to get his mind off himself. Individuals who are not intimately familiar with him will not be as likely to recognize that he is ill and will not question his level of functioning.

> Take him to social situations with people who do not know him.

Dancing

Dance with him. Some men hate to dance because they feel incompetent or out of control. Some think it is a feminine activity. You might be able to talk your man into taking private dancing lessons with you. He will find that when he is thinking about the steps, he isn't thinking about his depression. The exercise will be good for both of you. If he sees you are enjoying it, it will make him feel better knowing he is doing something to make you happy. As an aside, Louis XIV of France used this technique to distract his courtiers from plotting to overthrow him.

When he let it be known that he favored the best dancers, the members of his court soon grew preoccupied with taking dance lessons and practicing their steps instead of hatching rebellion.

I can personally attest to the benefits of dancing and dance lessons. I was once practically phobic about dancing. I knew my wife liked to dance and I wanted her to enjoy herself, but I felt extremely self-conscious, awkward, and generally inept on the dance floor. I would sit with her at a table next to the floor watching our friends dance and break out in a sweat: I knew I should ask her to dance, but every bone in my body resisted. Finally, she talked me into private lessons, and I developed a (false) sense of competence. Now I look forward to dancing with her. Yes, I'm still challenged as a dancer, but I realize that everyone is out there to have fun. This is not a competitive event.

Singing

Try singing. As a nation we seem to be inhibited when it comes to group singing. When our Tae Kwon Do team was in Mexico, each team sang some folk songs from their country. The Americans were at a loss when it was their turn. They sang "Row, Row, Row Your Boat" and "Home on the Range" and felt uncomfortable doing it. Karaoke, church, choir, piano bars, barbershop groups, and Christmas caroling are all possible venues in which you and he can sing. You can sing along with the radio in the car. The ancient Greeks observed that singing and dancing were therapeutic; they still are.

> The ancient Greeks observed that singing and dancing were therapeutic; they still are.

He may resist because of the inertia that accompanies his depression and because he fears he will not perform well. Accompany him and assure him that there is no competition or concern about his performance.

Athletics

Athletics can provide a great diversion from depression. Golf, tennis, pool, bowling, horseshoes, croquet, badminton, volleyball, martial arts—whatever has some appeal and is low-pressure will get his mind off his negative thoughts and give him some physical activity. In golf, you can encourage him to get excited about the good shots he makes and forget the bad ones. Then tell him to do the same thing in life.

Exercise in any form offers benefits for depressed men. It relieves tension, seems to speed recovery, and provides concrete evidence of progress. In addition, it helps the sufferer get his mind off his illness. Take him out for walks. The activity will be good for you as well. (See the next chapter for more on this subject.)

Charity and Service to Others

Helping others is a reward in itself. In addition, it forces your depressed man to focus on others rather than his own suffering. Encourage him to take some food to a shut-in, shovel a widow's sidewalk, mow a lawn, take toys to underprivileged kids, or serve a meal to the homeless. Years ago, one of the senior attorneys in town told me that his practice had dwindled down to a few older clients he had looked after over the years. "My practice is getting to be like yours," he said. "My elderly clients complain about their pains and losing their friends from illness. Most of them seem depressed. I tell them to make a bowl of soup and take it to one of their neighbors—it seems to work." Karl Menninger was once asked what people should do if they were on the verge of a nervous breakdown. He advised, "Lock up your house, go across the railroad tracks, find someone in need, and do something for them." Most religions, including the Christian faith, preach the idea of service to others. If you do something for someone else, without expecting anything in return, you will be rewarded by good feelings. Loving gestures benefit both the donor and the recipient.

Chores

As I've mentioned, compulsive work can be a manifestation of depression in men. Chores, on the other hand, provide distraction, activity, and, at the end of the day, a sense of accomplishment. Depending on the degree of depression he is suffering, the chores may be simple or more complex. You will need to break them down into simple steps and write out a detailed "honey-do" list for him.

Personal Hygiene

Everything is an effort for a depressed man. He has to push himself to get out of bed, to take a shower, to brush his teeth, and to put on proper clothing. Nurses in the hospital have to urge their depressed patients to carry out these routine tasks. You are his nurse at home and will need to coax him to follow a schedule of getting up, showering, brushing his teeth, shaving, combing his hair, and getting dressed each day.

→←

In addition to home-based activities to occupy and distract him, a number of formalized, nonmedical, nonpsychological treatments are available that are purported to help relieve depression. I'll describe and discuss some of these in the next chapter. In my opinion their principal value is distraction as well. In some cases, these approaches may have a placebo effect. I do not mean to belittle or minimize their importance in your depressed man's recovery, however. Anything that will encourage him, provide temporary relief for his suffering, and keep him occupied until he regains hope is of value.

CHAPTER SIX

Other Activities
That Help Depression

I shall pass through this world but once, therefore, if there be any kindness I can show or any good thing I can do let me do it now, let me not defer it or neglect it for I shall not pass this way again.

— *De Grellet*

The current accepted treatment of clinical depression consists of antidepressant medication and cognitive-behavioral therapy (CBT). At the least, it takes two to three weeks for the medications to start to work, and longer to see results from therapy. The purpose of this chapter is to describe other activities that may facilitate recovery and will serve to distract your man from the internal suffering and negative thought patterns that are a part of his depressive illness.

Treating Depression without Medicine

Forty years ago, inpatient treatment programs involved various activities aimed at permitting patients to express their anger without feeling guilty. Patients sanded tables. They broke colored glass and then used

137

the broken pieces to make ashtrays and lamp shades. They chopped wood and beat rugs. They were instructed to ask for things they wanted and to say no to demands made by the psychiatric nurses.

In the 1970s psychiatrists learned, to their chagrin, that episodes of depression were usually self-limiting, and the average duration of a typical episode of the illness was six to nine months. Patients recovered in the same period of time whether they were involved in milieu therapy or not. The same lesson applied to patients taking medication. Typically, they started to respond in two to three weeks whether they were involved in activities or remained idle. In other words, the elaborate programs psychiatrists designed to help patients express their unconscious hostility had nothing to do with their recoveries.

Having said all this, there were anecdotal stories of depressed patients recovering as a result of therapeutic interventions by hospital treatment staff. From today's perspective, we would probably conclude that these patients recovered spontaneously and the actions of the staff were incidental—but at the time the cures seemed almost magical. I recall one such case that was particularly fascinating.

A sixty-year-old executive was referred to the Menninger Clinic for the treatment of his severe depression. He had not responded to therapy in his own community and had become so withdrawn that he stopped talking. He sat in his room with his head down day in and day out.

As was the case with most Menninger patients at the time, the staff received copious documentation of his previous psychiatric treatment records in advance. It was noted that his main hobby was horseback riding and that, prior to the onset of his depressive illness, he had enjoyed looking after his horses on the small ranch where he and his wife resided. In anticipation of his arrival at our hospital, an occupational therapist named Frank was selected to work with him one-to-one. Frank, too, was a horseman, and it was felt that he might have something in common with the patient and might be able to form a therapeutic relationship with him.

After the patient was admitted, Frank arrived at his room at 9:00 a.m. and introduced himself. He talked to the man about horses while the patient sat on the bed with his head down, giving no response. Frank came in from 9:00 to 10:00 a.m. daily for the first two weeks and talked about horses. The third week Frank began bringing in reins, harnesses, and saddles to talk about during his hourly visits. In week five Frank took the patient outside and put him on a horse. He then walked the horse, with the patient astride, around the hospital grounds. Frank continued this daily for the next month.

So far the patient had not spoken a word; nor had he appeared to respond to Frank in any way. On a Tuesday, after twelve weeks of hourly visits, Frank failed to appear at the patient's room at 9:00 a.m. At 9:05 the patient got up from his bed, walked to the door, and stuck his head out into the hall. Frank was standing outside the door with a bucket of cold water, which he threw on the patient. "I knew you would come looking for me!" Frank shouted and laughed. The patient began laughing along with Frank and started talking to him. He continued to improve and eventually recovered and was discharged home from the hospital.

This case was legendary during my time in Topeka. It is unlikely that you will find it reported in any psychiatric textbook. I have never heard of any other instance in which throwing cold water on a patient shocked him into health. This was something that Frank came up with independently. I think it does illustrate that compassion, concern, patience, and kindness are all important ingredients in a therapeutic relationship. Perhaps the patient would have spontaneously recovered without Frank's intervention, but the fact is he did it when Frank doused him with water and laughed.

This unusual treatment approach illustrates that, while today we believe depression is genetically determined and chemically based, there is still

Sometimes the Cure Is Worse than the Illness

I once spoke with a physician in Africa who'd witnessed psychiatric treatment by a witchdoctor specializing in the treatment of mental disorders. The witchdoctor-psychiatrist was called to diagnose and treat a psychotic villager. He instructed the local elders to have the patient under a particular acacia tree at sunrise and to bring along a live goat. At the appointed hour a group of villagers arrived with an agitated fellow and a goat. The witchdoctor asked them to dig a large grave and to put both patient and goat in it. They did so, then shoveled back the dirt and buried the goat and the man alive.

The witchdoctor danced, sprinkled herbs, and rattled a shaker over the grave. Then he had them dig up the goat and the man. The goat was dead and the man, nearly so. The witchdoctor proclaimed that the evil spirit had left the man, entered the goat, and killed it. He then turned to the man, who was just regaining consciousness: "How are you?" The man replied, "I'm cured." Everyone rejoiced.

My point is this: The man knew that if he hadn't been "cured," he would have been put under the ground with a new goat at sunrise. Who wouldn't have claimed recovery?

I am not sure if there is any parallel to this technique in modern medicine, but I know that some patients—on hearing a doctor say, "If you do not respond to this medication, we will consider electroconvulsive therapy"—have reported feeling much better on the prescribed drug.

much we do not understand—and each human being is a unique individual. If someone responds to being doused with cold water, so be it— the important thing is that he got better. Our job as caregivers is to offer lots of alternatives, distract the depressive from his negative thoughts, and extend hope.

Just as we sincerely believed in the 1960s that our elaborate treatment plans to help patients express their negative feelings were what made them better, some practitioners and some patients feel the alternative approaches listed in this chapter cure depression. In fact, we probably did save many lives back then by keeping patients busy and distracted until they recovered. Patients were supported for six to nine months by the attention they received from their compassionate caregivers. Who cares who is right? The important thing is the recovery of the patient. If your depressed

> **Our job as caregivers is to offer lots of alternatives, distract the depressive from his negative thoughts, and extend hope.**

man takes his antidepressants but is convinced that hot baths and massages brought him out of the doldrums—then agree with him. But make sure he keeps taking his pills.

Distractions and Options

Earlier I suggested that you needed to form an informal treatment team to help sustain you in your efforts to support your man throughout his illness. Think of a tree. The more roots a tree has to sustain it, the more likely it is to survive.

In the same way, it is helpful to offer many options and alternatives to help your depressed man during his recovery. This chapter will describe a few of the myriad treatments that have been suggested for the treatment of depression. Some provide short-term positive feelings, some inspire hope, many distract the sufferer from the pain of depression for a period of time, some probably provide a placebo effect, and some give the patient a feeling that he is in control of his illness. Our goal is to help the depressed man recover and not give up and harm himself before this happens. To the extent that these alternative methods aid us in this mission, we welcome their use.

Sex

I didn't plan to include the topic of sex here. Then I started talking to men about this book, written for women trying to help their depressed partner. Every single man I spoke to remarked in one way or another that he hoped I would urge the women to give their men more sex.

> Every single man I spoke to remarked in one way or another that he hoped I would urge the women to give their men more sex.

Sex is certainly a way of making a man feel loved as well as bolstering his feelings of adequacy and masculinity. Many depressed men find sex less pleasurable than usual given the anhedonia that accompanies the disease. Their need for sex continues at the same frequency, however. So sex and reassurance about your love and need for him are important. If he is having problems with erectile dysfunction, mention this to the doctor's nurse. The solution may be as simple as a prescription for Viagra, Cialis, or Levitra.

I should also add at this point that one of the women who reviewed this book commented that this section probably represented another pitiful attempt by men to get more sex.

Exercise

It is debated but generally accepted that exercise is beneficial for depressed men. When your man is using his body, he is resting his mind, and this provides relief from the negative rumination that is a symptom of his illness. Exercise has an antidepressant effect itself. One of my elderly depressed farmer patients was certain that he'd walked his way out of a depressive episode when he was younger. He had an identical twin brother who retired from farming when he reached seventy. The first year he walked to town to get his mail. The second year he hired a boy to get his mail, and the third year he died. My patient was in his nineties and still helping his son put up hay. He said that he saw what happened to his twin brother and was determined to remain physically active.

Exercise relieves tension. Depressed men experience a double whammy of tension: They're frustrated by the limitations imposed by their illness, while irritability is one of its symptoms. Physical exertion provides a means of releasing some of this stress and aggression. Bipolar men have difficulty with anger and irritability during the manic phases of their illnesses as well. Punching a heavy bag or working out on a speed bag are ways to get rid of some of the anger that often accompanies melancholy in men.

> Recovery from depression takes time, and progress in therapy can be vague. Physical activity, on the other hand, produces change that can be quantified.

Recovery from depression takes time, and progress in therapy can be vague. Physical activity, on the other hand, produces change that can be quantified. You can show him how he is walking farther in less time. He can see that he is lifting more weight and performing more repetitions. Concrete evidence of advancement is encouraging to your depressed man.

Exercise increases his metabolism and makes his medicines work faster. This can be a motivating factor for a man who wants rapid relief from his illness.

Men with chronic pain learn that they need to throw themselves into activities that distract them from the pain. Activity does not lessen the pain but does provide relief simply by diverting the individual's thoughts from the discomfort. Men who lie in bed ruminating suffer more than those who are up and about. You might say, "I have read, and Dr. Jones confirms, that exercise can make your medicines work more quickly and distract you from negative thinking. Come for a walk outside with me. Just being out in the sunlight will help."

A Reason to Get Up in the Morning

In addition to physical activity, mental activity is important. Men need a reason to get up in the morning. I read that the concept of retirement was developed after World War II in order to free up jobs for returning young veterans. Men over sixty-five bought into the idea and stopped working to play golf, travel, work on their lawns, and generally take it easy. Women, on the other hand, continued to follow essentially the same routine they did prior to sixty-five.

It has been observed that men are at high risk for illness immediately after retirement. It has been postulated that retirement plays a role in men dying earlier than women. I personally do not feel that men should retire. They may choose to change their vocational course late in life. Certainly they should try to eliminate the stressful aspects of their work and hold on to those they find gratifying and rewarding. They may choose to devote more time to recreation, hobbies, sports, and leisure activities. However, it is my firm belief that men need a purpose in life and must feel that they are contributing to society in some fashion.

In my own case, I eventually eliminated from my professional life the hospital work that was the most stressful aspect of my practice. I reduced my hours and the number of patients I saw daily. As a result, I feel that my life is balanced and rewarding. I tell others my practice is limited to nice people, and I look forward to seeing my patients during the three days I am in my office and the one day I consult at Sharon Healthcare. I feel that I am making a contribution by writing as well. I enjoy passing on some of the wisdom I think I have garnered over my years of practice. Hopefully, I will be of some help to patients and their families beyond the walls of my office.

> Men need a purpose in life and must feel that they are contributing to society in some fashion.

For men who do retire, for one reason or another, I believe it is very important to find activities that are meaningful. Men need a reason to get up in the morning and to have a sense of accomplishment at the end of the day. Hobbies, sports, and travel are entertaining and distracting, but I believe we need to be involved in projects that are of service to others as well. This may be as simple as taking a bowl of soup to a shut-in or mowing a widow's lawn.

Other Activities that Help Depression

Recent studies suggest that having a purpose in life can even stave off some of the effects of Alzheimer's disease. It makes sense that a man with a *raison d'etre* in life is going to be more active and less depressed than one who feels useless.

Looking Good

Depressed men may neglect their hygiene, grooming, and dress. Encourage your guy to take care of his appearance. You might say, "I un-

145

derstand that everything is an effort for you right now, but I know you'll feel better after a nice bath and shave. I laid out some clothes for you on your bed."

Support Groups

Many depressed men benefit from attending a support group. Look for a group that has members with whom he might feel comfortable. Suggest to him that he may feel anxious as to what he should bring up and regarding issues of confidentiality. Reassure him that all new group members have these feelings and that groups of this nature protect members' privacy. There are many support groups available for depressed individuals and their significant others. You might tell him that you would like him to attend for your benefit because you are interested in learning about depression so that you can be more helpful to him. Interacting with people he doesn't know will alleviate some of his embarrassment and will prevent comments about how much he has changed, or questions as to what is wrong with him, that are likely to arise among family and friends.

If he is deeply depressed, you may not be able to convince him to attend a social event. Support groups may have the advantage of exposing him to people he does not know who share the depressive illness in common with him. Attendance may help distract him and force him to get his mind off himself in a supportive atmosphere. These groups are good for emotional support but are usually not a good source of information about treatment. The same goes for support groups on the internet. There is a great deal of misinformation available, which may cause him to be confused about his own treatment and might undermine his faith in his professional caregivers. You will need to accompany him and help him ignore inappropriate treatment suggestions.

Twelve-step programs are a particular type of support group. The best known is of course Alcoholics Anonymous (AA), but this group's approach has been applied to many other disorders as well. Narcotics Anonymous (NA) is a similar self-help organization for individuals with drug addiction. Overeaters Anonymous (OA) is for individuals addicted to food. Alanon is for spouses and children of addicts. In addition, there are 12-step programs for adult children of alcoholics, sexual addiction, gambling addiction, work addiction, internet gaming addiction, and even shopping addiction. John Bradshaw, one of the experts in the field of addiction, believes that 12-step programs convert the toxic shame that many addicts carry into guilt, which is then resolved by working the steps. These steps are a good path for anyone—addicted or not—to follow in life. They create a structured self-help program that leads to self-improvement and serenity. The organization offers support and compassion from its members. Sponsors provide individual mentoring. Several of my patients who used alcohol to cope with their depressive illnesses have been active in AA and found it to be helpful beyond the control of their alcohol addiction. Some patients prefer to think of themselves as alcoholics rather than mentally ill.

Years ago I took care of a patient who experienced episodes of psychotic depression with paranoid features. He would be brought to the hospital by his family convinced that communists were following him and trying to kill him. He was extremely embarrassed about being on a psychiatric unit and concerned about the stigma associated with mental illness. He said that he would drink one or two beers a night and he wondered if this made him an alcoholic. On his third hospital admission, I asked him if he would prefer to be on the chemical dependency unit instead of psychiatric services. His eyes lit up, and he

> These steps are a good path for anyone—addicted or not—to follow in life. They create a structured self-help program that leads to self-improvement and serenity.

quickly agreed. He became actively involved in Alcoholics Anonymous and, although he continued to take his antidepressant and antipsychotic medications, proudly assumed the identity of a recovering alcoholic.

As we have discussed, many depressed men engage in compulsive activities as a way to cope with their depressive illnesses. Some of them will benefit greatly from involvement in a 12-step program.

Light Therapy

Seasonal affective disorder (SAD) is believed to be a subcategory of bipolar disorder. When the skies are overcast in fall and winter, SAD sufferers go into a funk. They oversleep, overeat, and feel depressed until spring, when they become hyperactive and filled with energy. In my experience, nearly all depressed patients feel worse when we have several overcast days in a row and perk up when we have bright sun and blue skies. Many of our patients have purchased therapeutic lights, which provide a spectrum of bright light that stimulates the hypothalamus, melatonin production, and the neurotransmitter systems involved in depression. Patients turn on their lights in the morning and evening and extend their exposure to light during the winter months. Nearly all have reported some benefit from this procedure. Just having more light in the house may help in this regard. Opening up the shades and letting as much light into the house as possible is probably a good idea for most depressives.

Herbal Preparations

Some patients are attracted to "natural" treatments as opposed to pharmaceutical products. A recent study suggests that as many as one third of senior depressed patients are using herbal nutritional compounds (HNC) to treat their depressive illnesses. The two most commonly used herbals for depression are St. John's Wort (the active ingredient may be hypericum) and SAMe (S-adenosylL-methionine). In my experience high doses of these preparations may, at best, be equivalent to low doses of antidepressant medications. When researchers at Harvard studied SAMe, they found that many of the preparations they purchased did not contain the active ingredient and that it required a high dose of the active ingredient to equal 75mg of imipramine (the usual dose is 100 to 300mg per day). When patients ask me about these preparations, I respond that taking them for clinical depression is, in my opinion, like hunting elephants with a BB gun.

Although the herbal preparations are, at best, weak antidepressants, there are precautions with some of them. St. John's Wort is a weak MAOI and, as such, should not be taken by anyone already on a MAOI. I should add that, during the years that I was immersed in martial arts training, I tried a number of herbal products at the master's recommendation. I drank ginseng tea daily and once ate a ginseng chicken. The master said his mother always prepared it for him prior to a tournament and, as a favor to me, she came to my house and cooked a chicken in ginseng in a Crock-Pot for over twenty-four hours. I was instructed to eat it all. It was the most vile-tasting thing I have ever ingested. He assured me that my chi would be flowing after this. I was unable to correlate temporary nausea with improved performance in the tournament, but I did find that eating kimchee prior to a match tended to keep my opponent at a distance. (Garlic breath is potent!)

Martial Arts

Many martial arts practitioners feel training in their particular art relieves depression as well as other mental disorders. When I was involved in Tae Kwon Do, the master asked me to test the students using the Minnesota Multiphasic Personality Inventory (MMPI), a standardized psychological screening test consisting of 567 items. The results showed that the group was somewhat higher than normal on the anxiety scales.

> Martial arts training offers many positive benefits. Stretching provides greater flexibility, and meditation teaches calmness and focus.

The master then had the students line up and announced: "You are a very unique group. You have more anxiety than normal—therefore breathe out when you punch. HUH!"

I do believe martial arts training offers many positive benefits. Stretching provides greater flexibility, and meditation teaches calmness and focus. Martial arts involves strenuous exercise. Practitioners yell when they hit or kick (kiap), which creates a great outlet for frustration and aggression. I am certain that, if you can get your depressed man to participate, he'll benefit in many ways from the activity. There are excellent female practitioners, but it is a macho activity and may reinforce his masculinity—if he is able to do it.

Meditation

Some references suggest that depressed individuals might be helped by meditating. It is not easy to learn or to do. Sports psychologists found that athletes had more difficulty meditating than carrying out the strenuous physical workouts their sport required. Yoga, Buddhism, and the martial arts all emphasize and provide training in meditation. This provides relaxation, improves focus and concentration, and can lead to greater personal insight.

Meditation grows even more difficult to do when concentration is impaired by depression. In addition, there is a danger that your depressed male will ruminate on negative topics rather than counting his breaths or clearing his mind with meditation.

Biofeedback

Biofeedback is a method to provide feedback to the patient from his efforts to relax and control various aspects of his autonomic (involuntary) nervous system. A famous guru who visited Dr. Green's biofeedback research laboratory at the Menninger Clinic years ago took several biofeedback machines with him when he returned to India. He said that by using the machine, individuals were able to establish control over body temperature, blood pressure, and other autonomic functions much more rapidly than meditation practitioners were able to do by traditional methods.

When learning a new skill, the natural tendency is to try harder. With meditation and biofeedback, the novice must learn not to try, but to let go. Monitoring pulse and blood pressure allows an individual to see when he is relaxing and when he is tensing up. In time he learns to relax and develops control of his autonomic nervous system. In this way he is able to lower his pulse and blood pressure and reduce muscle tension.

> With meditation and biofeedback, the novice must learn not to try, but to let go.

EMDR

Eye movement desensitization and reprocessing (EMDR) has been shown to be helpful in the treatment of post-traumatic stress disorder and has been applied to the treatment of depression. In his book *The Noonday Demon: An Atlas of Depression*, Andrew Solomon says, "While many therapies—psychoanalysis for example— comprise beautiful theories and limited results, EMDR has silly theories and excellent results." I agree. The theoretical explanation for EMDR doesn't make much sense, but the therapy itself appears to be helpful to patients. Googling EMDR on the internet will provide a list of institutes and websites offering additional information and referrals to practitioners specializing in this approach.

Vitamins and Supplements

Vitamins and supplements are appealing to some as adjuncts to their treatment. It would seem logical that taking amino acid precursors of norepinephrine and serotonin would benefit depression. However, attempts in the early 1970s to load depressed patients with L-phenylalynine, DL-phenylalynine, L-tyrosine, and L-tryptophan failed to provide relief of their symptoms. B vitamins, magnesium, calcium, zinc, methionine, and folic acid are recommended for depression by some holistic practitioners.

It seems to me that when families and patients begin to feel frustrated and discouraged, they start buying vitamins and listening to outside advice from friends and health practitioners. There is no shortage of individuals willing to provide suggestions for recovery from depression in person and on the internet. I do not try to dissuade my patients or their helpers from following these suggestions as long as the patient continues to take antidepressants and follow my treatment recommendations.

Acupuncture

Acupuncture, a 2,000-year-old technique of inserting thin needles into various points of the body to alter the flow of chi (life force), has been touted as a treatment for depression. The practice's mechanism of action has not been determined by Western researchers, but it has been found to be helpful for some patients for a variety of disorders including depression. I have heard testimonials from reputable individuals who say that acupuncture made them feel better when they were depressed.

Music

The Greeks in 500 B.C. had their melancholic patients listen to music. For some patients, loud, upbeat music can help get them going. Turning on the lights, opening the windows, and turning on loud music can sometimes help get a depressed man out of bed in the morning. Like his reading and entertainment, keep the music positive.

Humor

The ancient Greeks also recommended that their melancholic patients attend comedic plays. I tell patients to watch and listen to comedians. I also suggest they read cartoons and joke books. As I was leaving my dermatologist's office one day, he said, "Stay out of the sun." "Why?" I asked. "Do I have some condition that would require me to avoid ultraviolet light?" "No," he replied. "I say that to all patients—don't you have some general advice you give to all your psychiatric patients?" I thought for a moment and then said "Well, maybe—*don't watch the news.*" As I will discuss in the chapter on humor, I am a strong believer in laughter as medication and avoiding preoccupation with stressful current events.

Massage

No matter what illness you have, massage usually makes you feel better. There are many types of massage. Swedish massage is the most common type in the United States. Typically Swedish massage therapists use long smooth strokes on superficial layers of muscle along with massage lotion or oil. It is gentle and relaxing. When scented plant oils are added, it is referred to as aromatherapy massage. When heated, smooth stones are employed to warm and loosen up tight muscles, it is referred to as hot stone massage. Deep-tissue massage involves deeper layers of muscle and connective tissue. My favorite form of massage is shiatsu—

a Japanese bodywork that uses localized finger pressure on acupuncture meridians. Thai massage is similar to shiatsu but, in addition, the therapist stretches you into a sequence of postures similar to a passive yoga exercise. Reflexology applies pressure to points on the foot that correspond to systems and organs in the body.

> No matter what illness you have, massage usually makes you feel better.

There are many other types of massage that are relaxing and helpful in relieving tension in the muscles as well. My suggestion for the novice would be to ask individuals who have massage on a regular basis which practitioners they feel are most skilled and most helpful.

Baths

Hydrotherapy has been around since ancient times. Spas, hot baths, and whirlpool baths are all relaxing and generally make people feel better. Many depressed individuals neglect their personal hygiene, and a hot bath will reduce their body odor in addition to helping them relax. For men with arthritis or other problems that prevent them from walking, jogging, biking, or performing other aerobic forms of exercise, water aerobics may be an alternative. Most YMCAs or YWCAs and health clubs offer this activity. The upbeat group atmosphere may provide an additional boost for the men who participate.

Sleep Deprivation

Sleep deprivation is an experimental treatment for depression. Typically depressed people feel their worst in the morning and better as the day progresses. Extending the day by not going to sleep as early may extend their hours of feeling a little better. There have been attempts to

Does He Have a Sleep Disorder?

If your man snores loudly and seems to gasp at times during the night, you might think about having him see a sleep specialist. Sleep disorders can cause daytime drowsiness, which will add to his lack of energy and dysphoria. Sleep apnea can be greatly improved by the use of a C-PAP machine. There are medicines that help restless leg syndrome. In any event, a sleep study will help determine if a sleep disorder is present.

treat depression by keeping patients awake for extended periods of time. When the patients are finally permitted to sleep, they often have more rapid eye movement (REM) sleep, which may increase the release of neurotransmitters in the brain that are low in depression. In the short term, these patients seem to experience some antidepressant benefit from this procedure, but it is not effective in the long-term control of their depressive illnesses. When depressed patients take a nap, they typically feel worse when they awaken (similar to the nadir they experience when they awaken in the morning).

Nexalin Treatment

A few patients from our area have traveled to California to have Nexalin treatment, or transcranial stimulation. Several, including some fibromyalgia sufferers, have been enthusiastic about the results they have achieved. Electrodes are placed on the head, and while the patient feels nothing from the treatment itself, it reportedly stimulates the hypothalamus to release neurotransmitters and endorphins. It has recently been approved by the FDA, it is a safe procedure, and there are a number of testimonials about its effectiveness. It's a new procedure, and as of this writing the company is seeking a CPT code and insurance coverage. Apparently it has been successfully used in Europe. For more information and a chance to read the studies attesting to its effectiveness, visit www.nexalin.com.

Other Holistic Approaches

There are other holistic therapies that have been advertised as cures for depression. The Alexander Technique, the Feldenkrais Method, the Mitzvah Technique, Rolfing, drumming therapy, movement therapy, dance therapy, detoxification, and allergy treatments are all nontraditional remedies that have been said to help depression.

Francis Matthias Alexander, an Australian actor, had difficulty reciting in public. He observed himself in multiple mirrors and realized that his body stiffened when he prepared to speak. Instead of approaching the problem via the psychological aspects of his anxiety, he worked on correcting his posture and physical tension. The Alexander Technique was developed from this experience. This educational approach led to the Feldenkrais Method, the Mitzvah Technique, and Rolfing, in which tight muscle groups are identified and massaged while patients recall the events, conflicts, and emotions that led to each area of tension.

Andrew Solomon in *The Noonday Demon* reports some unusual suggestions he received to relieve his depression: making yarn objects, avoiding toxic chemicals, replacing his RNA, moving, watching videotapes of talking heads, energy therapies from a mystic, chanting, diet, Outward Bound–type activities that encouraged self-discovery and self-confidence, hypnosis, homeopathy, journaling, and an aminist ritual called *ndeup*, which he went through in Senegal.

None of these adjunctive activities is, in my opinion, effective in alleviating the symptoms of clinical depression. However, none of them is particularly harmful, either, and many seem to make people feel better. Their primary value may be to distract, occupy, and help patients maintain hope until their medicines and therapy begin to work and they eventually recover from their depressive illnesses. On a short-term basis, they may provide a little relief. The belief of the practitioner and the belief of the patient are both important factors in the results achieved.

The Main Goal Is to Help Your Man Feel Better

Depression is, as I have noted, a self-limiting illness. It could well be that an individual was coming out of depression at the time he took up knitting or walking or whatever he then credited for his recovery. For example, Jack Dreyfus, the "Lion of Wall Street" and breeder of race-horses, had been through numerous unsuccessful attempts to relieve his depression when he decided to try Dilantin (phenytoin, an anti-epileptic medication that has been on the market since 1938). He recovered and sponsored a research program on Dilantin, sending a copy of his book *The Story of a Remarkable Medicine*—describing the wonders of Dilantin—to every physician in the country. I received a copy. Personally, I've never seen a depressed individual respond to Dilantin, nor have I met a doctor who had a depressed patient who was successfully treated with it. Mr. Dreyfus also wrote *Written in Frustration*, documenting how information about the marvelous effects of Dilantin has been kept from the public. It may have been that Mr. Dreyfus was coming out of depression at the time he convinced his doctor to give him Dilantin; it's also possible that this drug worked for him and not for most other people. Mr. Dreyfus went through a long, painful bout of depression, and I am glad that he found relief with Dilantin.

➤✦

Things are seldom simple in life, and depressive illness is no exception. I have asserted that depression is a genetically determined illness caused by a chemical imbalance, and is best treated with antidepressant medication and cognitive-behavioral therapy. In this chapter we have examined a number of alternative approaches that have been reported

157

helpful for depressed individuals. It is unknown if these approaches offer an innate curative effect or if their palliative effects are due to distraction, a placebo effect, or simply paying attention to the patient. In the long run it probably doesn't matter. If your man is helped by one of these approaches or activities, then it's worthwhile.

CHAPTER SEVEN

More Than One Problem

Mysteriously and in ways that are totally remote from natural experience, the gray drizzle of horror induced by depression takes on the quality of physical pain.

—*William Styron*

Medical and psychological problems frequently accompany depression. Treating professionals need to recognize and treat these conditions in order to achieve complete remission of the depressed man's symptoms. If your man's recovery isn't progressing quite as well or as quickly as you'd anticipated, you might think of the possibility of other problems being present in addition to depression. In this chapter I will briefly describe some of the psychiatric and medical illnesses that commonly accompany depression. Later in the chapter I will discuss some of the pervasive personality patterns that may interfere with the diagnosis of or recovery from depression as well. The purpose of this information is not to make you into a junior psychiatrist, but to help you sort out the factors that may interfere with your man's speedy recovery from his depressive illness.

Just as other illnesses can interfere with recovery from depression, depression, especially if unrecognized and untreated, can complicate the recovery from other illnesses. The American Heart Association (AHA) recommends that all cardiac patients be screened for depression. Men who have heart attacks, strokes, cancer, diabetes, and Parkinson's frequently have depression as well. It is understandable that the suffering, anxiety, and limitations imposed by these serious illnesses might cause psychological distress. It is important to recognize the presence of depression in these men and treat it as soon as possible. The medical profession is aware that depression occurs with these disease states, but sometimes the initial focus is on the cardiac, neurological, or endocrine problem; the developing clinical depression is overlooked.

It Is Possible to Have More Than One Illness

In medical school we used to write, "innately obvious to the most casual observer" (IOMCC). Attorneys write *res ipsa loquitur*: the thing speaks for itself. Either way there are some things in life that would appear to be self-evident. One of these would be that your man could have more than one illness—and yet, in my experience, this is one of the most frequently overlooked realities in medicine.

One cause of this diagnostic error is that specialists tend to view the patient through the bias of their particular area of expertise and think of treatment in terms of what they do best. For example, if an internist is evaluating a depressed man and finds that he is anemic or has a low-functioning thyroid, he or she is likely to tell the patient, "No wonder you are feeling depressed, you are anemic." Or, "You aren't depressed; you are suffering from hypothyroidism." In the same vein, a sleep expert might say, "No wonder you're feeling low, you have sleep apnea." My experience treating depressed patients has taught me that these patients usually have both anemia *and* depression, low thyroid function *and* depression, and sleep apnea *and* depression. Zeroing in on the newly discovered medical problem and treating it to the exclusion of the depression only delays the treatment of the depression and full recovery.

I hospitalized one young man for treatment of an episode of severe (psychotic) depression. He went home, felt better, and began to wonder if he really needed to take the antidepressant and antipsychotic medication he had received. He stopped it. Not surprisingly, in two weeks his symptoms returned and he was readmitted to the hospital. I emphasized the need to stay on the medication to both the patient and his wife. He again went home and, after a longer period of time, once again weaned himself off his medicine . . . and ended up back on the psychiatric ward. I went over with him his history of stopping the medications twice and both times experiencing an exacerbation of his depression that required hospitalization. This time both he and his wife were convinced of the need for him to stay on his medicines. A year later his family physician noticed that this young man's SGOT and SGPT liver enzymes were slightly elevated. This is not unusual in patients who are taking drugs that are metabolized in the liver. The man's generalist referred him to a liver specialist, who promptly stopped his antidepressant and his antipsychotic medication. Two weeks later his symptoms returned and, for the third time, he returned to the psychiatric unit.

> It is self-evident that your man could have more than one illness—and yet, this is one of the most frequently overlooked realities in medicine.

Unfortunately this situation is not unusual in this era of specialization. Experts focus on their own area of expertise and fail to realize how serious and debilitating depression can be. A similar scenario occurred when a sleep expert stopped my patient's antidepressant without checking with me. The man ended up in the hospital with a recurrence of his depressive illness. I once referred to a surgeon a patient who had presented with symptoms of panic disorder but was found, by me, to have a pheochromocytoma. This rare benign adrenal tumor secretes hormones that cause a sudden rise in blood pressure and symptoms that mimic panic disorder. The surgeon who removed the benign tumor lectured his medical students and residents on the need to think of this tumor when patients present with symptoms of panic disorder and noted that he had cured a psychiatric problem with surgery. A few months after surgery the patient returned to my office with symptoms of panic disorder and responded to psychiatric treatment of the illness—at that time Nardil, a monoamine oxidase inhibitor (MAOI). He had both a pheochromocytoma and panic disorder.

The purpose of including these examples is not to criticize other specialists, but to support my earlier statement that there is a tendency to try to explain all findings on the basis of one illness when it is more likely, especially when depression is involved, that more than one illness is present. When patients suffering depression are not responding to treatment as anticipated, we begin looking for the possible presence of another illness. For example, hypothyroidism, anemia, and sleep apnea will all cause loss of energy and daytime fatigue that will not be helped by antidepressant medication or psychotherapy.

When You Hear Hoofbeats on the Bridge . . .

When I was a medical student, the professors told us, "When you hear hoofbeats on the bridge, don't think of unicorns." This admonishment is important to new students of medicine, who have been reading about all the rare medical and neurological illnesses that may present with symptoms similar to the much more prevalent illness of depression. The warning implies that while doctors should be aware of the existence of the unusual disorders, they need to think in terms of what is most likely to be the cause of the patient's symptoms and not waste time and money ruling out diseases that are extremely unusual. In my experience, elaborate work-ups of this nature are often the result of insecure new physicians trying to impress others with their knowledge of medicine—or of a patient's desire to have a diagnosis other than depression. One depressed patient proudly told me that his physician was in the process of evaluating him for "periodic, relapsing familial hypokalemia." He responded to standard antidepressant medication. Fans of the television show "House" may be attracted to rare, complicated diagnoses to explain their symptoms as well.

Conditions commonly associated with depression include migraine headaches, panic attacks (PD), obsessive-compulsive disorder (OCD), fibromyalgia, post-traumatic stress disorder (PTSD), multiple chemical sensitivity (MCS), chronic fatigue syndrome (CFS), and some gastrointestinal problems. The connections are so prevalent that a common chemical substrate is suspected. We know that these disorders frequently respond to antidepressant medications. Panic disorder, OCD, social anxiety, and PTSD respond to medications that block the reuptake of serotonin in the brain.

Let's look at some of the common co-morbid conditions that may accompany depressive illness in more detail.

Panic Disorder (PD)

Nearly one-third of young adults experience at least one panic attack, and approximately 2 percent of people worldwide develop a panic disorder during their lifetimes. It appears to be biologically based—there is a genetic factor of nearly 25 percent among close relatives. Two-thirds of individuals with panic disorder will experience an attack if given sodium lactate intravenously.

PD patients suddenly feel as though they are going to die or go crazy. Most have medical evaluations for heart disease, seizures, or other physical problems before getting to a psychiatrist. The details surrounding the first or "herald attack" are typically etched in the patient's memory due to the release of vasopressin in the brain, which is typical of peak experiences in our lives. Once a patient has his first attack, anything that reminds him of that event can key another attack. For example, if the patient is in the doctor's waiting room and starts smelling the chemical odors, feels light-headed, and starts worrying that he might pass out—he then either faints or jumps up and runs out of the office. After this, smelling chemical odors, being in closed spaces, going to the doctor's office—anything that reminds him of the attack—can initiate a new episode. Even the symptoms of rapid heartbeat, hyperventilation, dizziness, sweating, nausea, and shakiness can precipitate another attack. Nearly all of these patients undergo multiple medical evaluations before they arrive at our office. Frequently they are initially convinced that they are having a heart attack or a seizure. We had a support group for these patients and one individual, who was a professional musician, brought his guitar and sang a song about his ailment to the group entitled, "Gee, I'm a Hypochondriac." The song concluded, "… but my doctors like me and they even like my ills, because I'm a hypochondriac who pays his medical bills."

> Once a patient has his first panic attack, anything that reminds him of that event can key another attack.

Some patients find that working out in a gym causes them to hyperventilate and to perspire freely, their hearts beating rapidly. These physical events remind them of their previous attacks and can key a new one. Patients who become panicky in malls do so typically because they are afraid they can't exit quickly if they want to. Bridges, bathtubs, barber chairs, closed-in spaces, airplanes, and elevators all can evoke anxiety because the patient feels he can't easily escape. Sufferers of panic disorder in church or theaters can be quickly identified because they sit in the back corner close to the door. Panic disorder patients sometimes get into difficulty with alcohol when they discover that it relieves anticipatory anxiety. Frequently, after an evening of binge drinking, patients experience a panic attack the following morning when their alcohol level drops.

Panic disorder usually responds to low doses of a selective serotonin reuptake inhibitor (SSRI) and a benzodiazepine that they can take as needed for anticipatory anxiety.

Before the advent of effective medication for panic attacks, I had patients work with psychologists and support groups. They would have patients name the ten most frightening situations they could think of (elevators, bridges, closed spaces, malls, restaurants, doctor's waiting rooms . . .) in order of fear; the therapist would then have them visualize themselves in each situation and teach them to relax. (One of my most honest patients listed "Your fee of $120" as one of his most frightening situations.) When patients could relax while visualizing all ten scenarios, the psychologists would have them go out and actually put themselves in these situations and relax. I prescribed minor tranquilizers to use to help them control their anxiety and had them attend a support group that would cheer them on in their efforts.

This treatment approach changed in the late 1970s when a British psychiatrist published a paper describing a large number of patients with panic disorder who responded to the monoamine oxidase inhibitor Nardil (phenelzine). This was unheard of in the United States, where MAOIs were used as backup treatments for serious, resistant cases of depression and for atypical depression. When I read the paper, I pulled the charts on our patients with panic disorder and told them that while I had no experience using MAOIs for this problem, it appeared to be effective, and if they wanted to try it they could. They all wanted to try it, so apparently they were not too pleased with what we had been doing. To my surprise, they all got better.

Initially I had some difficulty getting patients to take the medicine. Anyone with panic disorder is already fearful and mistrustful of any new drug. The first question my patients asked was, "What are the possible side effects?" When I mentioned that one potential side effect was death due to cerebral vascular accident, their anxiety went through the ceiling. I did my best to educate them about the diet and precautions, but they would inevitably go home, sit on the edge of the bed, take their pill, and wait for bad things to happen. Unsurprisingly, many then experienced a panic attack and concluded that they were reacting to the drug. They would check and, sure enough, there was monosodium glutamate in the peas they'd eaten for supper, and they'd read that monosodium glutamate can cause protein breakdown, and if you have protein breakdown, you could have tyramine, and if you have tyramine, you could have a reaction.

To counteract their apprehension, I organized a support group consisting of "veteran" patients who were doing well on Nardil. These patients were, prior to their recoveries, socially isolated by their panic disorders and welcomed the opportunity to meet with a group of individuals who had common experiences. I introduced each new patient to a veteran I thought he would like and could relate to. New patients did not trust me completely, but they *would* listen to another panic sufferer who was actually taking Nardil. When they took their first pill and started thinking they might be having a reaction, they could call their "prayer partner," who would tell them, "Heck no, that's not a reaction, you're just afraid you're going to have a reaction. It takes four to six weeks for this stuff to work. Keep taking it—you'll love it."

> Anyone with panic disorder is already fearful and mistrustful of any new drug.

I used Nardil successfully to treat hundreds of patients with panic disorder for several years. Then psychiatrists began switching to the use of

SSRIs like Prozac or Zoloft along with benzodiazepines like Xanax or Ativan for the treatment of panic disorder; these are effective without most of the MAOIs' diet issues, side effects, or dangerous interactions with other medications. The MAOIs continue to be the most effective drugs for the treatment of panic disorder but are seldom used today because of the difficulties associated with their use.

Post-traumatic Stress Disorder (PTSD)

Post-traumatic stress disorder has received considerable publicity in recent years as combat veterans from Iraq and Afghanistan have returned and sought assistance from the military and Veterans Administration health services. Depression and PTSD are frequently connected among returning combat veterans. There is an association as well among civilian survivors of disasters and severe trauma. PTSD was described as a psychiatric disorder in 1980 among Vietnam combat veterans. It is estimated that six of ten combat veterans returning from Iraq and Afghanistan suffer from psychological problems. Most of these experience symptoms of PTSD and/or depression. There are some estimates that up to 30 percent of disaster victims experience symptoms of PTSD.

These individuals experienced, witnessed, or were confronted with severely traumatic events that evoked intense fear, helplessness, or horror. They re-experience the traumatic event in the form of recurrent distressing thoughts or dreams. An example would be a veteran dropping to the ground when a car backfires or attacking a waiter who surprises him from behind.

They avoid stimuli associated with the trauma. One combat veteran from Afghanistan, who had been a gunsmith and an avid hunter before deployment, avoided any contact with weapons after his return. Others have amnesia around the traumatic experiences.

An individual suffering from PTSD may experience psychic numbing and feel detached or estranged from others. He may have a sense of a foreshortened future. He may show signs of increased arousal. Difficulty falling asleep, increased irritability, hypervigilance, and exaggerated startle response are common symptoms.

> It is estimated that six of ten combat veterans returning from Iraq and Afghanistan suffer from psychological problems.

The combination of symptoms may significantly impair his social, occupational, or other important areas of function. During World War II, a researcher named Grinker used sodium amytal interviews to help soldiers re-experience the trauma that had led to their symptoms. I used this method and hypnosis at Fort Knox and in Vietnam and, like Grinker, found that this dramatically alleviated many of the soldiers' symptoms—but not sufficiently to return them to combat. Today the military is experimenting with virtual reality equipment to help combat veterans relive their battlefield trauma. Counseling for trauma victims and their families is helpful. Eye movement desensitization and reprocessing (EMDR) has been found to be of use. Zoloft is the only Food and Drug Administration–approved drug for the treatment of acute and chronic PTSD. Paxil is approved for the treatment of acute PTSD. From a practical standpoint, the other SSRIs and even the dual-acting antidepressants are effective for PTSD as well. The benzodiazepines may be used to reduce associated symptoms of anxiety. Inderal given near the exposure to the traumatic event has been shown to diminish the long term effects of PTSD in many cases.

Generalized Anxiety Disorder (GAD)

Nearly 3 percent of the population experiences symptoms of generalized anxiety disorder (GAD) in any one-year period; the lifetime prevalence is 5 percent. This translates into six to nine million individuals. These sufferers experience chronic, irrational worry to the extent that they feel physically ill.

Many of the antidepressant medications will also help anxiety. For example, the old tricyclics, the SSRIs, and the MAOIs are all useful in relieving anxiety as well as depression. Antidepressants that do not elevate the levels of serotonin in the brain—such as Wellbutrin and Strattera (atomoxetine)—do not alleviate symptoms of anxiety in patients. Those that block the reuptake of serotonin are useful, however. It is not uncommon to prescribe benzodiazepine medications on an as-needed basis as well to treat anticipatory anxiety.

> GAD sufferers experience chronic, irrational worry to the extent that they feel physically ill.

Obsessive-Compulsive Disorder (OCD)

Two to 3 percent of the population develops symptoms of obsessive compulsive disorder during their lifetime. This translates into nearly four million Americans. Prior to the introduction of Tofranil into the market, people were tortured by the symptoms of this disorder. Those who were treated with psychoanalysis acquired great insight into themselves, but their OCD symptoms remained unaltered. In the past, patients were so tormented by their illnesses that they sought frontal lobotomies, which left them free of anxiety but flat and emotionless in many cases. Tofranil was the first medication that appeared to help relieve symptoms of obsessive-compulsive disorder in patients. Anafranil was even more effective, though many patients were unable to tolerate its side effects when adequate treatment doses were reached.

Then it was discovered that high doses of SSRIs, along with behavioral therapy, were effective and better tolerated by many patients with OCD.

When obsessive-compulsive disorder is associated with clinical depression, both problems must be addressed in treatment. Generally OCD responds to higher doses of an SSRI, in some instances augmented with Anafranil.

Migraine Headaches

There is a connection between migraine headaches and depression. The two disorders tend to run in families. Frequently both are present, and sometimes the treatment of depression relieves the headaches as well. A recent study notes a seeming correlation among migraines, left-handedness, and bipolar disorder. In the old days, many patients from our area who suffered from chronic headaches were sent to the Diamond Headache Clinic in Chicago. The ones I saw in my practice were frequently put on lithium and Nardil for the treatment of their headaches. Lithium is a mood stabilizer used for bipolar disorder. Nardil, a monoamine oxidase inhibitor, is a powerful antidepressant used for depression, atypical depression, and panic disorder.

Fibromyalgia

Fibromyalgia is a relatively newly recognized disorder that responds to antidepressant medication. Sufferers are usually careful to point out that their difficulties are not due to depression. They emphasize that this is not a psychological disorder and that they must be treated by nonpsychiatric specialists who understand the disease and its treatment. I see a number of patients with this diagnosis in my practice. They benefit from antidepressant medications but typically require periodic changes in medication as the antidepressants that initially are beneficial appear to fade in effectiveness over time.

Chronic Fatigue Syndrome (CFS)

Four out of a thousand people in the United States report having symptoms of chronic fatigue syndrome. More are women than men, and they're typically in the forty-to-fifty-year age group. In my experience, CFS is often seen in conjunction with fibromyalgia. These patients also feel they are not depressed; nor do they have psychological difficulties. They initially feel their problems are due to Epstein-Barr syndrome, post-mononucleosis, or some other viral disorder. If the work-ups for these disorders are negative or inconclusive, they are diagnosed as having CFS. Twenty-five percent of these patients are unemployed or on disability. A small percentage (5 to 10 percent) achieve full resolution of their symptoms.

Multiple Chemical Sensitivity (MCS)

Multiple chemical sensitivity (MCS) is a rarer malady that may be associated with the problems above. MCS patients become ill if exposed to shaving lotion, smoke, cleaning solutions, or virtually any chemicals in their environment. This restricts their activities to a great extent. It can be troublesome when they visit our office—we have to extinguish any scented candles and air out any rooms people wearing perfume or shaving lotion may have occupied. Some of our patients had to wait in a clinic room instead of the waiting room because they could not tolerate the chemicals on other patients. The courts have not upheld disability claims on the basis of MCS because of a dearth of scientific evidence supporting it as a diagnosis.

Irritable Bowel Syndrome (IBS)

Irritable bowel syndrome (IBS) is generally thought to result from an interaction between the brain and the gut although, in some cases, an alteration of intestinal flora has been demonstrated. Many patients who

171

present with gastrointestinal problems are found to be depressed as well. Some of these patients find that their alternating symptoms of diarrhea and constipation respond to antidepressant medication.

Coronary Heart Disease (CHD)

Depressed men have a 71 percent greater risk of coronary heart disease; their risk of dying from CHD is increased by a factor of 2.34. This is another reason to have the family physician on the case: to rule out CHD and to treat any symptoms that may arise. It's also another reason to identify and treat depression in men. By controlling the depressive illness, the risk of CHD is reduced.

Attention Deficit Disorder (ADD) and Attention Deficit/Hyperactivity Disorder (ADHD)

ADD and ADHD are diagnoses that are typically associated with grade school kids, who are treated with Ritalin or amphetamines. It is an important diagnosis to make, as failing to treat the disorder can lead to problems with low self-esteem and self-confidence as well as poor academic, social, and vocational performance. On the other hand, it seems to me that, in recent years, kids who have behavioral problems in grade school are likely to be given a stimulant without receiving individual and family therapy. Managed care, expediency, parental guilt, and other outside factors appear to favor the prescription of a pill over a more holistic approach to the problem.

In recent years we have learned that attention deficit disorder frequently extends into adulthood. Because of their inattentiveness and problems organizing their lives, these individuals typically have problems obtaining and maintaining employment. They are restless and find it difficult to finish projects. They may interrupt others in conversations. They lose things. They are quick to anger and have problems in their relationships. They tend to get into legal difficulties. They get speeding tickets and are accident-prone. They may require both antidepressant medication as well as stimulants to address their attention disorder. Their academic, legal, vocational, and relationship problems may cause them to be psychologically depressed and, if they are genetically predisposed, clinically depressed as well.

> **Attention deficit disorder frequently extends into adulthood.**

If the problem of ADD or ADHD is not addressed it is likely that these men will not be completely relieved of their depressive symptoms with antidepressant medication alone. They will benefit from therapy to help them, and their significant others, understand and cope with their attention problems as well as those associated with depression.

Eating Disorders

Another category of illnesses commonly associated with depression is eating disorders. While more common in women, some men also have problems with anorexia, bulimia, and compulsive eating. Typically men have insomnia and weight loss associated with their depressive illnesses; more women have symptoms of atypical depression with weight gain and hypersomnia. If present, it is likely that your man showed symptoms of an eating disorder before the onset of his depressive symptoms. If this is the case, or if his depression appears to be responding to treatment but he continues to have symptoms of an eating disorder, this problem will need to be addressed in therapy as well.

Diagnostic Labeling

Rather than argue about the cause or cure of these problems or who can best diagnose and treat them, their frequent association leads one to suspect that there is probably a common chemical basis underlying all of them. As we reach a better understanding of the causes and cures of these illnesses, it is likely we will change their names to something like "serotonin and/or norepinephrine deficiency." At this point we lack the understanding required to give them diagnostic names with any real meaning.

The International Classification of Diseases, Ninth Revision Clinical Modification (ICD-9-CM) is the official system used in the United States for the coding of diseases. In addition, psychiatrists use *The Diagnostic and Statistical Manual* (DSM-IV-TR) which is an agreed upon set of criteria to describe the various mental disorders we are called upon to treat. Diagnoses are made on five Axes with Axis I being the primary psychiatric diagnosis and Axis II being any personality disorders that may be present. Axis III is a list of any physical problems, Axis IV is a listing of current stresses and an estimate of the severity of the stress and Axis V is a estimate of the patient's overall level of functioning, their baseline functioning and their best level of functioning in the last year. By using these agreed upon definitions, psychiatrists are able to communicate more accurately with one another. The criteria are also helpful in defining patient populations for research. However, psychiatry has not reached the point of scientific accuracy where we have a blood test, x-ray, or other objective means to establish our diagnoses. Our diagnoses are based on history and description. As a result, they are subject to the whim of majority opinion among psychiatrists. Homosexuality was eliminated from the DSM as a diagnosis because of social pressure and post traumatic stress disorder was included because of political lobbying. Medical and neurological diagnoses cannot be deleted or created in this manner.

Survivors of Abuse

I see a few depressed men who retain some degree of pain and sadness over years of treatment. Many of these individuals have histories of severe childhood abuse. I am able to control the symptoms of clinical depression with medication, but the childhood trauma they sustained requires lengthy therapy that, in some cases, amounts to re-parenting. Some of these men have benefited from 12-step programs, which provide peer support and unsolicited affection from individuals who have had similar childhood experiences.

> One out of four children in the United States is a victim of some type of abuse. Survivors develop patterns of behavior to cope with childhood trauma.

One out of four children in the United States is a victim of some type of abuse. Survivors of severe abuse develop patterns of behavior to cope with childhood trauma. They feel that there is something bad inside them, and that they deserved the treatment they received. They keep others at a distance. They like to be in control, fearing that they will be hurt if they are not. They have difficulty trusting. As adults they frequently repeat their childhood experiences and put others in a position of hurting them—or perceive them as doing so.

Personality Disorders

Personality disorders are enduring patterns of behavior that deviate markedly from the expectations of an individual's culture and lead to distress or impairment in social, occupational, or other important areas of functioning. The manifestations of your man's depressive illness and his reaction to treatment may be affected by the patterns of behavior he has developed to cope with the relationships and stresses he experienced during his formative years.

Individuals with paranoid personalities are going to have difficulty trusting caregivers. They may set up situations to justify their lack of faith in others. Individuals who are depressed tend to be somewhat clingy and desperate for attention, but those with a preexisting dependent personality disorder may have problems helping themselves in treatment. One such fellow told me that his best friend's wife had just died and he was jealous of the attention this friend was receiving. Schizoid men may avoid relationships with caregivers. Borderline individuals may idealize and then denigrate their caregivers and therapists. They may feel easily overwhelmed and make suicidal gestures. They and men with addictive personalities may seek out minor tranquilizers, sedatives, and pain medications. Many of these individuals were survivors of childhood abuse.

><

It is helpful to identify and treat any medical or psychological problems accompanying your man's depression; failure to do so may impede his timely recovery. With or without other diagnoses, some depressions are more difficult to treat. Treatment-resistant and pseudo-treatment-resistant depressions do not begin to respond within the usual two to three weeks on antidepressant medication. They may fail to show improvement even after twelve weeks at the maximum dose. These recalcitrant depressions may require a number of medication trials or other forms of treatment in order to recover. Delays in improvement may lead to discouragement, frustration, and loss of hope. I will next discuss how you can continue to bolster your man's morale should treatment seem to drag on.

CHAPTER EIGHT

How to Encourage Him if He's Not Responding to Treatment

Dum spero speri.
Where there's breath, there's hope.

—*Anonymous*

As I was going through the process of writing and publishing my first book, *Wizard 6*, I complained to my literary agent about the time it was taking. He said, "Publishing takes a long time—it isn't like the immediate results you are used to in psychiatry." This brought me up short, because, obviously, change in psychotherapy takes a long time. Treatment for depression used to be, and sometimes still is, a lengthy process as well.

When I began my psychiatric training, depressed patients were hospitalized for treatment; the average length of stay was six to nine months. Neither the caregivers nor the patients expected a quick cure. Most of us at that time could recall the care in the 1940s and 1950s, which was largely custodial. We were pleased to see that active treatment programs were in place and that there was hope for recovery.

We spent the first six weeks of a patient's hospital stay gathering information from our daily visits with him along with psychological test results, reports of the activity therapists, nursing observations, occupational therapy notes, and the social histories obtained from the patient's significant others. All this information was included in a case study, which was presented to a consulting analyst at the case conference. Included was a psychodynamic formulation of the patient's illness and treatment recommendations. Sometimes patients would report that they were better within a few weeks of their hospital admission. We would tell them they had not even had their six-week case conference yet and that they were probably experiencing a "flight into health." In other words, we thought their resistance to treatment caused them to act as though they were well in order to avoid dealing with the unconscious issues that caused their illness. Looking back, they had probably recovered on their own.

Today, patients and their families expect a pill that will alleviate their symptoms immediately. Treatment has not progressed to this point, of course, but many depressed patients do begin to feel better within two to three weeks and are pretty much over their depressive illnesses by six weeks. Some, however, do not respond to the first medicines we try. Treatment drags on as we experiment with other antidepressants and combinations of medications to control their depressive illnesses. Some

---

Remind Your Man That He Has a Recurrent, Self-Limiting Illness

You can tell your man that he is likely to recover eventually no matter what we do. I tell newly depressed patients and their families that depression is usually a recurrent illness and is usually self-limiting. We give antidepressant medications to speed up recovery, but sufferers will feel better eventually no matter what we do.

---

experience a partial response to treatment but continue to suffer from low-grade symptoms of depression for an extended period of time.

What Professionals Do When Patients Do Not Respond as Expected

Some depressed patients do not respond to the first medications that are prescribed. These individuals may be treatment-resistant depressions (TRD) or pseudo-treatment-resistant depressives (PTRD). PTRD are individuals who appear to have a treatment resistant depression, but who were not treated long enough or with a high enough dose of an antidepressant to allow the drug to control their depressive illness. My practice consists largely of patients who are considered "treatment failures" by other practitioners. The majority of these cases turn out to be PTRDs.

Here are some diagnostic factors to consider if your man is not recovering from his depression in a timely manner:

- Has he been compliant with his medicine? Is he taking it as directed? By managing his medicines, you can make sure that he takes the prescribed amount each day.
- Has he taken the maximum dosage of the medicine?
- Has he taken the maximum dosage for a period of twelve weeks?
- Are there undiagnosed medical problems present?
- Is there a history of childhood abuse that has not been addressed?
- Is he a rapid or slow metabolizer of his medication?
- Is he using nicotine, and could it be lowering the blood level of his medicine?
- Is he using drugs or alcohol to self-medicate?
- Is he suffering from chronic pain?
- Does he have an undiagnosed bipolar disorder? (He will require a mood stabilizer.)
- Does he have another psychiatric condition that has not been recognized?

- Has he demonstrated a partial response to his current antidepressant medication after two to four weeks? (This usually means that he will respond to the medication in time.)

Family physicians are usually the first professionals to see depressed patients. They may try several medications before referring a patient to me. More often, the patient and his family become discouraged and come to me on their own. The patient and the family may bring a list of medications they say did not work or that the patient was unable to tolerate. In going over the list, I often find that the patient was on a low dose of medicine, he was on it for only a short time, and frequently the side effects he claims to have had were due to psychological rather than physical factors. It is not uncommon for the patient and family to have noticed partial improvement with a particular medicine within two to four weeks. This initial response was an indicator that he was likely to respond to that medicine eventually. All too often this promising drug was discontinued because it did not completely relieve the patient's symptoms. Your man should be on the maximum dose of a particular antidepressant for twelve weeks before concluding that he is not going to respond to it. Any medicine that shows a partial response should be continued and augmented if necessary.

Some patients require higher doses of medication, while others are extremely sensitive to low doses. Response to medication can be plotted on a bell-shaped curve. The recommended dose is based on those under the bell—the majority of patients. If an individual is not responding as expected, it may mean that he's not under the bell but at either end of the graph.

Slow metabolizers reach a high blood level of the drug on a low dose of medication. These are the individuals who experience side effects and even toxic effects from a starting dose of medicine. In order for them to benefit from the drug, they have to be started on an extremely low dose of medicine and maintained on a low dose as well.

At the other end of the spectrum are the rapid metabolizers. These are people whose livers crank out the drug at a rapid rate; it takes a very high dose to achieve a therapeutic blood level. I once used electroconvulsive therapy to treat a young man whom the anesthesiologists could not seem to put to sleep. They had to call down for another bottle of Brevital because they could not get him under. I later asked him if he had a high tolerance for alcohol. He told me that he could drink his fraternity brothers under the table. Needless to say, we had to treat him with an exceptionally high dose of antidepressant medication to control his melancholia. This is something to be kept in mind if your guy is not responding to treatment. He may be one of those individuals who require a higher dose of medication than is typically recommended.

If things are not going as expected with the family physician's initial medication, it is the psychiatrist's job to find the right medication or combination of medications for your man. Your guy's job is to take his medicine(s) as directed and try to do what the professionals advise. I tell new patients these facts because I know that depressed patients tend to blame themselves and feel hopeless when they do not respond quickly to treatment. I remind them that I am the hired help whose job it is to find the drug that works. If they feel frustrated, and griping about my failure makes them feel better, great.

Even though it is the doctors' job to discover the right medication or combination for him, I believe it is helpful for you and your man to understand the way doctors go about finding the best drug. If you or he notices some improvement with a particular medicine, you want to let the doctor know so that he or she can increase the dose and, at least, not discontinue something that appears to be helping. Some common errors in treating depression are underdosing with the antidepressant (which happens less often with the current medicines, but may occur in the case of rapid metabolizers) and giving up on a drug before it has a chance to work. In many cases the medication starts to work within two to four weeks, but it may take up to twelve weeks to achieve full benefit. If the doctor moves on to another drug too quickly, he or she may be discounting a medication that would work eventually.

If your man has not responded to a selective serotonin reuptake inhibitor (SSRI) like Prozac, Zoloft, Paxil, Serzone, Luvox, or Lexapro, then the doctor may want to add one that raises norepinepherine, such as Strattera or Wellbutrin. He or she may want to try a dual-acting antidepressant like Effexor, Cymbalta, Remeron, or Pristiq. If these do not appear to help, it may be time to go back to one of the older antidepressants like Elavil, Tofranil, Aventyl, Anafranil, Norpramin, Sinequan,

> It is the psychiatrist's job to find the right medication or combination of medications for your man.

or Vivactil. These have more side effects but sometimes work where newer drugs fail. Some studies suggest that the older antidepressants may be more effective for the more severe depressive illnesses. The older ones offer the advantage of allowing doctors to check a patient's blood levels and adjust his dose more accurately.

If the conventional antidepressants do not work, the doctor may want to try a monoamine oxidase inhibitor (MAOI) like Parnate, Nardil, Marplan or the new Emsam patch. These are frequently effective but have the disadvantage of requiring a special diet and many precautions because they interact with many other medications. Nonpsychiatric specialists hate to see patients on MAOIs because it's difficult to find drugs compatible with them.

If your man experiences a partial response to any of these medicines, then that medicine's dose can be increased to the maximum. If his symptoms still are not completely controlled, other medicines can be added to augment the effect of the partially effective antidepressant. Lithium, thyroid preparations, antipsychotic medications such as Abilify or any of the atypical antipsychotics, and testosterone have been used for this purpose, as have combinations of antidepressants. Make your fellow aware of the many treatment options for depression that have not been tried, including electroshock therapy, vagal nerve stimulation (VNS), and inpatient programs.

What You Can Do When He Does Not Respond as Expected

Check His Family Tree

Depressed patients usually respond to the last drug that the drug salesman left at the family doctor's office. Some individuals, however, simply have more resistant forms of depression. Prescribing antidepressant medication is largely a trial-and-error process, but you can help the professionals by doing some research into your man's family tree. If a blood relative is depressed and is doing great on a particular medicine, then this would be the one to try. Response to medicine, like vulnerability to depression, is genetically determined. What helps one family member will likely help another. Remember the bell-shaped curve of dosing. Perhaps he is a rapid metabolizer and requires a higher than normal dose. If he has side effects with every medicine tried, he may be a slow metabolizer and require a smaller dose of medication.

> Response to medicine is genetically determined. What helps one family member will likely help another.

Stay Positive

Encourage him: "Some depressive illnesses are more resistant than others. Yours is one of the tough ones that didn't respond to the first medicine the doctor tried. Dr. Jones is going to have Dr. Smith, a psychiatrist, help find the right medicine for you. Dr. Smith specializes in the treatment of depression and is more experienced with these medicines. Both Dr. Jones and Dr. Smith feel you should also see a therapist, because statistics show that the combination of medication and therapy is more effective than medication alone. They're going to discuss which therapist is likely to be best for you."

Like it or not, you have taken on the role of cheerleader. Hang in there with him and do not pull back or withdraw. Many caregivers report that there is a kind of emotional wall between them and their depressed men. Anyone constantly confronted with a negative, resistant, unfeeling, hopeless, withdrawn, irritable man who defeats every effort at encouragement can become drained. You may feel like withdrawing or be tempted to vent your frustrations at your depressed man. This would not be helpful; it could even be dangerous. Instead, remember that you feel angry with the illness, not the man. Don't let the illness defeat you. If you find yourself wanting to pull away, call in some of your treatment support group to spell you until you can recharge your batteries. You cannot do it all. Call in the reserves frequently to give you some relief from his demands and negativity. This is not being selfish. No one, not even professional psychiatric nurses, can continue to support a depressed man 24/7 for an extended period of time.

You can say, "I know you're frustrated and that my encouragement irritates you at times, but I love you and I'll be here with you until you recover. You don't see it, but I can tell that you're getting better all the time. Hang in there. I can't imagine what you're suffering, but I admire your courage and perseverance." He may not outwardly respond to your comments, but he hears them.

Keep a Diary

Keeping a diary will help your man see progress in treatment and help the professionals evaluate his response. The record does not have to be detailed or extensive. Just jot a few notes each day as to how your guy is feeling and what he was able to accomplish. This will provide a record for the doctor to evaluate his response to medication and also help him see that overall he is making progress. Ask him to graph on a scale from 1 to 10 how badly he is feeling each day. This will give him a record of his moods and how he is responding to the medications. If he is unable to keep a record, ask him how he's doing each morning and evening, and keep the graph yourself. Remind him that the doctor said it takes a minimum of two to three weeks for the medicines to start to work, and several more weeks to recover.

Follow a Daily Schedule

Set up a regular schedule for him. Nearly everyone likes predictability. In our family, changing a single dish at Thanksgiving or Christmas leads to an overwhelming outcry. Routine gives us security. The same is true for your depressed man. Depression forces him to be dependent, fearful, and needy. He may not want to admit this to himself or to you, but being able to rely on events occurring in a predictable pattern each day is reassuring.

In the pre-medication days, depressed patients were in the hospital, where nurses made them get up, take showers, brush their teeth, and go to their various activities. Patients are now treated at home. They can learn to follow a programmed schedule in order to overcome their urge to regress to their beds and neglect their day-to-day activities. Help him make out a daily schedule and then follow it. The hour-by-hour schedule should include getting up, taking a shower, brushing his teeth, dressing, and

> Depression forces him to be dependent, fearful, and needy. Being able to rely on events occurring in a predictable pattern each day is reassuring.

eating breakfast, as well as daily tasks he can accomplish. Include some positive, gratifying activities as well as chores. Remember to be specific when you give him chores.

The schedule is the modern version of being in a hospital with nurses encouraging patients to follow a therapeutic agenda of activities. You can say, "I know depression is a painful illness and that you'd just as soon pull the covers over your head and shut out the world, but from what I've read and what the doctors have told me, that will just make you feel worse. Following a schedule should give you a little short-term relief. I can make out the schedule for you. All you have to do is follow it."

Encourage Healthy Habits

Depressed patients neglect their personal hygiene, their nutrition, and their daily exercise. Getting out of bed, taking a shower, brushing their teeth, getting dressed, and taking a walk will make them feel better. Still, all these things require effort, and your guy is going to resist doing them. You might say, "You'll feel better after you take a shower and brush your teeth. I can fix you anything you want for breakfast. Then we will take a walk together to get your juices flowing."

It is difficult for men to see progress in treatment. As I've noted previously, the recovery course waxes and wanes and the positive changes in therapy are hard to recognize. Exercise, on the other hand, produces concrete, objective improvement that can be measured and graphed. Post a chart with the distance walked, the number of situps, push-ups, weight lifted, repetitions, and any other measure of exercise completed on a daily basis. Point out the gains he is making. If possible, exercise with him. The workout will be good for you, too, and he'll appreciate your support and sharing the time with him.

One male patient was a beer drinker who could not seem to get himself going on an exercise program. His therapist told him to drink one beer for every quarter mile he walked. (Obviously, this prescription would not be appropriate if your man has been self-medicating with alcohol.) The first day he was on this program he walked a mile and a half and drank six beers. The next day he walked three miles but decided he did not need twelve beers and limited himself to a six-pack. Gradually he found that he enjoyed walking more than beer drinking; he cut out the beer altogether but continued to walk.

Keep notes and give him positive feedback daily. For example: "Today you walked half a block more than you were able to do last week. You did five more push-ups, three more sit-ups, and you're lifting more weight more times than you did a week ago. Have you noticed that your mood numbers are better in the evening? As you recover, you'll notice improvement earlier and earlier in the day. Keep up the good work!"

> Exercise with him. The workout will be good for you, too, and he'll appreciate your support and sharing the time with him.

Make Changes and Provide Options

If treatment drags on, you will want to introduce options and changes that will keep hope alive. In the next chapter I'll discuss the role of hope in the treatment of depression. It is important to change things and provide options when you sense that your man is becoming discouraged. If he is starting to lose hope, it's time to take a new treatment tack. If treatment is dragging on and your professional seems to be running out of new ideas, find a new professional.

Family physicians and even psychiatrists may become discouraged when illness does not seem to respond to treatment. The professionals may lose enthusiasm and appear to stop trying to find a successful approach.

Worse, some may begin to blame the patient. This tendency is ubiquitous in medicine, even among our colleagues, the witchdoctors. The study of primitive cultures can teach modern doctors some humbling lessons about their so-called modern methods of treatment. I once attended a lecture by a speaker who studied African witchdoctors. He told the group of Western doctors in the audience that African natives had faith in their witch-doctors but didn't trust the missionary hospitals. This was because the witch doctors would accept patients with acute illnesses that had good prognoses who were likely to recover quickly. Chronic and terminal cases were referred to the missionary hospitals. As a result these institutions had the reputation of being places where people didn't recover or died.

> If treatment is dragging on and your professional seems to be running out of new ideas, find a new professional.

Families would sometimes refuse to go to the missionary hospitals and insist that the witchdoctor take on a patient with a chronic condition. When this happened, the witchdoctor would give the afflicted individual the following prescription: "Don't step on any twigs." The patient would protest, "But I live in the jungle." The doctor would shake his head. "Do what I say, I am the doctor. Don't let any rain fall on your head." Again the patient would object, saying that he lived outdoors. Finally the doctor would conclude, "No sex, see me in six months."

When the patient returned, if he was doing well, the doctor would tell him to continue to follow his recommendations. If the patient or family complained, the doctor would ask, "Did you step on any twigs?" The patient would say he couldn't help doing this. "Did you let any rain fall on your head?" Again the patient would admit he did but that he couldn't avoid it. Finally the doctor would say, "I'm not even going to ask you about sex."

The audience of Western doctors laughed, but the speaker said, "I don't know what you guys are laughing about—you do the same thing. When you get a patient with a chronic problem you tell him, 'Diet, exercise, and quit smoking.' You know he's not going to do any of these things and you can blame him if he complains when you see him for follow-up."

If you detect that the doctor is beginning to blame your man for his failure to respond to treatment, find a new, enthusiastic, optimistic physician immediately. Do not let your loved one lose hope. If he is becoming discouraged, make changes in his treatment plan and offer alternatives.

- If he is under the care of your family physician, encourage the doctor to refer him to a psychiatrist.
- If he is under the care of a psychiatrist, discuss the various medicines that have not been tried and particularly any that have helped other family members.
- Ask the doctor for a referral to a therapist—or a new therapist. It's easy to conclude that therapy isn't helping when, in fact, the approach was flawed, the therapist was incompatible, or the patient was not motivated to receive assistance at the time.
- If the psychiatrist seems to be losing enthusiasm for your man's treatment, start looking for a new, energetic professional.
- Many patients with severe depression respond better to the older first- and second-generation antidepressants.
- Some patients will do better on monoamine oxidase inhibitors (MAOIs). The most common is Nardil. Some patients fail to respond to it but will respond to Parnate, Marplan, Sertraline or an Emsam patch.
- Ask about augmentation therapies such as adding lithium or another mood stabilizer, or adding an atypical antipsychotic medication such as Abilify, Geodone, Respirdal, Seroquel or Zyprexa to boost the effect of the antidepressant. Adding thyroid extract

(Cytomel) or testosterone may make the antidepressant work faster or better and may increase the patient's energy level.

- Discuss electroconvulsive therapy.
- Discuss vagal nerve stimulation (see Chapter 13).
- Get a second opinion. Have another respected psychiatrist review your man's case and make suggestions. His current psychiatrist will not take umbrage at this. It is common practice in medicine for doctors to consult with one another when things are not progressing as they'd hoped in treatment. It is always helpful to have additional, outside observations and suggestions. If your doctor objects to a second opinion, that is a red flag.
- You might want to take your man to a major center like the Menninger Clinic in Houston, Harvard's McLean Hospital in Boston, or, if occult medical problems are thought to be involved, the Mayo Clinic in Minnesota.

Let your depressed loved one know that there are many medications and many combinations of medicines that have not yet been tried. If he doesn't believe he's progressing in therapy, ask him to discuss this with his therapist and to consider seeing someone else. Remind him that the doctors are his hired help. If the ones he has currently employed aren't doing the job, there are others out there who may bring a fresh perspective and new ideas to the table.

Selecting Your Professional Caregivers

The Family Doctor

Be discriminating in your selection of your caregivers. Hopefully you have a family physician whom your partner knows well and trusts. If this is the case, it will be easier to convince him to make an appointment. You will be able to ask the doctor which psychiatrist and therapist to contact.

If you do not have a family physician, ask your friends and family for professional reference. You can check his or her credentials online and through the local medical society office. Of course you want someone who has good training and is probably board-certified by the family practice or internal medicine board of examiners. You might want to inquire in advance if the doctor is experienced working with depressed patients and if he or she likes treating depression.

Think of your first visits as a probationary period in which you decide if this doctor is going to be good for your man. Does he or she appear to be competent? Does the doctor seem to know about depression and its treatment? Does the doctor spend time with both of you and is he or she willing to include you in the treatment? Does the physician listen to you and respond to your ideas? You are the expert on your depressed man's current level of functioning. You are also the best source of information as to his response to treatment. Does the doctor seem to realize this?

Is he or she willing to refer you to a psychiatrist if the drugs he or she prescribes do not appear to work? You don't need the smartest doctor in the world, but it is important that your caregiver knows his or her limitations and is willing refer to an expert if things are not going well. Does he or she appear comfortable referring and working with psychiatrists and psychotherapists? Just as I have encouraged you to be optimistic, unambivalent, and positive toward your man, make sure that his professional caregivers have the same confident attitude. If a physician seems to you to be unsuccessfully trying the same approach or to be pulling back and becoming discouraged—get another opinion. Your depressed man will sense the doctor's discouragement, and this will confirm his conviction that he is hopeless.

> You are the expert on your depressed man's current level of functioning.

> ## How Important Is Board Certification?
>
> Board certification is not an absolute requirement for your family physician or your psychiatrist. I have been certified in general psychiatry and in additional requirements in geriatric psychiatry. I also served as a board examiner for the American Board of Psychiatry and Neurology for many years. Nevertheless, I have worked with many fine physicians over the years who, for one reason or another, were not board certified. I personally know one of the top psychiatrists in the country who failed the boards and refused to retake them. In other words, board certification may mean something, but it is by no means the primary standard by which you should make your selection.

Tell him that you are planning on getting a second opinion to review his current treatment and that you're looking into other professionals to give a fresh look at his case and try new approaches to his care.

The Psychiatrist

Ask your family physician about psychiatrists he or she has worked with in the past. Who does your doctor think would be good for your man? Do not rely entirely on the generalist's suggestions, however. These days many doctors are salaried and required by their employers to refer within their professional groups. Check around and see what other patients think of the recommended psychiatrist and whether he or she is a good match for your loved one. Is the psychiatrist enthusiastic and optimistic? Is he or she board-certified in a specialty? Does he or she come from a background similar to his? Does your guy appear to relate to the psychiatrist? Is the professional willing to include you in the treatment? Is he or she willing to have you seek a second opinion if things are not going well?

The Therapist

Take a survey of therapists by seeking the recommendations of your friends, your religious leader, your family physician, and your psychiatrist. Once you have a name, determine if the therapist has experience working with depressed men. For depression you will probably want someone skilled and experienced in cognitive-behavioral therapy (CBT). If your loved one has problems in addition to depression, you may consider a gestalt or Freudian psychotherapist. Evaluate his response to the counselor. See if the therapist is willing to include you in the treatment. Does the therapist appear comfortable in his or her professional role? Therapists who want the medical doctor to adjust the medication or who want to prescribe vitamins or wish they could write prescriptions are sometimes insecure in their professional identities as talking doctors. Be wary if a therapist wants to talk about topics other than therapy, such as changes in medication. The counselor's focus should be on what can be done in therapy to help. For your depressed man you want a therapist who understands the pain he is suffering but is energetic, upbeat, and optimistic about his eventual recovery.

Another caution to observe with psychotherapists is their ability to deal with negative feelings. Experienced therapists make it easy for patients to express their frustration and anger. Less experienced counselors want the patient to like them and avoid topics that seem to irritate their clients. As a result, in a few weeks the patient, who is unable to express his negative feelings to such a nice person, will say something like, "I think we have pretty much covered things, we seem to be going over the same material." An inexperienced counselor might agree with him and suggest they begin to space out the interval of their visits. This type of therapist would not comment about a patient being late or canceling an appointment. He or she might be reluctant to discuss the patient's fees. When a patient is doing poorly, he or she may opt to see him less frequently.

A better-trained, more experienced therapist would hold on to the structure of the therapy. This therapist would want to know why a patient is late, would question the cancellation of a session, may charge the patient for it, and would probe into the meaning of the patient's statement that the same topics were being repeated in therapy. The therapist cannot provoke the patient but he or she can make it easier for him to express his negative feelings. One of our therapists told the story of his own analysis. He had been seeing his analyst four times a week for over a year. He said that he was unable to pay for his session but would make it up the following week. The analyst said that he had agreed to pay each visit. The therapist/patient said, "I know we had that agreement, but I just bought a car and I don't have the cash today." The analyst repeated the original agreement. The patient said, "I just don't have the money." The analyst said, "Sell the car." The therapist/ patient said he had to sell his new car at a loss and was furious—but this ended up being a positive turning point in his therapy. Although CBT therapists do not deal with transference issues as part of their treatment, experienced, well-trained CBT therapists are aware of these factors and their influence on their relationship with their patients. For example, if your man voices his discouragement with treatment and hints that he is having suicidal thoughts, you do not want the counselor to increase the intervals between his visits. Similarly, when your man complains about the therapist's shortcomings, you don't want the therapist to immediately suggest he go elsewhere for treatment.

> You want a therapist who understands the pain he is suffering but is energetic, upbeat, and optimistic about his eventual recovery.

Religious Faith

Recent studies suggest that patients who have a strong religious faith may respond more quickly and more fully to treatment for depression.

In some cases religion can become a resistance to treatment. Some individuals feel that seeking help would signify a lack of faith on their part. Others feel they need a therapist who is a member of their faith and refuse to consult with anyone who is not. When I run into a patient who feels seeking professional help is a sign of weakness or lack of faith on his part, I tell him the following story: A town was hit by a flood. A deeply religious man climbed to the roof of his church to evade the rising waters. A rescue boat approached him and he waved them away, "The Lord will protect me," he said. The water continued to rise and a helicopter dropped a ladder nearby. "Go on," he shouted, "I am a man of faith, the Lord will look after me." The water continued to rise and the man drowned and went to Heaven. He turned to St. Peter and said, "I prayed and am faithful, why didn't you save me?" "Didn't you get the boat and the helicopter we sent?!" asked the saint. I then explained that God created doctors and medicines to help people. We are instruments that He made to help the faithful when they need assistance.

In my experience, patients who have a strong religious faith rarely take their own lives. In the studies of captured soldiers who were subjected to Chinese brainwashing during the Korean conflict, those who had strong religious beliefs were better able to withstand the torture and stress imposed by their captors. In the same way, men who are religious have more strength to endure the suffering associated with a bout of depression. Because of the negative thinking associated with the illness, they may see themselves as being sinners and their illness as a punishment for their transgressions. In these situations, your minister, priest, or rabbi can help him with his irrational guilt. You might say, "I spoke with the Reverend Vaughn about your depressive illness and your concerns about your faith. He's very familiar with depression and he'd be happy to talk with you."

Some studies have suggested that religious men are less likely to become depressed. It is postulated that people of faith think that things happen for a reason; that God has a plan that we do not understand and we are to learn a lesson from the adverse experiences we inevitably encounter in life. From my experience, I would say that religious faith may better enable you to cope with painful experiences in life, but it does not inoculate you from depression.

I see a number of Apostolic Christians (ACs) in my practice. Their marriages are arranged by church Elders, and they marry within their church. Because of my lengthy time in practice, I have seen three generations of some of the families, and it is clear that depression runs in some of the families—as does their response to particular medications. These people are faithful members of a Christian community and are devout in their beliefs. Nonetheless, many suffer from severe episodes of clinical depression due, no doubt, to their genetic predisposition to the illness. The AC faith does sustain them, however. I have yet to see a depressed Apostolic Christian patient who took his own life. In general ACs are compliant with treatment, and their Christian community supports them through their recovery. I have had Elders accompany patients to my office to convince them that they need to see a psychiatrist and to reassure them that they will recover from their treatable illness.

Attitude Therapy

Depression is an illness, and your man cannot snap himself out of it. However, attitude is an important factor in coping with stress. Viktor Frankl was a Jewish psychoanalyst who was incarcerated in a death camp in Germany during World War II. He witnessed the murders of his closest family members. He decided that his captors could torture him and kill him—but they could not control his attitude. He started smiling and helping other prisoners. His fellow captives responded to his compassion and positive attitude. The guards felt guilty when they witnessed his acts of kindness in the midst of the misery of the camp. Frankl observed that he began to feel better as a result of his conscious decision to maintain a positive attitude. After the war he wrote a book about attitude therapy.

The well-known melancholic Abraham Lincoln said people are as happy as they want to be. This may appear to contradict my earlier statements about depressives having negative filters, but it does not. Individuals with depression do screen out any positive statements and magnify any negative information that comes their way. However, cognitive therapists encourage depressed patients to try to change negative thoughts into positive ones. Frankl's attitude therapy may have been a precursor of this approach. It does help many patients.

> He began to feel better as a result of his conscious decision to maintain a positive attitude.

I have had some practical experience with Frankl's approach. My wrestling coaches in high school and college told me to jump up and act like I wanted to go several more periods even though I felt physically drained. They said my appearing energetic would demoralize my opponent. I don't know if my behavior affected other wrestlers, but I do know it had a positive effect on me and caused me to feel as though I did have more energy.

Some of my kids played tennis. When it was a blistering hot day on the courts, I encouraged them to tell themselves that they loved heat. By doing so they would eliminate having their heads down griping about the temperature and would feel better themselves. When our son played football in freezing weather, he told himself he loved the cold and couldn't wait to hit someone and to be hit himself on the icy field. While your man cannot relieve his depressive symptoms with a change in attitude, he can act as though he is feeling better and, on a short-term basis, actually experience some relief. Alcoholics Anonymous refers to this as "Fake it until you make it."

Because of the inertia that goes with depression, it is an effort for your man to push himself to do anything. He is frustrated and discouraged by the limitations that are imposed by his illness. Tell him about Frankl's experience in the concentration camp and how a positive attitude helps athletes under adverse conditions. Encourage him to make a conscious effort to think positively about his recovery. You might say something like: "Okay, handsome, say it with me, I am getting better every day in every way. Tell yourself you can't wait to force yourself out of the sack in the morning. Drag yourself to the shower, brush your teeth, and then make yourself take a walk with me. Tell yourself you like to push yourself."

➢✦

Helping a depressed man whose depressive illness drags on is an exhausting assignment. In Chapter 12, I'll suggest some ways that you can take care of yourself through this ordeal. In the next chapter I'll turn to the important role hope plays in your man's recovery.

CHAPTER NINE

The Role of Hope in Depression

Depression is the inability to construct a future.

—Rollo May

My experience with depressed patients over the years has taught me that hope is the most important signal of their impending recovery. Loss of hope is the greatest danger.

Borrowing Three Principles from Military Psychiatry

Three important principles of psychiatric treatment arose from military psychiatry. During World War I, Colonel Thomas W. Salmon, chief psychiatrist of the American Expeditionary Forces, developed the principles of proximity, immediacy, and expectancy. By this he meant, treat the solders near the place where their symptoms developed, treat them right away, and treat them in an atmosphere where they are expected to recover. These principles can be applied to your efforts to help your depressed man. You are there. You can intervene immediately to help him see a medical professional for evaluation and treatment. And, most important for friends and family, you can create a positive atmosphere in which recovery is expected.

One of the earliest cases of depression I treated in my private practice ended tragically. An elderly, retired librarian was referred to me by his family doctor. He had evaluated his physical complaints and concluded that he might be depressed. The patient was resistant to the idea of seeing a psychiatrist and felt that the referral meant his family doctor thought he was crazy and had given up on him. I explained that his physician was very interested in him and had in fact insisted that I report my findings and recommendations immediately following our initial consultation. After explaining that his symptoms confirmed the diagnosis of depression, I told him what antidepressant medications did and described the side effects he might encounter. I started him on Elavil. Despite his aversion to psychiatric medication, he took it and got better.

> Hope is the most important signal of impending recovery. Loss of hope is the greatest danger.

Once he was over his depression, he asked if he could follow up with his family physician and have him prescribe the Elavil. He said this would be less expensive for him, but we both knew that he didn't like the stigma of the diagnosis and seeing a psychiatrist. In any event, I agreed to let him return to his family doctor for follow-up. After a few months he discontinued the Elavil on his own. A few weeks later he began to develop depressive symptoms again. He returned to his general practitioner and said: "I know the psychiatrist thought I was depressed, but do you think the problem could be hardening of the arteries?" The busy family doctor said: "At your age, yes, it could be." The gentleman drove to a nearby lake and walked into it, drowning himself.

I've always felt guilty about allowing this man to follow up with his family physician. I know that, had he asked me the same question, I would have told him: "Absolutely not. You have exactly the same symptoms you had before you started on Elavil in the past, and if you get back on it, you'll soon be over them once more." Instead, the depressed fellow had gone to his family doctor looking for confirmation that his illness was hopeless. The busy practitioner failed to recognize what he was doing and told him that his problem could be (hopeless, incurable) hardening of the arteries.

The lesson here is to be positive and optimistic in your statements to your depressed man. If he asks "Do you think I have Alzheimer's disease?" or "Do you think I have cancer?" do not obsess over details or become wishy-washy. Your response is to say: "Absolutely not. You have symptoms due to depression and, while this is a painful condition, the prognosis for complete recovery in the near future is excellent. You are definitely going to get better."

Side Effects as Instruments of Hope

Medication side effects can be used to inspire hope. In general it's a good idea to predict side effects in advance. Newer antidepressants have fewer side effects than the old ones, but if your man realizes he may temporarily experience an upset stomach, jitteriness, sedation, delayed ejaculation, or whatever—he'll be less likely to get upset if it happens.

Psychoanalytic influence in the United States slowed American psychiatrists from getting started using psychotropic medications. English psychiatrists were not caught up in the Freudian movement and had more experience prescribing medicines over the years. In addition, the British have fewer lawyers and are less litigious. Our English colleagues are more positive when they give prescriptions. I always thought their approach was better than ours. Instead of cautioning and creating a dread of side effects, they tell their patients to look forward to them as positive events. English psychiatrists tell their patients, "After a few days taking the tablets, you will experience a dry mouth, blurred vision, constipation, and hot flashes. That means that the medicine is building up in your system and starting to work." You might borrow from the British and, when your loved one complains about side effects, tell him: "I just read that the side effects you're having are transitory, and they're actually a good thing—they tell you that the medicines are building up in your system. Which means that any minute now, you'll be seeing the positive benefits of your medications."

He Will Look Better Before He Feels Better

Depressed patients frequently look better before they feel better. Nurses on the psychiatric unit would reflect how much better a depressed individual on the ward looked—which would only irritate the patient, who didn't feel better at the time. Again, it is good to anticipate this event. "I read that depressed patients treated with antidepressant medications often look better before they feel better, so if I tell you that you're looking better and you don't believe me—it's still a good sign. It means you're about to feel better."

Recovery Is an Up-And-Down Course

Depression waxes and wanes. If you graphed the symptoms, it would look like a roller coaster. The depressed patient may start to feel better and think that perhaps you and the doctor knew something after all, only to feel worse than ever the next day. This does not mean he's slipping or back at zero—it is the natural course of recovery. Overall the low periods will be shorter and less intense as he recovers.

Predict setbacks in advance. You can say, "You'll start to feel better, and then the next day you'll be down in the dumps again. Remember, it was an up-and-down course going into the depression, and you'll come out of it the same way. If you chart it, you'll see that the lows aren't as deep and don't last as long."

When the First Pill Doesn't Work

Sometimes the first medicine tried isn't effective. If the family physician's first medication choices do not relieve your man's symptoms of depression, he will likely refer him to the psychiatrist in your area whom he feels will be the most helpful.

It's important that the doctor conveys his interest in what the psychiatrist recommends and expresses his continued wish to see him in the future. If not, your guy may feel that his doctor has given up on him, think he's crazy and is rejecting him by banishing him to a "shrink." You can reinforce the concern of the primary doctor by saying, "Dr. Jones told me he's referring you because he wants you to have the best possible treatment. The psychiatrist treats depressed patients every day and is the best qualified medical specialist to help you. But Dr. Jones wants to keep following your care, too, and he'll be in touch with us throughout your treatment."

> Because of his tendency to convince himself that he's hopeless, it's important to let your man know that many options are available.

Because of his tendency to convince himself that he's hopeless, it's important to let your man know that many options are available. There are many antidepressants and combinations of antidepressants. What fails to work for one man may be the just the ticket for the next fellow.

In the same light, the psychiatrist whom the family physician selects may be great for one man but not on the same wavelength with another. If your man feels he is unable to relate to the specialist selected, reassure him that there are many more to choose from. Remind him that the professional caregivers are the hired help whose job it is to find the treatment that relieves his symptoms. If the doctors are not accomplishing this goal or doing the job quickly enough, then you'll find others who can.

You might intervene by saying: "Dr. Jones picked a psychiatrist he thought would be of help to you. I spoke to him about your frustration, and he said that you should go right ahead and look for another doctor you're more comfortable with. What matters is finding the psychiatrist who finds the medicine that works best for you."

He Has Negative Filters

It is the nature of depression to cause sufferers to perceive the world negatively. Depressed men think their brains are not working. As I've noted, this isn't true. Their perceptions, however, are nearly delusional.

Melancholic patients can turn any positive into a negative. It's as if they walk around with a dark rain cloud over their heads. If you introduce your depressed man to someone who has recovered from depression, instead of feeling hopeful about his own situation, he will think, *Everyone gets better but me.*

Pointing out that others have more serious problems in life does not encourage a depressed man, who will hear this statement as criticism of his inability to function that implies he is weak. Unless you have experienced a depression yourself, the statement that you know how he feels will likely be rejected by your depressed man. Better to say that you understand that he is suffering more than you can imagine, but you love him and will be close by until he recovers. Listen and be empathetic, but recognize you cannot truly understand the depth of his despair unless you have been depressed yourself.

As hopeless as he feels, you must maintain a positive outlook yourself and continually reinforce the fact that his illness is common, it's treatable, and he is going to recover. It is important to emphasize that there are many alternatives available. Depressed individuals tend to paint themselves into a corner and convince themselves the only way out is suicide. You do not want this to happen. There are lots of medicines, and what works for one person may not work for another. There are lots of psychiatrists, and if one isn't doing the job then it's time to find another. There are numerous treatments in addition to medication. For example, some patients go into the hospital for treatment in specialized programs.

> Reinforce the fact that his illness is common, it's treatable, and he is going to recover.

You might want to say: "I realize that it doesn't do any good to argue with you about your negative perception of the situation, but your outlook will get better as you recover from the illness. You don't realize it, but right now you aren't thinking straight due to your depression."

He Will Likely Blame Himself for His Illness

Other characteristics of depression are irrational guilt and self-blame. I was making rounds on the psychiatric unit with a group of medical students one morning. I told them that depressed patients turned their frustration inward and beat themselves up for being ill. Depressed patients saw their inability to function as weakness on their parts. To illustrate this point, I asked the students to accompany me on rounds when I visited an elderly patient of mine who happened to be a retired farmer. He was a man in his seventies who had suffered from recurrent depressive episodes since childhood. He had responded to antidepressant medications and limited psychotherapy in the past and was compliant with his treatment, but the therapeutic effect of his selective serotonin reuptake inhibitor (SSRI) Prozac had faded in time (as occurs in 20 percent or so of those who are taking these medications) and he was back in the hospital. He sat in his darkened room slumped, tearful, head down, and obviously depressed.

I said: "Are you depressed again?" He nodded. "Well," I said, "I can't understand it. You are on the best medicine, you've had the best therapy, and you have the best psychiatrist in the world. Yet you're depressed." The depressed man nodded and said, "Yes, I know it—it's all my fault." I hastened to explain, "No, it is not your fault, Joe, you have an illness and the medicines that helped you earlier stopped working. I said these things to you to illustrate to these medical students how depressed patients tend to blame themselves for their illnesses. Most nondepressed individuals would be complaining that the medicines and the psychiatrist were not doing their job. They would blame the caregiver rather than themselves, so relax and leave the driving to us."

> Depressed patients have difficulty saying no to the demands of others and difficulty asking for help for themselves.

Joe was not a unique case; nearly every depressed man feels that he is weak or deficient for not being able to pull himself out of his depression. If others share this view and tell him he needs to pull himself up by his bootstraps or "get right with the Lord," he will agree and berate himself for being weak and nonfunctional. Instead you want to reassure your guy. "From what I've read and from what the doctor told me, this is a chemical imbalance and it's the doctor's job to find the medicine that pulls you out of the depression. If you feel frustrated with someone about the illness or your recovery, direct it at the doctor and cut yourself some slack. It's an illness that runs in your family. You can't pull yourself out of it any more than you can make your thyroid level go up or your blood sugars go down. So relax and let the doctor find the drug that works for you."

As part of the self-blame, depressed patients have difficulty saying no to the demands of others and difficulty asking for help for themselves. This pattern was so prevalent that we had an assertiveness class for our hospitalized depressed patients. I saw a patient for follow-up who had been recently discharged from the hospital. Prior to the onset of his depression, he had been working many hours of overtime without additional pay because his boss told him how much the company needed him. I noticed that he had a book with him titled *When I Say No, I Feel Guilty*.

I asked him if he felt the book was helpful and something we should recommend to other patients. He said he hadn't read it yet but had purchased it because he thought he needed additional help with his assertiveness. At his next office visit, I again inquired about the book. He still hadn't read it. I asked him why not. He said, "My buddy borrowed it and when I asked for it back—he said no!"

Depression Is Not the Blues

Most of us try to understand depression by drawing on our own earlier experiences with the blues. Clinical depression is not the same thing. I used to ask hospitalized depressed patients if they would trade their depression for any other illness. They all answered, "In a minute." They didn't care which illness—cancer, heart disease, stroke—anything but depression. If you tell a depressed man, "We've found that cutting your arm off will help," he'll stick out his arm immediately in the hope of relief.

Clinical depression is not, as nonsufferers assume, sadness—it is an absence of feeling. As a caregiver, you may feel that your loved one no longer loves you. He does, but his illness prevents him from feeling the emotion.

Do Not Imitate the Professionals

It's not a good idea to try to slavishly imitate the professional caregivers. The suggestions and advice contained in this book are valid and the product of years of experience working with depressed patients and their families, but they also reflect my personality. Use the information in this book, but the style in which you approach your depressed man must reflect your unique individual personality. Interventions must be tailored to fit his characteristics and needs.

Use your own words. The examples given are not a magic spell to be repeated word for word like an incantation. An extreme example of a mistaken attempt to directly apply a psychological intervention occurred during my residency training. A senior psychiatric resident had been on call and had consulted with a young woman whose roommate had committed suicide. She was distraught and sought help at the Menninger Clinic. The resident tried to convince her to come into the hospital for admission. The depressed young woman refused and went on to California. Dr. Karl Menninger suggested that the resident play the part of the young woman while he took the role of the resident. The interaction went something like this:

> **Dr. Karl (in the role of the resident):** What are you going to do?
> **Resident (in the role of the depressed young woman):** I'm going to California and start over with my life.
> **Dr. Karl:** Run away.
> **Resident:** What?
> **Dr. Karl:** You can't run away from a broken heart.

At this point we all sighed. The resident playing the part of the depressed young woman admitted that his eyes welled up with tears and he nearly wept. He said that, had he used the words that Dr. Karl had uttered, he was sure the young lady would have come into the hospital. One of the first-year residents, Dr. Bill Schulz, ran back to his ward in the Topeka State Hospital to apply his new knowledge to a difficult case there. He had a sociopathic patient named Dewey who had been causing problems on the unit. Dewey was a biker and, among other things, had blown his fingers off with a pipe bomb. Dr. Schulz took Dewey out of seclusion and sat him down in a chair facing him.

> **Dr. Schulz:** Dewey, you can't run away from a broken heart.
> **Dewey:** Huh?

Looking back, it is was humorous to think of Bill's naive attempt to directly apply the "magic"of Dr. Karl's words to cure his problem patient. The lesson of this story is: Don't apply the suggested words rigidly. Incorporate the spirit of the interventions, but use the words that fit your personality and the needs of your depressed man.

My approach to new depressed patients is to be positive, energetic, and optimistic. However, the melancholic man does not know me. He sees me as an authority figure and a specialist in the treatment of depression. I do not have to sustain this enthusiasm as he is not going to be around me for extended periods of time. In most cases, I will see him for thirty minutes a week or less. If you try to emulate this approach at home, your guy will likely think that you are patronizing him, and eventually your own enthusiasm will wane. Your man will use your ebbing efforts to support his contentions that he's a burden, you're losing hope, and there is no chance for his recovery. It is important to remain positive, exuding confidence and the knowledge that he is going to recover. Still, for family and friends, this approach needs to be more subtle and geared for the long haul.

I like to kid people, telling jokes and lots of stories. This is part of my personality. I am cautious about this with depressed patients because they tend to interpret nearly every comment in a negative way and beat themselves over the head with it. However, I have been able to effectively employ some humor and teasing with depressed men over the years. I think humor can be helpful, even with depressed patients, but I would not recommend using humor unless it is part of your personality. If your man knows that you're aware of his suffering and accepts your joking as a loving gesture, then it is helpful. If he sees it as a criticism or a put-down, avoid it at all costs.

It is acceptable to quote the doctor and to remind your fellow what the psychiatrist has said. However, your efforts to encourage him will likely differ from those of the professionals.

First of all, you need to remind yourself that depression is a curable illness and that your loved one is going to get better. Read again the introduction of this book to reinforce your own conviction that depression is a chemically-based illness not unlike thyroid disease or diabetes. Medication usually relieves the symptoms within a few weeks. The prognosis is good. You do not need to state this conviction, but you need to believe it in your heart. Others can sense our convictions.

In addition to your own internal optimism, get the message across that you know your man is a good person, that he is ill and not weak, and that he is going to recover. Encourage him to be physically active. Tell him that exercise relieves tension, it makes the medicine work quicker, and it has an antidepressant effect itself. My neurologist brother saw two marathon runners at the Mayo Clinic who became depressed when minor injuries forced them to stop running. At first he thought the depression was psychological since they both were unable to do the thing they loved most in life. However, he soon discovered that both were clinically depressed. Apparently the continuous, intense exercise had elevated the neurotransmitter levels in their brains; the sudden halt to their exertion led to a drop in these brain chemicals. The result: depression.

> If you tell a depressed man, "We've found that cutting your arm off will help," he'll stick out his arm immediately.

An old saying notes: *The reality of sweeping the floor is better than the fantasy of being the king of England.* Permit your depressed man to have as much control and as much responsibility around the house as possible. Jumping in to take over his household chores may confirm to him that he is useless and a burden to the rest of the family. Tough love is an overused phrase these days, but it probably has some application to your interaction with him. However, you are walking a tightrope. You do not want to try to push him into an activity he is unable to perform because, when he fails, it will confirm his conviction that he is useless. On the other hand, it isn't good for him to lie around ruminating on negative topics. At the end of the day, the fellow who has mopped the floor or done some mundane household chores can look back and think, *At least I helped out a little.* Whereas the man who remains on the couch believes, *I didn't accomplish a thing all day—I am truly worthless and a burden to my family.*

You might want to acknowledge his illness, but also encourage activity: "I know you're feeling crummy but come on, get up, we're going to go for a walk together." Or, "How about helping me clean the kitchen?" These statements express empathy for your man's pain as well as your confidence that he can do more. And since you'll be doing it with him, you are conveying your interest and support.

Do Not Let His Depressive Illness Push You Away

It is important for you to hang in with your depressed man and resist the temptation to withdraw. Depressed men are not good company. They lie around and, when you try to encourage them to be more active, they snap at you or whine that they can't. Their self-esteem and self-confidence are low, leaving them cynical and belittling toward those around them. They are hyper-irritable and react defensively to any comments as though you were criticizing them. They are preoccupied with themselves and their illnesses and oblivious to the negative reactions they may engender in those around them. They have little energy to expend and are unable to empathize with others. They may seem to be taking advantage of your goodwill with little acknowledgment of your efforts on their behalf.

As a result of these porcupine behaviors, you may tend to avoid your depressed man's company altogether. This would not be helpful. Remember, the times when people are least lovable are often the times when they need love the most. Let him know you realize he is suffering. Continue to encourage activity even though it requires effort on his part. Tell him that you do not take his rejection of your efforts personally. Remain upbeat and cheerful yourself.

I once saw an attorney's wife who reported that her husband had been an active, athletic individual most of his life but recently, due to osteoarthritis, had suffered from chronic pain and limited movement. She said that initially, when he would come home at the end of the day, she would fluff pillows for him to make him comfortable and ask him if she could get anything for him. His response was to become angry and yell, "I'm no damn baby—cut it out." Thinking that he wanted her to leave him alone, the next day she stayed in the kitchen when he returned from work. He again became angry and said, "Apparently you don't give a damn about how I'm feeling." The woman was convinced she couldn't do anything right. I pointed out to her that her husband wasn't angry with her—he was frustrated with his painful illness and the limitations it imposed upon his life. He was directing his frustration at her, but it wasn't her problem. As your melancholic's caregiver you are in the same boat and may find yourself the target of his frustration. Don't take it personally.

> The times when people are least lovable are often the times when they need love the most.

212

The Greeks in 500 B.C. encouraged their depressed patients to watch comedies. I still think this is a good idea. I tell my depressed patients jokes and, in the depth of their depression, they are still able to laugh most of the time. Patients who suffer from pain benefit from distraction. If they can get their mind off their aches and pains they don't seem to suffer as much. The same applies to the pain of depression. Physical activity shuts down mental activity and provides some relief for the depressed patient.

It is important to remember that recovery takes time. He did not become depressed overnight and he is not going to recover immediately. It takes weeks, sometimes months.

Point out areas of improvement that you observe. "You read the newspaper today." "You were up more today." "You smiled last night." All of these are concrete examples illustrating that he is heading in the right direction on his road to recovery. Now, most likely your man will disagree with you or trivialize your observation—but he hears it and it is a positive, hopeful message. He wants to believe he's going to get better, but he's unable to do so because of his illness. When you can't think of anything to say, just listen. Noncritical, nonjudgmental, empathetic listening has a positive influence. You can say: "I know that you're suffering and that it's hard for you to accept the positive things I tell you—but I love you and I'll always be here for you." Dr. Ernst Ticho, a brilliant Viennese psychoanalyst, once said; "If you can't think of anything to say to your patient, you can always say, 'You aren't telling me everything'—and you will always be right."

> **When you can't think of anything to say, just listen. Noncritical, nonjudgmental, empathetic listening has a positive influence.**

Maintain Your Own Hopefulness

Stay hopeful. Depressed patients defeat the efforts of the caregivers who then become frustrated and depressed themselves. I've worked with many psychiatric nurses to prevent them from becoming discouraged.

While exercise and activity have positive benefits for depressed individuals, you are involved in a balancing act as you try to help them. If you push him to do something he is unable to do, he will feel as though he has failed (again) and this will make him feel more worthless and depressed. It's therefore important to encourage (rather than force) him to do a little more than what he is currently doing. You want him to succeed and be able to accomplish what he sets out to do. If he declares that he is going to clean his room, suggest that he straighten up a few things—if he does more than this he will feel good about it and if he doesn't, he won't feel as though he failed.

As mentioned above, give your depressed man concrete examples of his improvement that show that he is going in the right direction on his road to recovery. We used to put patients in a physical therapy program where they could see that they were able to do more sit-ups, more push-ups, lift more weights more times, etc. this week than they were able to do the week before. This was encouraging because they saw progress. You can do the same with your walks or with simple tasks around the house. For example, "You walked further today." "You swept the floor last evening." "You got cleaned up and dressed today." If he responds with, "Well, I don't feel any better—if anything I feel worse." You can say: "The doctor told me, depressed patients look better to those around them before they feel better. To me you look better and I think this is a sign that your medicines are starting to work."

> If you push him to do something he is unable to do, he will feel as though he has failed (again).

Psychotherapy is Frequently Helpful, but with Initial Caution

Psychiatrists agree that a combination of psychotherapy and antidepressant medication is the most effective approach to the treatment of depression, especially mild to moderate depression. However, it may be necessary to caution your fellow when he begins therapy. There is a risk that as he starts dredging up negative memories, he'll beat himself over the head with his magnified sins and transgressions. He may attempt to confirm the negative conception of himself that is the product of his depressive illness.

Therapy and psychopharmacology have the same goal—to help your man recover from his depressive illness. However, it may seem initially that these treatments are at odds. The medicines are working to provide symptom relief while therapy seems to stir up painful memories that are upsetting to the patient. The type of therapy employed and the therapist conducting treatment are both very important variables in the effectiveness of the treatment. Cognitive-behavioral therapy, which focuses on the correcting the patient's negative thought patterns and essentially ignores childhood trauma, is the treatment of choice.

Prepare your loved one for therapy by saying: "From what I've read about depression, people who see a therapist and take antidepressant medicine do better in the long run than those who just take the medicine alone. One caution is that depressed men tend to magnify the negative and screen out the positive. Because of this tendency, depressed men who start psychotherapy have to be warned not to dwell on the negative aspects of their past and beat themselves over the head with all the things they think they've done wrong. In fact, the goal of most helpful therapies is to help change negative thought patterns into positive."

The Antidepressant Outpatient Treatment Regimen

Encourage your man to write out a schedule and then follow it. Put in actions that are pleasurable as well as activities that are distracting or demand physical activity. Tell your guy to jot a note as to the depth of his depression by putting a number between 1 and 10 for each date.

Make Sure Your Loved One Knows He Has Many Options

Some patients benefit from hormonal therapy (testosterone or thyroid). Stimulants help others. Light therapy is of help for those who have seasonal affective disorder. Electroconvulsive therapy, vagal nerve stimulation, and transcranial magnetic stimulation are further treatment options. Many therapists and therapeutic approaches are available. Inpatient treatment on the psychiatric unit of a general hospital or in a pri-

Journaling

I encourage patients to keep a diary of their thoughts and feelings during their depressive episodes. I tell them that many famous writers have been bipolar; one theory is that, during their episodes of depression, they are brutally honest and critical of their thoughts and feelings. During this negative period they will admit to thoughts and feelings that the average person tends to suppress. When they recover from their illness, they put these admissions on paper in an interesting fashion, and their writing resonates with the readers who recognize thoughts and feelings that they have secretly harbored but were afraid to admit to themselves. I tell the patients that, later on, they may be interested in what they have discovered about themselves or, at the very least, in the frame of mind they had during their illness.

vate psychiatric hospital is a possibility. Exercise, good diet, and relaxation techniques might be helpful as well. The idea is to keep him aware that—although he has not started to feel better yet—given the myriad approaches available to treat his illness, eventually he will recover.

> The idea is to keep him aware that eventually he will recover.

When Hope Returns, He Has Turned the Corner in Treatment

When a depressed man sees that he is getting better, he begins to have hope. At this point he has turned the corner, and everything will start progressing in the right direction. Depression is a negative downward spiral. When men begin treatment, start on medication, and begin to see a therapist, they continue to spiral downward until the medicines begin to work.

Nearly every man has a symptom in the back of his mind that he uses to tell himself he really is getting better. For some it's an improvement in appetite, for others it's socializing in public without pushing themselves. Some men mark when they can begin to have fun, and still others note when they are able to read and concentrate on technical material. Whatever this milestone is for your man, when he sees improvement in it, he begins to have hope of recovery.

This is when he begins to believe that the encouragement you and his doctors have been giving may be valid. With the return of hope, everything starts going in a positive direction. He does more things, which provides more evidence that he's getting better and is a worthy individual. This encourages further activity and socialization.

I tell patients that one indication that they are over their depression is when their families get angry with them. I point out that their loved ones have been worried and stressed by their illness, but walking on eggshells for fear they will make them worse. Once family members are certain the patient has recovered, they feel safe venting their frustrations. One fellow told me that, following his discharge from the hospital, his wife and children brought him breakfast in bed each morning. The family's unusually solicitous behavior caused him to wonder if he might have had a terminal illness in addition to his depression. "Then, one morning, my wife shouted up the stairs that I could come down and fix my own breakfast. I perked up. Things were back to normal and I knew I was not going to die." He smiled as he recalled this sign of his recovery.

➤‹

Lack of hope is a symptom of depression and one to be monitored closely. Caregivers need to be vigilant for signs of suicidal thoughts. The next chapter will discuss how to talk to a depressed man about his self-destructive impulses and how best to reduce the risk of self-harm.

CHAPTER TEN

Assessing and Reducing
His Risk of Suicide

*It is always consoling to think of suicide: in that way one gets through
many a bad night.*

— *Friedrich Nietzsche*

Lack of hope is the greatest signal of danger in depression. Do all
you can to protect your depressed man from self-harm. Over the
years I have heard the argument by some that it was an individual's
choice to take his life; to interfere was being paternalistic. I disagree ve-
hemently when it comes to individuals who are depressed. These men
are not making a logical decision but one based on their distorted view
of reality. I have seen a number of men who survived lethal suicide attempts; all were grateful that they did not complete the act.

One middle-aged man was brought to the emergency room by the police. He had a .32 caliber bullet sticking out of his forehead. He had
become depressed and, feeling hopeless, impulsively took an old loaded
pistol down from a closet shelf and shot himself in the head. The bullet was so old that it did not have enough force to pierce his skull com-

pletely. The projectile was removed, the skin sutured, and he was admitted to the psychiatric unit. The gentleman later recovered from his depression and was grateful to be alive.

Another case was particularly frightening. This man was not aware he was depressed and gave his family no clue as to his mental state. He had dinner with his family, left his home, and took a boat out to the center of a nearby lake. He then drank a fifth of vodka and ingested a lethal dose of sedatives and pain pills. He was accidentally discovered by a passing boat that nearly ran into his unlighted vessel. He was rushed to the emergency room and, after several days in intensive care on a respirator, he recovered from the overdose. The day he left intensive care, he participated in a therapy group on the psychiatric unit. He was advising and supporting other patients in the group, one of whom asked him if he was part of the psychiatric staff. He still had no awareness of his depression or, for that matter, any of his feelings. We transferred him to the Menninger Clinic. They found that the only way he was able to express his feelings was through art. After several months of intensive treatment with art therapists, he was finally able to recognize and verbalize his emotions. He was eventually transferred to a traditional psychotherapist, who was able to continue working with him in the conventional manner. He was grateful that he did not succeed in taking his life.

A third example was a bipolar patient who was not recognized as such. I inherited this fellow from another psychiatrist who had been treating him for clinical depression for a number of years. None of the multiple antidepressant medications that had been tried was effective in alleviating his depression, and he remained dysphoric with periods of extreme irritability. His wife of many years was threatening to leave him. I had the benefit of being able to review the previous unsuccessful attempts to give him relief. Noting his periods of irritability and his failure to respond to conventional antidepressants, I prescribed a mood stabilizer.

He responded dramatically and both he and his wife said that he was a new man. He then saw me for brief appointments at infrequent intervals. He was under my care for several years before he brought me a large vial containing a lethal dose of tranquilizers, sleeping medications, and pain pills. He said he kept it in his safe in case his life became absolutely unbearable. Knowing that he could take his life, he told me, gave him some feeling of control.

There is considerable evidence that most individuals who are stopped from acting on their suicidal impulses do not carry out the act later on. Ninety percent of those who were prevented from killing themselves by jumping off the Golden Gate Bridge in San Francisco ended up dying of natural causes later on.

Here are some statistics to think about: The suicide rate for men in their 40s is 3.5 times higher than for women. It is four times higher for men in their 50s, and men in their 60s are five times more likely to commit suicide than women. There is a correlation between low serotonin levels in the brain and suicide. Men have lower serotonin levels than women. Approximately seventy-one men kill themselves each day. White males are twice as likely to take their own lives as men of color. The incidence is 0.5 percent in the general population and esti-

> I have seen a number of men who survived lethal suicide attempts; all were grateful that they did not complete the act.

mated to be as high as 3.5 percent among individuals suffering from affective disorders. In the old days, before mood stabilizers, the incidence was 20 percent among individuals with manic depression (bipolar disorder). There are approximately 31,000 suicides each year and 425,000 visits to emergency rooms for self-injurious behavior.

Risk Factors for Suicide

- A history of previous attempts.
- A family history of suicide or violence.
- Talk about suicide.
- Giving away possessions.
- Talking about plans after death.
- Writing instructions in the event of death.
- No future plans.
- Suddenly visiting old friends and family members.
- Sudden changes in mood or behavior.
- Risk-taking behaviors.
- Agitation or violent behavior.
- Stopping or changing medications.
- A history of depression.
- Chemical dependency.
- Being male.
- Being teenaged or over sixty-five.
- Being Caucasian.
- No progress in treatment for a while.
- Presence of physical illness.
- A major loss.
- A significant life change.
- Feeling alone.
- Other friends, relatives, or acquaintances committing suicide—there is an infectious aspect.

Signs to Look For

Depression

Your depressed man has two risk factors already: He is depressed and he is male. Because of this, he should be considered at jeopardy for self-harm. In my experience, about a third of depressed patients have suicidal thoughts at some time during their illness. You will not know what he is thinking if you do not ask him. Inquire directly as to the depth of his despair and whether he ever thinks about giving up. If so, does he think about suicide? Does he have plans how he would do it? Does he have the means to do it? Is he making arrangements for the future?

A Sudden Change in Behavior

Be alert for changes in his behavior, such as an ordinarily cautious man taking risks. When a depressed man takes up motorcycle riding, scuba diving, mountain climbing, or some other risky behavior, it doesn't take a psychologist to recognize that he's engaging in activities that are potentially self-destructive. Be especially vigilant when a normally animated, outgoing man withdraws or when you sense a change in your relationship with him. As I mentioned previously, sexual indiscretion, gambling, impulsive investing, compulsive work, and disregard for personal health are examples of potentially self-destructive behaviors.

A Sudden Shift in Mood

A sudden shift in mood from depression to apparent happiness may be a warning sign. The idea is that a depressed patient who finally decides he is going to commit suicide becomes relaxed and happy now that he knows he will obtain relief (through death) from his suffering. In my experience this sign is overemphasized. Most depressed patients who suddenly seem better are better, and are starting to recover from their de-

Antidepressants and Suicide

Warnings have recently been issued that antidepressants may cause suicidal thoughts in the minds of some patients. Concern began when a Harvard psychiatrist reported that a few of his patients on Prozac expressed suicidal thoughts and that these thoughts went away when they stopped the medication. The Scientologists attempted to pursue a class action suit against Eli Lilly claiming that Prozac caused people to become suicidal and homicidal. Harvard, the National Institutes of Mental Health (NIMH), and Eli Lilly then conducted controlled studies, all of which concluded that Prozac did not cause people to become suicidal or homicidal and that many depressed patients experienced suicidal thoughts at some time during their illness.

My experience is that in most cases the antidepressant is not to blame. It is valid that severely depressed individuals may be so ill that they cannot formulate (because of impaired concentration) or carry out (because of inertia) a suicide attempt. As these patients begin to respond to the antidepressant medication, they begin to have the energy and the mental capacity to carry out a suicide plan.

For this reason you need to be on alert as your man recovers and also suggest to him that he may be at greater risk for self-harm. You might want to say: "Dr. Jones told me to keep an eye on you when your antidepressants start to work. As you begin to have more energy and your brain starts working, you might be at greater risk to impulsively hurt yourself. Of course, I want you to tell me if you have suicidal thoughts. Remember, improvements in your energy and concentration are positive signs that mean you're starting to recover."

The issue remains controversial and bears further research.

pression. However, if you suddenly see his mood alter for the better, it is still a good idea to make sure he does not have some secret plan for self-destruction that he has not revealed to others.

Talking About and Making Plans for Death

Men who seem to be making arrangements for their deaths are obviously serious about suicide. These behaviors are ominous. Talk to your man if he is giving away possessions, checking his will, getting his life insurance policies in order, or other behaviors that suggest he is planning for the end of his life. Contact your professional treatment team for help. It is likely that your depressed man is going to require hospital treatment if he is preparing for his death. On the other hand, if he is making plans for the future and he is present in them — going to school, changing jobs, changing locations, or whatever — the risk that he is planning to take his own life is lessened.

Talking About Suicide

The reality is that a third of depressed patients experience the thought of suicide at sometime during their illness. It relieves them to talk about these thoughts, because expressing a thought reduces the anxiety associated with it. They know that people who care about them and who are in better control are aware of the depth of their despair. Most people know they should ask depressed individuals about suicidal thoughts and that talking about their self-destructive urges is helpful in lessening them. Loved ones, and sometimes professional caregivers, are reluctant to discuss this topic with depressed male patients. They fear that they will put the idea of suicide into the depressed man's mind or that the depressed guy will admit he is suicidal and then they won't know what to do with this information.

Contrary to popular opinion, men who commit suicide have frequently talked about it prior to their deaths. Nevertheless, it is important to discuss this topic: Talking about suicide does reduce the risk to a degree, and also makes it easier for him to let you know when he is having urges to harm himself. Start out by asking how bad he feels. Ask him if he ever feels like giving up. If he says yes, ask him if he thinks of suicide. Again, if he answers affirmatively, ask him if he has thought of how he would do it. Does he have the means to do it? Does he feel he can control these thoughts and urges? Would he let you know if he had these impulses?

> Expressing a thought reduces the anxiety associated with it.

You then want to discuss with him how you can deal with the situation together if he feels the impulse to harm himself. Discuss the options you might pursue. You might call the doctors. You could go to the hospital emergency room. You or another family member could sit with him. If he feels that he may act on his impulses, or doubts that he would let you know, contact the professionals. They may want to see him on an emergency basis or tell you to take him to the nearest hospital with a psychiatric unit. A national hotline is available for depressed men having suicidal thoughts as well as caregivers seeking guidance: 800-273-TALK.

Removing the Means to Commit Suicide

One of the most important interventions you can make is an obvious one: Remove guns, drugs, poisons, or other means by which he could impulsively end his life. It may seem simplistic, but eliminating access to a means by which an individual can impulsively kill himself can make a difference.

A few years ago psychiatrists in England observed that suicide rates had dropped dramatically. Initially they thought this was due to improved educational and preventive programs that had been established. They

The No-Suicide Contract

Contracting with an individual not to commit suicide is popular among crisis workers and some therapists. In my opinion, this isn't much of a deterrent. If the fellow has already decided to take his own life, he will lie to the caregiver to accomplish his goal. If he is not suicidal at the moment, he may agree to tell the caregiver if he becomes suicidal—but then in the depths of depression, in a moment of impulsivity, or while intoxicated with drugs or alcohol, he may forget his earlier promise.

When I had a hospital practice, I received calls from the hospital emergency room from crisis workers who would assure me that the depressed, suicidal patient had contracted with them not to kill himself and did not need to be admitted. I was loath to accept this recommendation. I always felt it was better to err on the side of conservatism and admit the patient for observation. The reasons for my thinking were that the patient or the patient's loved ones were concerned enough about his self-destructive risk to bring him to the hospital. I also felt that to disregard what seemed to be an obvious cry for help might precipitate a self-destructive act. In some cases I had not evaluated the patient and, because of the threat of suicide, I felt it would be prudent to keep him under observation until I had a chance to take a detailed history and examine him myself. Even if the patient was known to me, it was obvious that he was experiencing a crisis that brought him to the hospital emergency room. Finally, should the patient take his own life, you can bet that the crisis workers and the emergency room personnel would quickly point out that it was the doctor (me) and not them who gave the order to let him go home from the hospital. In other words, it is the medical doctor who is always responsible should something go wrong.

were surprised to discover that the decreased mortality was in fact related to the gas companies switching from coke gas to a less toxic cooking gas for homes. Death by sticking one's head in an oven was a popular form of suicide in England, and the ability to impulsively take one's life in this manner had been eliminated.

The author Tolstoy asked his wife to hide the ropes in their home to prevent him from impulsively hanging himself when he was depressed. More than half of all suicides in this country are carried out by firearms; obviously, you should get all guns out of the house until he recovers. I suggested earlier that you should take over his medications because of his impaired concentration and so you can make sure he is taking his drugs as prescribed. Another reason is to make sure he does not have a lethal dose at his disposal that he could take impulsively when he feels suicidal.

Control Chemical Dependency

Chemical dependency is frequently associated with suicide. One-third of all suicides are committed by men addicted to alcohol. Chemical dependency increases the risk for suicide five times in depressed men. A depressed man who is self-medicating with drugs or alcohol has a much higher risk of impulsively taking his own life because his inhibitions are lessened, his judgment is suspended, his impulsiveness is increased, and his depression is probably deeper.

> One-third of all suicides are committed by men addicted to alcohol.

While it may not be possible in all cases, it's important to try to control this factor in order to reduce the risk of suicide. Alcohol is a depressant. Stimulant drugs have a shortterm antidepressant effect but then lead to increased depression when they wear off. It is like beating a tired horse. You are pushing out what few neurotransmitters are available at the synapse, and you then end up with even less than you had to start with. Sedative and tranquilizing drugs reduce anxiety but increase depression.

Physically Restrain Him from Self-Harm

In some instances it may be necessary to physically restrain your man from harming himself. A depressed man who is acutely suicidal may need to be hospitalized; there he can be watched closely and physically prevented from injuring himself. This is a temporary measure to delay and prevent his impulsively harming himself while caregivers help him regain some glimmer of hope for the future.

Provide Options

If you sense your man is becoming discouraged with his treatment, point out the numerous treatment options that are available that have not been tried. Show him the many antidepressant medications and combinations of drugs that have been successfully used for depression. Talk about the various therapeutic options other than drugs that have been helpful for depression. Discuss getting second opinions or seeing other caregivers. You are trying to help him see that there are many alternatives that have not yet been explored and many caregivers he has not seen who may be able to provide relief from his illness. The idea is to try to kindle some hope for the future.

Websites

There are many sites on the internet that inspire hope and encourage depressed individuals. One is www.mengetdepression.com; several others are listed at the end of this book. You can show him the many medicines and treatments that will soon be available for depression. A word of caution: If you are going to have him read this material, you should inspect it yourself in advance. Some websites might have an adverse effect and even encourage self-harm.

Make Sure He Understands You Would Not Be Better Off if He Died

Spend time talking how his suicide would adversely affect you, his family, and his friends. Depressed men convince themselves that everyone, and especially you, would be better off without them. You would have his insurance money and you would no longer be burdened by his negative attitude, irritability, withdrawal, and non-productiveness. You know this is not true and that his death would result in a lifetime of pain, guilt, and suffering.

Do not tell him these things, however. Instead say, "You are magnifying the negative and screening out the positive because of your depression right now. I love you and I don't want anything to happen to you. I would never get over it if you harmed yourself. This is a very painful period in your life but we will get through it together. After you recover, you'll wonder how you ever could have thought this way." You might also add, "Don't worry, I am keeping track of everything. I have several ideas as to how you can make it up to me when you recover."

When Your Morale Suffers, Get Help for Yourself

It is understandable that your own morale might begin to suffer. You are carrying a heavy burden. You have been trying to maintain a cheerful, optimistic, hopeful attitude while being bombarded with irritability, hopelessness, and negativity from your depressed partner. I'll discuss this further in Chapter 12, but, unless you're Wonder Woman, it's almost certain that you're going to feel drained, frustrated, angry, and discouraged at times during his illness.

Nearly every caregiving woman I know has reached the point where she has had intrusive thoughts: "Quit talking about it and do it if you're that discouraged. I wish you would die and this would all be over. Everything is about you—what about me?"

These thoughts are normal for this situation, but should be regarded as signals that you need to recharge your emotional batteries. Block out some time to do things that make you feel better. Get away from your depressed man to exercise, enjoy yourself, and talk with close friends and family. Ask some of your informal treatment team friends and family to relieve you. A change with some energetic, optimistic caring companions taking over

> Unless you're Wonder Woman, you're going to feel drained, frustrated, angry, and discouraged at times during his illness.

for you will provide a boost of energy for him and a respite for you. Make appointments with his psychiatrist and therapist and talk about your feelings with them. Listen to their suggestions as to how you can deal with your negative feelings toward him and how you can reenergize yourself.

This is not selfish on your part. Your guy needs you to be on top of your game, and if he senses that you're pulling away, he may conclude that you'd be better off without his presence on earth.

An important caution: Make sure to have one of your informal treatment team members fill in for you when you are taking care of yourself. Your depressed man is likely sensitive to any withdrawal on your part. He may interpret this change as his causing you stress and your being better off without him, which would increase the risk of impulsive self-harm. Make sure someone is keeping an eye on him while you are restoring your morale.

Some Suicides Cannot Be Prevented

Sadly, it is not always possible to prevent suicide. Do everything in your power to keep your depressed man safe, but recognize the fact that some suicides cannot be stopped.

Many can. If you can get your man through the danger period until he recovers his hope, the risk is alleviated. Some patients, however, do not reveal their plans and intentions to caregivers. It is nearly impossible to prevent these individuals from self-harm. It is often difficult to detect what a depressed man is thinking. There are no discernible clues. William Styron described how he had dinner with his family and guests and then went upstairs intending to take his own life. (He failed.) The best clinicians acknowledge that we cannot keep anyone from killing himself. What we can do is try to physically prevent the patient from taking his own life and give him time to come out of his depressive illness to the extent that he rediscovers hope for the future.

The survivors of a completed suicide are affected for the rest of their lives. They are guilt-ridden over their inability have prevented their loved one from killing himself. They punish themselves for not acting differently, saying something different, or somehow keeping the deceased from carrying out his self-destruction. My decision to train in psychiatry and my younger brother's to go into neurology were in part influenced by our desire to understand the illness that caused our brother's suicide and, hopefully, to keep other families from going through what we experienced through his illness and suicide.

Karl Menninger told us the story of one of his early depressed patients in the 1930s. He had tried to persuade the family of the need to hospitalize the young man. The family was opposed on the grounds that patients went to the hospital to die. Dr. Karl was eventually successful in accomplishing the patient's admission to the hospital. There the patient put his head in the toilet and drowned himself. The family told Dr. Karl, "We told you he would die in the hospital."

I recall a patient who was known to be extremely suicidal. He was admitted to the hospital, and because of his high risk three staff members were kept in the room with him at all times. He rocked forward on his chair and then threw himself backward, sustaining a skull fracture and brain hemorrhage that caused his death in front of the three staff members. Another fellow sitting in a chair in his clinic room was on close suicide watch. He suddenly slumped over in front of his caregivers, who discovered he had a hat pin that he had pushed through his chest wall and into his heart while under observation. In 1964 my younger brother was hospitalized for the third time for his bipolar disorder. He barricaded the entry to his room on the psychiatric unit and hanged himself while his psychiatrist was talking to him through the obstructed door. His last words to the family were "Three strikes and you are out."

I give these sad examples to illustrate that hospitalization, even in the best hospitals with the most intense patient supervision, can be insufficient to prevent a determined patient from taking his own life. I have seen other patients over the years who have given no warning of their plans for self-destruction. I have conducted psychological autopsies on suicide cases to determine if something could have been recognized or done to prevent the death. Nearly always I have had to conclude that nothing could have been done to save them. These are individuals who are not psychotic or delirious and are capable of understanding the dangers of withholding information from the caregivers. In most instances they carefully planned their suicides.

> Fortunately, most patients retain some hope and want to be kept from self-harm.

Fortunately, most patients retain some hope and want to be kept from self-harm. The cases I describe are relatively rare. I mention them because families and friends blame themselves when successful suicides occur when nearly always, there is nothing they could have done to prevent their loved one's death. A determined patient who plans his demise and keeps his intentions hidden is nearly impossible to save.

Giving Up: Passive Suicide

It has been my observation that individuals, especially as they age, have the capacity to release their grip on life and die nearly at will. We are all familiar with elderly couples who have enjoyed an especially close, loving relationship throughout their lives. When one of them dies, we are not shocked to learn that the other has passed away soon afterward. When I was a medical student in Chicago, one of my duties was to interview elderly patients who were scheduled for elective surgery the following day. As instructed, I asked them if they thought they were going to make it through their surgery. If they said no, the surgeons would not operate: They had found that older patients who believed they wouldn't survive an operation seldom did. They called this "the X factor" in surgery.

Similarly, I believe that depressed individuals, who feel they have no reason to get up in the morning and are convinced that their families and the world would be better off without them, have the capacity to let go of life and die. Death may be attributed to infection or some medical cause, but the primary factor leading to their demise is, in my opinion, their wish to die. For this reason, as caregivers, it is important that we seek to impress depressed individuals with their importance to us and to society. Everyone needs a reason to get up in the morning, and we need to try to help our loved ones discover their raison d'être.

✣

We will shift from the frightening and depressive topic of suicide to the use of humor in the treatment of depression. Laughter can be useful in the treatment of depressed men if it is natural for the caregiver using it. A sense of humor can also be a way to help you maintain your positive spirit as you care for your depressed man.

CHAPTER ELEVEN

Humor: A Double-Edged Sword

The wink of the comedian lets the audience know that the comedian knows that the audience knows that the comedian is playing a role.

—Diderot

One definition of *psychotherapy* is "telling people things about themselves they do not want to hear in a way that they can hear them." Kidding is a technique to communicate unwanted information in an acceptable manner to men who have a sense of humor. If humor is a part of your personality and an ingredient in your relationship, it can be an effective way to reduce tension and reach your man.

Humor in Our Practice

You might surmise from the fact that I am a psychiatrist who has chosen to practice in Normal, Illinois, that I tend to look for humor in life. The license plate on my truck reads NORMAL 1. I treated a depressed man on the psychiatric unit in Normal whose surname was Looney. He was concerned that he might not be released in time to attend his son's marriage. I suggested they might want to hold the ceremony on the unit.

"Why would we want to do that?" he inquired. "Well," I said, "just think of the headlines in the paper—'Looney man marries Normal woman on psychiatric unit.'"

I agree with the ancient Greeks that it is therapeutic to be exposed to comedies when suffering from melancholia. We have joke books in our waiting room. State Farm Insurance Company was started in Bloomington-Normal and remains the major employer in the twin cities. As a result, we see a number of its employees. One of them told me that if I wished to understand corporate life, I should start reading Dilbert cartoons. I followed his advice, and we have several of the Dilbert cartoon books in our waiting room for the benefit of our corporate patients. Far Side remains one of the most popular cartoon books. Charles Addams's cartoons from The New Yorker are among the well-thumbed volumes as well. My brother sent me a couple of John Callahan's cartoon books, which are popular with some of the patients. Mr. Callahan is a recovering alcoholic and a paraplegic. There are no limits to his targets for humor.

Story and joke telling are part of my personality. My patients recognize this and tell me jokes and put up with my teasing. The humor I use is never intended as a put-down of a patient or his actions. Most of my humor is self-deprecating and gives the message that I am a fellow sinner. Of course, my old patients kid me in return. One man, after listening to my latest joke, looked at his watch and said, "Do you suppose I could come in for follow-up visits a little less often? I would prefer a little less exposure to your crummy jokes."

Kidding is so much a part of my personality that my patients give me considerable leeway with what I say to them. I sometimes tell patients that I went into psychiatry because it enables me to get away with saying things other people can't without being socially ostracized. They respond that psychiatrists are already socially ostracized and I am merely demonstrating why.

In any event, I had a paranoid male patient who was very concerned about what people were thinking and saying about him. He said that he had informed his neighbor that he and his wife were going on a trip and the neighbor replied, "Again?" The patient found this disturbing and could not quit thinking about the remark. "Does he think we travel too much?" he asked. "Do they think we are putting on airs and showing off because we frequently go on trips?" I assured him that this was a harmless comment that probably had no hidden meaning. Some months later I happened to pick up a phone call to our office. It was this fellow, who was confused by my answering the phone instead of the office secretary. "Why are you answering the phone?" he asked suspiciously. I said that sometimes I picked up the phone if no one was nearby to do it.

> The humor I use is never intended as a put-down of a patient or his actions.

"Oh," he answered, not completely convinced. "Well, I was calling to have my medications refilled because we're going out of town for two weeks," he went on.

"Again?" I asked. There was silence on the line for a minute or so, and then he gave a dry laugh that demonstrated he was not amused.

A young male patient on the psychiatric unit thought that another patient was Jackie Gleason. He would try to trick the other patient into admitting that he was the television star. He would ask him, "When were you in Las Vegas last?" The other patient denied having been there, and the young man smiled knowingly as if the fellow was just hiding his identity. The same patient would hug me when I came on the unit and loudly announce, "This is my wonderful Dr. Bey." I took him aside and said, "Would you mind getting well before you tell everyone who your doctor is?" He got a kick out of this and, eventually, he did get better.

239

Males Use Humor to Cope with Stress

I believe that humor can be especially helpful when dealing with male patients. Boys show their affection to one another by teasing and poking, and most men are still boys at heart. In Vietnam the docs and medical service officers in our battalion used to kid each other in a counter-phobic way that we referred to as "pimping." When one of us went on leave, we would complain to the others how we would probably have to eat steaks and drink fine wine and would no longer be able to enjoy the tasty green roast beef and iodine-treated Kool-Aid we so loved in the base camp mess. Those left behind would tell stories of guys being killed on the way to R&R.

> Boys show their affection to one another by teasing and poking, and most men are still boys at heart.

We had a policy in the medical battalion that the newest doctor would take the next assignment. One day in the mess hall, after we had finished our noon meal, Captain Guarino, medical Company A commander, spoke to Bob Anzinger, who was the newest doctor to arrive in the unit. The dialogue went something like this:

> **Guarino:** This assignment doesn't look too good. We have a policy that the newest doc in the unit gets the next assignment. You're the newest, so you get it.
>
> **Anzinger:** Uh, okay—what is it?
>
> **Guarino:** One of the units is requesting a doc. Their landing zone is too hot to land a helicopter, so the doc will have to be inserted by cable.
>
> **Anzinger:** When is it?
>
> **Guarino:** Right away, get your stuff.

The doctors gathered as Anzinger began stuffing his clothing and equipment into a duffel bag. He looked pale and ready to cry. The tension mounted as each doctor in the room thought about how glad he was that he hadn't pulled the assignment ... and how bad he felt that Anziger did. No one seemed to know what to say to Bob. Finally I spoke, and the doctors looked up expectantly, sure the psychiatrist would know the right words.

Bey: Bob.
Anzinger: Yeah.
Bey: If anything happens to you—can I have your Nikon?
Anzinger: (laughing) What? You SOB!

The tension was broken, and Anzinger got into the copter with a smile on his face.

Humor with Patients

My practice is in the Midwest, and I see quite a few farmers. They are independent, self-made, religious individuals who are aware that they are not in control of the forces of nature. As a group they tend to be pessimistic. I believe this characteristic comes from a European peasant heritage in which optimism was considered bragging and could evoke the evil eye and tragic consequences. In any event, the typical farmer complains about too little rain, too much rain, too much wind, hailstorms, the cost of fertilizer, the price of herbicides, the expense of farm equipment, the cost of having the equipment repaired, and the price of grain. As he gets to know me, he will also complain about my fees and how little I do for him.

One family brought in a depressed uncle for consultation. They described how negative he was about everything; they could not seem to cheer him up no matter how hard they tried. I told them that he was probably depressed, but we had to rule out "normal farmer" because they are all negative.

So a Farmer Walked into a Psychiatrist's Office . . .

I ask my farmer patients if they know why farmers do not wear green tennis shoes. The answer I give them is, "Because the seed companies don't give them away." I inquire if they know the difference between a farmer and a 747 and then tell them, "A 747 stops whining when it lands in Florida." I quiz them why the Cadillac glove box is the particular dimensions that it is and then explain, "It's that size so the government cheese will fit in it." I query them, "Do you know what the '4x4' stands for on the side of your truck?" When they say, "Four-wheel drive?" I answer, "No, it stands for working four weeks in the spring, four weeks in the fall, and having forty-four weeks off." I ask them what you call a basement full of farmers and then tell them, "A whine cellar." Of course my farmer patients kid me in return. One said that his definition of a psychiatrist was a chiropractor with tired hands!

Humor in Your Interaction with Your Depressed Man

Humor can be very useful in working with depressed men, but it depends on your personality and how natural it is for you to joke and tease. It also depends on the type of relationship you have with him. If it is an ingredient of your nature and part of your relationship, then by all means inject humor into your interaction. If it is foreign to you or your relationship, then don't try it and skip this chapter.

If you do not feel comfortable using humor, think of his male friends. Do his golf buddies kid one another? Is there a male friend who could "pimp" him in a positive way? Richard Pryor told how his buddy James Brown came to his home when Richard was struggling with drug addiction. James continually asked him, "What are you going to do?"

Richard said he was still hanging on to his addiction and tried to avoid answering his friend, but eventually capitulated and agreed to go into rehabilitation.

> Your guy may find it easier to accept advice from his male friends than from you.

Your guy may find it easier to accept advice from his male friends than from you. Use your informal treatment team to accomplish your goals of getting him into treatment and supporting his compliance with treatment recommendations.

> ✄

If humor is part of your usual modus operandi and is part of your relationship with your guy, it can be useful in your efforts to support him. It can also help you if you can laugh at yourself. It's important to take care of yourself throughout your man's diagnosis, treatment, and recovery from depression. This is a stressful, emotionally draining process, and you need to put limits on the demands put upon you and find ways to recharge your emotional batteries.

In the next chapter I will make some suggestions as to how you can protect your mental health and keep up your morale while trying to look after your depressed man.

CHAPTER TWELVE

Maintaining Your Morale

In life, the difficult periods are the best periods to gain experience and shore up determination. As a result, my mental status is much improved because of them.

—The Dalai Lama

This is one of the most important chapters in this book. It is directed at helping you maintain your mental health while going through the arduous task of supporting your depressed man. You have taken on this difficult job because you love him, but it is important that you love yourself as well. Caring for a depressed man is a wearing and often thankless task. It is not selfish to make plans to look after your own well-being. If you get down, you won't be of much help to him. I have included some suggestions on telling jokes and a few jokes I thought might bring a smile while you are going through this ordeal.

You Are at Risk for Reactive Depression

Depression is infectious. We know that psychiatric nurses, who have a professional relationship with their depressed male patients and have a limited exposure to them, become depressed. When I treated depressed psychiatric patients in the hospital, I spent a good deal of time talking to the nursing staff to keep them from becoming depressed themselves. Knowing this, what is the likelihood that you—who are working with a man you love twenty-four hours a day, seven days a week—will get down? The answer is that you *will* become depressed unless you make a proactive, serious effort to take care of yourself. Marriages where one spouse is depressed are nine times as likely to end up in divorce. College students whose roommates suffer clinical depression are at high risk for psychological depression themselves. The danger to your mental health is clearly present if you do not take steps to look after yourself throughout this ordeal.

> # Depression is infectious.

I should add, at this point, that many of my medical colleagues over the years have questioned my choice of specialty. "Don't you get depressed talking to all those depressed patients every day?" they ask. I tell them that I do not because I know my patients are going to get better. I point out that their patients with chronic conditions—hypertension, respiratory problems, diabetes, arthritis—are going to worsen over time and will continue to complain of their symptoms, while my patients can be restored to their previous level of functioning and are pleased and grateful for their recoveries.

Separate the Illness from the Man

Remember Flip Wilson's character Geraldine? She was always saying, "The Devil made me do it." One important key to maintaining your sanity and preserving your relationship through all this is to see depression as an entity apart from him. Whether you refer to it as "the Devil" or make use of Winston Churchill's wisdom and humor by referring to it as a black dog, visualize your guy's affliction as being separate from him. Doing so will help you protect yourself from the personal injury to your self-esteem and self-confidence that results from trying to help an unfeeling, negative, irritable, resistant depressed man you love. You might be able to agree with him on a name for the illness and talk about it in the third person. This can lighten up your interchange and help focus on the illness as something you and he are battling together. For example, "Hey, I think your black dog just bit me! I asked you to take a walk with me and he snapped back to leave you alone."

Of course you will feel frustrated and irritated with your depressed man at times. You will be reluctant to express your negative feelings toward him because he is ill and you don't want to make him feel worse. It is possible for you to talk about how you feel about his illness, however. You might say, "I feel hurt when your depression causes you to be critical of me. I know it's your illness and not you talking, but it's still hard. If I see that your illness is making you irritable, I'll stay away from you until you get your feelings under control."

Depressed patients are afraid of abandonment, and you want to take care that your depressed man doesn't think that you feel you'd be better off without him. You can safely express your frustration toward the illness apart from him and set some limits on how much negativity you are willing to tolerate from his tormentor.

> Looking after your own well-being is a requirement, not a suggestion, for being a caregiver to your depressed man.

Many caregivers feel guilty when they try to set limits on the demands of their sick loved ones or take time out to engage in gratifying activities for themselves. I am reminded of the advice one of my psychotherapy supervisors gave to me years ago: "If you don't take care of yourself, you won't be of much good to anyone else." Looking after your own well-being is a requirement, not a suggestion, for being a caregiver to your depressed man. This chapter will offer a strategy for you to use to keep your batteries charged as you undertake the draining task of helping and supporting him through his recovery from depression.

Find Outlets for Your Frustrations

You need to think about outlets for your frustrations. Consider keeping your own secret diary in which you write down the feelings that arise from dealing with him each day. Perhaps there is a close friend, mentor, priest, therapist, or other individual you can speak to in confidence about your feelings of anger and frustration as you help and support your depressed man. Some caregivers go to a private, secluded place and scream out their frustrations. Some do it in their cars as they commute. Exercise is an outlet for frustration for many. Some take up martial arts and find the screaming, kicking, and punching involved in this training make for a relaxing outlet.

Develop Your Sense of Humor

I've discussed the use of humor with your depressed man. Humor can be therapeutic for you as well. Laughter is good for you because:

- It gets rid of frustration.
- It relieves tension.
- It allows a release of your negative feelings.
- It has an antidepressant effect.
- It gives you energy.
- It helps you keep things in perspective.
- It enables you to laugh at yourself.

Humor helped me get through my year in Vietnam and helped me cope with the stresses of life over the years. No matter what stresses I am facing, if I put on a Louis Black or Rodney Carrington CD I will start laughing and the pressures are diminished. I listen to Bob and Tom every morning they're on, then switch to comedy on satellite radio. I watch stand-up comedy on television and read joke books. I used to read Dave Barry's column and still read his books. To me, humor is the yeast that leavens the bread of life.

I adhere to the Chinese philosophy that the mind is a flexible container that conforms to what you put in it. I try to fill mine with funny stuff. As a result, I tend to look for and find humor in life. For example, I wasn't in very good shape when I arrived for my second open-heart procedure in 1996. The surgeon said, "I'll do my best," which didn't sound too promising to me. As I lay on the gurney in the cold operating room, the staff prepared for my procedure. I was wondering if I would survive or if this was it for me. As I contemplated my demise, the anesthesiologist approached and said, "I have to tell you this—your anesthesia could make you sterile." My reverie about death thus interrupted, I looked up at him and said, "That's the last frigging thing I'm worried about at this point!" This got a laugh from the surgery staff, and I went under the anesthesia with a smile.

> The mind is a flexible container that conforms to what you put in it. I try to fill mine with funny stuff.

Call on Your Team

You can use members of your informal team as well as your guy's professional caregivers to reinforce what you are saying. He may accept some advice better from his buddies than from you, and this is okay as long as he accepts it. The doctor or nurse may tell him things you have been harping on every day and he may act as though it's new information. That's okay as well—as long as he gets it.

Edie was the housekeeper on our psychiatric unit. New patients some-times asked Edie if depressed people ever recovered. Edie, who was sweeping the floor of their room, would look up, and without missing a beat, say "Oh, yes, I see them get well all of the time." The patients would believe her and feel more hopeful. This is the key. It doesn't mat-ter who gets through to the patient, the important factor is that we reach them with a message that inspires hope.

Call in your informal helpers to be with him when you begin to feel drained and need a break. Make them part of your schedule so you can plan on times you can spend recharging your emotional batteries and doing things you want to do.

Remember, too, that the professionals who are working with your de-pressed man can help you as well. Ask for appointments for yourself. Re-mind them of the stresses you are dealing with as you aid and encourage him through his illness. Ask them for suggestions as to how you can maintain your equilibrium through this arduous task. You have gotten his permission to exchange information with the professionals on the case, and part of this information has to do with you and your well-being.

Let The Professionals Be the Bad Guys

Use the professionals to tell him things he doesn't want to hear. They are only with him for limited periods of time. Quote them for the same pur-pose. If he is griping about getting up in the morning, you can tell him, "Dr. Jones said it was very important that I saw to it you were up, show-ered, and dressed each morning by eight."

Reduce Your Time Pressure

The number one source of stress in our society is time pressure. We try to pack too much into one day. Everything has to go right in order to complete our list of daily to-dos, and it never does go right—which causes stress. When you undertake to help and support your depressed man, you need to recognize and convey to your helping team that this is a full-time job. Put limits on other demands on your time. Block out time for yourself to meditate, have a massage, get a pedicure, have your hair done—whatever will keep your emotional batteries charged. Stephen Covey in his bestselling book *The Seven Habits of Highly Effective People* suggests that you put an appointment with Mr. Nike in your appointment book and schedule time to take a walk or some other break for yourself.

Find Groups That Will Understand and Support You

Groups such as the Manic Depressive Support Group and National Alliance for the Mentally Ill have been established for families of patients with psychiatric illnesses. Here you'll find other women who have supported their men through recovery from depression and some who are doing it at the same time you are. You may decide to meet with the group of helpers you have organized, or you may have a Bible study group, golfing group, bowling team, or card club that provides you with support and understanding. If your guy is self-medicating with alcohol or drugs, Alanon is an excellent resource. In addition to friendly caring support, these groups will help you set limits on the demands placed on you, and encourage you to take time out for yourself.

Reduce Your Workload

If you work outside the home, you might want to consider taking some leave from work while you take on the full-time job of helping him with his depression. On the other hand, some women find work a refuge from the demands of caregiving at home. They point out that they receive positive feedback from their bosses and colleagues, as well as concrete rewards in the form of paychecks and bonuses. This is your call. If working is restorative for you, then by all means continue on the job.

If you have children, you may want to make arrangements for help with their care and with your housekeeping duties. Do not see these steps as being self-indulgent on your part. Think of it as your taking on full-time psychiatric nursing duties for an ill man while he recovers from a very serious debilitating illness.

Have Fun

Find ways to laugh and have fun on a regular basis. Constantly trying to buoy the spirits of a negative, depressed man will get you down if you're not careful. Turn the job over to some fresh, upbeat members of your informal treatment team and go do something that cheers you up. Go out with some of your positive friends and engage in activities that make you laugh. Listen to and watch comedians if you like them.

> Find ways to laugh and have fun on a regular basis.

Go to upbeat plays and movies. Get into fun groups playing cards, playing sports, taking trips.

Exercise

Walking with your guy and cooking him nourishing meals will ensure that you are active and eating properly as well. In addition, see to it that you have some stress-free exercise of your own: aerobics, yoga, or whatever interests you. Make sure you see your doctors for regular checkups.

Faith and Fellowship

If you are able to turn to a higher power, it can be a great source of strength and support to you throughout this ordeal. I remember the first Bible study group I attended. The gentle people in the group appeared to me at first glance to be somewhat passive and weak. As I got to know them better, I realized that many were very strong individuals bearing tremendous burdens in their daily lives. Their faith allowed them to endure overwhelming stresses. Their approach to life was, "Let go and let God." They turned their lives over to Christ and tried to follow his teachings. They accepted the burdens they had been given in life. The fellowship with other church members provided love and support for them. The ministers of the church helped them with their caregiving tasks at home.

I believe in the power of prayer as well—I have seen this power over the years. One of the best examples happened to a psychotherapist who does not consider herself to be religious. She flew into Chicago's O'Hare airport in January in the middle of a blizzard. She was frightened as she began her drive home to Indiana just before 1:00 p.m. Roads were icy, visibility was poor, and tractor-trailers lined the ditch. Then, she said, she felt suddenly at peace. In what seemed like no time at all she found herself in front of her home at 3:00 p.m. She thought that this was a strange phenomenon but was unable to explain it. The next day, back at work in her office, her first client was an Apostolic Christian woman. This woman began her therapy session by saying: "Oh, Doctor, I was so worried about you coming in yesterday in that storm that I prayed for you from one o'clock straight through until three."

Avoid Co-dependency

By co-dependency, I am referring to the need to provide everything in a relationship without regard to your own needs. Co-dependency is a problem for most women who are attempting to care for a depressed man. Because of the nature of depression, women are doing nearly all of the giving in the relationship. You did not cause his depression and you cannot fix it. You cannot control his feelings or his behavior. Your happiness does not depend on his. You are not responsible for his happiness. It is okay to think of your own needs. All these things would seem to be logical, but it is easy to become co-dependent when you are trying to help and support your loved one through his recovery.

I followed a man for a number of years who suffered from a severe recurrent depressive illness. His son was an army officer who told me that he had returned from his military assignment after being away from home for several years. The soldier asked his mother, "How are you, Mom?" She answered, "He had pork chops for supper." The officer said, "She was so enmeshed with my father's illness that she could not even think of her thoughts, feelings, or behavior. All her thinking revolved around him."

> You did not cause his depression and you cannot fix it. You cannot control his feelings or his behavior.

If you decide that you are co-dependent, think of what you would tell someone in a situation similar to yours. Imagine a woman friend who came to you and told you she was trying to help and support her depressed man and that she was becoming burned out in the process. What would you advise her to do? Write down the suggestions you would give her and then apply them to yourself.

Some Good May Come from This Experience

This section is for you and not something you should convey to your man. It's important for you to remember that if you look back over your past, the best changes you've made were likely preceded by the worst times in your life. Why? We all cling to our usual ways of doing things because they are predictable. We may be miserable, but we know what to expect. Change is scary because it is the unknown. Think of the alcoholic who has to hit bottom before he is willing to give up the booze and seek help. It is only when things become intolerable that we are forced to climb out of our ruts and try something new.

Depression is the pits. People will do anything to get relief. Your macho, independent, stoic man is forced by his illness to depend on you. He will find out that you are there for him; you continue to love him when he is irritable, negative, even obnoxious. You have hung in there with him when he was ready to throw in the towel. He has had to admit his vulnerabilities and weaknesses to you, and you have continued to love him. All of this will strengthen your relationship in the long run.

> It is only when things become intolerable that we are forced to climb out of our ruts and try something new.

In addition, he may have, out of desperation, agreed to see a therapist. In my opinion, therapy is good for everyone and especially men. All males can all benefit from getting in touch with their feminine sides. The process of introspection, identifying feelings and expressing them, will make him a better man after he recovers from his depression. No doubt he will be more empathetic toward others who suffer from mental afflictions, having been through depression himself. Learning to admit his vulnerabilities, depending on you and the doctors, talking instead of acting—all are good changes for him to make.

Again, this is not something you should say to him while he is depressed. He is in the throes of a painful illness and the last thing he wants (or needs) to hear is that it is good for him.

After He Recovers, Seek Joint Counseling

Once he has recovered from his bout of depression, it would be help-ful for the two of you to attend couples' therapy to reestablish your com-munication and discuss the effect that his illness has had on your relationship. Depressed men withdraw, are irritable and angry, and lose their capacity to feel. Although you tried to separate his illness from him as a person, chances are that you've been frustrated and pulled back from the relationship emotionally to protect yourself. It's also likely that he has said and done things hurtful to you. You have had to keep your own frustrations and negative feelings in check. When he is well it is time to discuss these things and get your relationship back on track. Pro-fessional assistance will facilitate this process.

CHAPTER THIRTEEN

The Future of Depression

There is no medicine like hope, no incentive so great, and no tonic so powerful as expectation of something tomorrow.

—O. S. Marden

The display cases in my office waiting room are filled with antique curiosities that were thought to be the cutting edge of medical treatment years ago. No doubt our current pills and treatments will be on exhibit in the future. New diagnoses and treatments will obviate many of our current drugs and management approaches—even our understanding of mental illnesses.

Medicine is improving all the time. Surgeons tell patients to wait as long as possible before having surgery because techniques are improving so rapidly. The same is true for every medical specialty, including psychiatry. Research in medicine is, in part, financially driven. The pharmaceutical companies know that any new psychotropic drug that is faster acting, has fewer side effects, and is more effective will capture the market and result in huge profits. As a result, research is tireless and never ending. New medicines and new delivery systems are constantly being developed; many are in the pipeline for release even as I write. The profit motive also influences the development of improved methods of diagnosis and novel physical treatment approaches.

New Methods of Diagnosis

Researchers seek to develop diagnostic tools to help professionals identify specific neurobiological defects in depressed patients and also spot precise remedies for these individuals. Positron emission tomography (PET) analysis suggests that increased activity in the brain's limbic system—specifically the amygdala—may indicate vulnerability to depression. PET scans of patients with obsessive-compulsive disorder (OCD) reveal similar changes in the frontal lobes among individuals treated either with medicine or with cognitive-behavioral therapy (CBT). PET scans of depressed patients, on the other hand, demonstrate changes both from antidepressant medication and from CBT—but in different areas of the brain. This may account for the observation that patients treated with antidepressants and CBT do better than those treated by either alone. PET scans may lead to a more objective means of evaluating psychotherapy and psychotherapists in the future as well as the development of more effective psychological treatments.

> Medicine is improving all the time.

Recent research has begun to identify areas of the brain that are responsible for specific symptoms of depression. Genetic studies have identified individuals likely to respond positively to particular medications as well as those likely to react adversely. Treatment-resistant patients are responding to new somatic treatment approaches.

New Information about Old Medicines

The newer serotonin reuptake inhibitors (SSRIs) and dual-acting antidepressants are as effective as the old tricyclic antidepressants in mild to

Mind versus Body

Throughout history we have debated the mind–body dichotomy as it applies to mental illness. The roots of psychiatry lie both in philosophy and in physical medicine. This split may soon be resolved. One of the most exciting prospects for the future is based on PET scan evidence that psychological treatment and biological treatment *both* act to produce physical changes in the brain and in brain chemistry. Findings such as these may end the centuries of debate between the psychological and biological causes of mental illnesses and their treatment.

moderate cases of depression, but there is recent evidence to suggest that the older drugs are more effective in severe forms of clinical depression.

New Delivery Systems

Medicines don't have to be taken in pill form. New routes of delivery are being developed. Drugs absorbed through the skin bypass the gut and, in some cases, enable patients to tolerate higher and more effective levels. In some situations, new forms of delivery lead to improved compliance.

Patches

Some new medicines are delivered using patches. Medicines for depression, attention deficit disorder, and Alzheimer's are currently available in this form. They offer the advantage of delivering higher blood levels of the medications with fewer side effects.

Emsam is a patch that contains a MAOI antidepressant. On the lowest dose (6mg) patients do not have to be concerned with the dietary precautions that are required with the oral forms of the medication. Some

259

patients who could not tolerate higher doses of MAOIs are able to do so with the patch. It is frequently easier for caregivers to put a patch on the back of a patient with Alzheimer's disease than to try to get him to take his pills by mouth. I have a few treatment-resistant patients who appear to have benefited from Emsam patches.

Hormones

Some investigators feel that the future of psychiatric treatment lies in the use of hormones to control conditions of the brain. One new cream containing estrogen and progesterone specifically targets depression. The estrogen provides increased energy and elevated mood, while the progesterone reduces anxiety and calms the individual. These preparations are aimed at anxiety and depression in women. However, investigation into hormonal treatment may lead to effective treatments for men as well.

Extended-Release Products

As we've seen, noncompliance is the most important factor leading to treatment failure in depression. Anything that increases compliance will also improve the chances of treatment success. Studies have shown that the fewer doses a patient is required to take each day, the greater his compliance. A number of medicines have been developed that are released over a lengthy period of time. These extended-release drugs improve compliance because they only require one dose per day.

Aerosols

A form of insulin in a nasal spray has just entered the market. This is obviously more convenient than giving yourself an injection. No doubt other drugs, including those used in psychiatry, will be put in aerosol form. Just like patches, nasal sprays bypass the gastrointestinal tract and may lead to higher blood levels with fewer side effects.

New Treatments

Vagal Nerve Stimulation (VNS)

Stimulation of the vagal nerve has been used for some time in the treatment of seizure disorders. It was noted that some seizure patients who also suffered from depression responded to this treatment. VNS involves a relatively simple surgical procedure that usually takes about forty-five minutes in which the stimulator, known as the NeuroCybernetic Prosthesis System (NCP), is inserted under the skin on the chest, and the stimulating connection is made to the left vagal nerve in the neck. It is sometimes referred to as a "pacemaker for the brain." It consists of a pulse generator and a nerve stimulator electrode usually programmed to send a thirty-second electrical impulse into the left vagal nerve every five minutes. It has been reported that some treatment-resistant patients have responded to vagal nerve stimulation. I have to say that the ones who have tried it in our practice have not responded dramatically.

Transcranial Magnetic Stimulation (TMS)

Transcranial magnetic stimulation (TMS) involves exposing the patient's head to a strong magnetic field. It appears that the effect is similar to that of electroconvulsive therapy, but the process is much less invasive and has fewer side effects. It is currently being used for treatment in Canada and is poised for release in the United States when it has FDA and insurance coverage approval.

Cingulotomy

Hyperactivity in the anterior cingulated cortex of the brain has led to the surgical removal of this area in some severely resistant cases of depression. The procedure involves cutting two white matter tracts just below the anterior cingulate gyrus. Researchers in Scotland noted that three of eight patients who had the surgery were relieved of their depressive symptoms; improvement was observed in two more. The conclusion was that this procedure might help patients who have failed at all other treatments.

Harvard neurosurgeons have treated a limited number of resistant patients with this experimental surgery as well. Some carefully selected patients have received benefit from the procedure. I do not have any patients who have undergone this procedure.

Deep Brain Stimulation (DBS)

Researchers have found that planting an electrode deep in the brain that is connected to a stimulating device under the skin of the chest helped some patients with treatment-resistant depression as well as some with obsessive-compulsive disorder. The procedure is based on the finding that a very specific area of the brain—Brodmann area 25—appears to be overactive in patients with treatment-resistant depression. These findings are still preliminary as I write.

Diet and Environmental Factors

I was discussing what appears to be an increased incidence of autism among children in recent years with a retired professor of veterinary medicine. He was inclined to think that the changes in the food of the animals whose meat we eat might be responsible. He noted that these animals used to graze and eat alfalfa; now they are usually enclosed and given feed made from ground-up corn and soybean products. All he had to do was walk onto a farm, he told me, and he could immediately tell whether the livestock was al-

> We are exposed to more toxins in our environment these days.

The Future of Depression

lowed to graze or kept penned up. Those animals allowed to graze walked up to him and sniffed him in a friendly way. Those who were confined stood off at a distance and shied away when he approached. In addition to the differences in diet, confined animals are subjected to more stress, and it is likely that the hormones and physiological changes that accompany stress will also affect the chemistry of the animal's meat.

In addition to what appears to be an increase in autism, there seems to be more cancer among younger individuals of late. We are exposed to more toxins in our environment these days. As we become more aware of the food we eat and air we breathe, we may be able eliminate some of the influences that are producing disease. We may also identify environmental factors that would lessen or improve chronic illnesses like depression and bipolar affective disorders.

Genetics

The future of medical diagnosis and treatment is in the field of genetics. It is likely that the genes involved in depression and bipolar disorder will someday be identified, and treatments aimed at correcting their dysfunction will be developed. This will lead to more accurate diagnoses of psychiatric illnesses as well.

Ethical considerations regarding gene manipulation are critical, though. The University of Iowa has noted that many of the great writers invited to its summer writers' seminar through the years have been bipolar. We would not want to stifle artistic creativity in an effort to control bipolar illnesses.

We are beginning to locate which structures in the brain are responsible for specific symptoms of depression. Current neuroanatomical findings suggest that the neocortex and hippocampus may direct the cognitive aspects of depression such as memory impairment, suicidality, and feelings of worthlessness, hopelessness, and guilt. The hippocampus volume has been found to be reduced in patients with depression, and the amount of reduction is proportionate to the number and severity of their untreated episodes of depression. The amygdala and striatal areas are important in emotional memory and may be related to anhedonia, anxiety, and reduced motivation. The neurovegetative symptoms of decreased sleep, appetite, and energy are probably associated with the hypothalamus.

> We are beginning to locate which structures in the brain are responsible for specific symptoms of depression.

Further recent findings help us understand why untreated patients seem to get worse in time. Recurrent or prolonged bouts of depression, it's been learned, may produce structural changes in the brain. These may be mediated by neurotrophins such as brain-derived neurotrophic factor (BDNF).

This is only the beginning. Many other recent discoveries represent new directions in research that may lead to a better understanding of the more severe and resistant forms of depression.

Cortical Releasing Factor (CRF)

Studies suggest that cortical releasing factor (CRF) concentrations are elevated in some patients treated with antidepressants, and high CRF concentrations appear to normalize with treatment. The significance of these changes is as yet unknown, but it's possible that adjusting CRF levels may assist in the amelioration of depressive symptoms in the future.

Serotonin Transporter Gene (5-HTTLPR)

It's been discovered that individuals having the short variant of the serotonin transporter gene (5-HTTLPR) suffer a greater incidence of depression and more suicidal thoughts and behaviors following stress in life. Children with this variant tend to be more negative. Hyperactivity of the amgdyla is associated with this genetic variant, as is an increased sensitivity to negative stimuli and a negative bias in the interpretation of stimuli.

Hypothalamic-Pituitary-Adrenal Axis (HPA)

Current research is helping us understand the relationships between stress and depression, as well as the decrease in immunity that appears to accompany depression. The brain reacts to stress via the hypothalamic-pituitary-adrenal axis. We've known since the 1970s that in major depressive disorder (MDD), an alteration in the HPA axis occurs. Recent research has suggested that a category of signaling proteins known as cytokines link the non-specific immune system to the HPA axis. These proteins could be involved in the development of depression by activating the HPA axis; the activated HPA axis seen in MDD could, in turn, suppress the activity of the immune system.

> Current research is helping us understand the relationships between stress and depression, as well as the decrease in immunity that appears to accompany depression.

Methylation

A recent Canadian study of the brains of a relatively small sample of individuals who had committed suicide suggests that their DNA was being chemically modified by a process normally involved in regulating cell development, called methylation. The methylation rate in the suicides' brains was almost ten times that seen in brains of individuals dying from other causes. The gene that was being shut down was a chemical message receptor that plays a major role in regulating behavior. The study suggested that "this reprogramming could contribute to the protracted and recurrent nature of major depressive disorder."

Predicting Response to Specific Antidepressants

Better diagnostic methods will result in more individualized approaches to the treatment of depression. Genetic analysis and frontal quantitative electroencephalopathy may enable us to predict a patient's response to a particular antidepressant as well as the likelihood of adverse reactions to the medication. Better diagnostic tools would obviate the current trial-and-error treatment methods and enable the practitioner to prescribe the specific drug that will be best tolerated and most effective. Indeed, one recent study appears to move the field closer to the identification of individuals who are responsive to a particular antidepressant. The Sequenced Treatment Alternatives to Relieve Depression (STAR*D) study suggests that response to citalopram (Celexa) is associated with genetic variations in DNA segments that control the expression of the serotonin transporter gene SLC6A4.

>‹

If your man has one of those tough depressions that is not responding or only partially responding to current treatment choices, encourage him to keep trying the treatments available and assure him that more effective treatments are near at hand. Some of the material in this chapter is very technical and the medical terms used are difficult to understand. It is not crucial that you fully grasp these concepts. The main message is to hang in there. Things are getting better and better.

Resources for Caregivers

Well, Art is Art, isn't it? Still, on the other hand, water is water. And east is east and west is west and if you take cranberries and stew them like applesauce they taste much more like prunes than rhubarb does.
Now you tell me what you know.

—*Groucho Marx*

Fortunately, there are many resources to provide information and support for women who are trying to help the depressed man in their lives. In this final section I will mention a few that I have found useful and that I have recommended to depressed men and their caregivers over the years. There are many more available that you will no doubt find on your own on the internet and through community support groups. In addition to the references below, if you send me an e-mail at my website www.dougbey.com I will do my best to respond to your questions.

Books

General Help for Caregivers

What to Do When Someone You Love Is Depressed by Mitch Golant and Susan Golant (New York: Henry Holt, 1996). This book contains helpful advice for families of depressed patients. It appears to be directed more toward female patients and the more typical symptoms of depression. The authors consider clinical depression on a continuum with grief and "the blues."

When Someone You Love Is Depressed by Laura Epstein Rosen and Xavier Francisco Amador (New York: Simon & Schuster, 1997). Suggestions for both sexes as to how to recognize and assist individuals with depression.

How You Can Survive When They're Depressed by Anne Sheffield (New York: Three Rivers Press, 1998). Advice to help families of depressed patients understand the illness and how to maintain their own mental health as their loved one recovers from the illness. Sheffield is an excellent writer and has personal experience both growing up with a depressed mother and participating in a support group for families of depressed individuals.

Depression Fallout: The Impact of Depression on Couples and What You Can Do to Preserve the Bond by Anne Sheffield (New York: HarperCollins, 2003). A sequel to the book above focusing on how spouses of depressed individuals can pull together instead of apart under the stress of the illness.

Talking to Depression: Simple Ways to Connect When Someone in Your Life Is Depressed by Claudia J. Strauss (New York: Penguin Group, 2004). The author is a communication consultant and uses her training and experience to suggest how best to communicate with a depressed loved one.

Undoing Depression: What Therapy Doesn't Teach You and Medication Can't Give You by Richard O'Connor (New York: Berkley Books, 1997). Suggestions as to how to change the negative patterns of thinking that accompany depression.

I Am Not Sick, I Don't Need Help! by Xavier Amador with Anna-Lica Johanson (Peconic, NY: Vida Press, 2000). How to help seriously mentally ill patients accept treatment.

Voices of Caregiving, edited by The Healing Project (Brooklyn, NY: LaChance Publishing, 2009). Individuals who have experienced the challenges of caregiving share their insights.

Gender Differences

The Pain Behind the Mask: Overcoming Masculine Depression by John Lynch and Christopher Kilmartin (New York, London, and Oxford: Haworth Press, 1999). An excellent presentation of the factors underlying men's difficulties identifying and verbalizing their feelings. The authors note the problems recognizing depression in men who frequently express their distress through self-medication, violence, excessive work, womanizing, and physical complaints. Their focus is on the psychodynamics and psychological treatment of male depression. They also offer preventive measures to try to alter the resistance men have toward recognizing and expressing feminine aspects of their personalities.

If Men Could Talk: Translating the Secret Language of Men by Alon Gratch (Boston, New York, and London: Little, Brown, 2001). This book describes some of the distortions that occur in male communication and the psychological reasons behind them.

Men Are from Mars, Women Are from Venus by John Gray (New York: HarperCollins, 1992). This well-known volume describes the way men tend to verbalize their thoughts while women express their feelings.

The Complete Guide to Guys by Dave Barry (New York: Ballantine Books, 2000). A humorous but valid description of some of the differences between men and women.

Is He Depressed or What?: What to Do When the Man You Love Is Irritable, Moody and Withdrawn by David B. Wexler (Oakland, CA: New Harbinger Publications, 2005). This book contains many practical suggestions for using psychological techniques to encourage and support depressed males.

How Men Think: The Seven Essential Rules for Making It in a Man's World by Adrienne Mendell (New York: Fawcett Columbine, 1996). A book written for women to help them understand men's language and behavior in the business world.

His Needs, Her Needs: Building an Affair-Proof Marriage by Willard F. Harley, Jr. Written by an experienced marital therapist, the book zeros in on the different needs men and women have in a marriage and what happens if the needs are not recognized or met.

For Women Only—Discussion Guide by Shaunti Feldhahn with Lisa A. Rice (New York: Multnomah Books, 2005). A companion to the bestseller The Inner Lives of Men. Understand the thinking and behaviors of your man.

Depression and Its Treatment

The Noonday Demon: An Atlas of Depression by Andrew Solomon (New York: Scribner, 2001). This National Book Award winner is a comprehensive discussion of depression by an brilliant wordsmith who suffers from bouts of depression.

From Sad to Glad by Nathan Kline (New York: Ballantine Books, 1987). One of the classic books on depression, with an emphasis on the biochemical basis for the illness.

Personal Experiences of Depression

Darkness Visible: A Memoir of Madness by William Styron (New York: Vintage Press, 1992). A classic description of the author's experience going through depression. He is an excellent writer and is able to vividly describe what depressed men feel.

A Season in Hell by Percy Knauth (New York: Harper and Row, 1975). Another classic description of one man's experience with depression.

Personal Experiences with a Depressed Spouse

Living with a Depressed Spouse by Gay Ingram (Mustang, OK: Tate Publishing, 2007). Ingram watched her husband develop, live with, and recover from a bout of depression. She suggests what to say and what not to say to a depressed man. She lists resources that may be of assistance and gives suggestions as to how the caregiver can take care of herself during the ordeal of helping a depressed mate.

Morning Has Broken: A Couple's Journey Through Depression by Emme and Phillip Aronson (New York: New American Library, 2006).

Undoing Depression: What Therapy Doesn't Teach You and Medication Can't Give You by Richard O'Connor (New York: Berkley Books, 1997). Personal experience coping with depression.

Bipolar Disorder

Mood Swing by Ronald Fieve (New York: Bantam Dell Publishing Group, 1989). A classic book on bipolar disorder and its treatment with lithium.

Bipolar Depression: A Comprehensive Guide by Rif S. El-Mallakhand and S. Nassir Ghaemi (Washington, DC: American Psychiatric Publishing, 2006).

Loving Someone with Bipolar Disorder: Understanding and Helping Your Partner by Julie A. Fast and John D. Preston (Oakland, CA: New Harbinger Publications, 2004).

Voices of Bipolar Disorder edited by The Healing Project (Brooklyn, NY: LaChance Publishing, 2009). Individuals with bipolar disorder, their loved ones and caregivers speak candidly about their experiences.

DVDs

Depression: Out of the Shadows. This is an excellent overview of our current knowledge of depression and its treatment narrated by Jean Pauley, who suffers from bipolar depression. It features Andrew Solomon, author of *The Noonday Demon,* and a panel of prominent psychiatrists. It is a 120-minute DVD produced in 2008 and available from Public Broadcasting System (PBS) for $24.99.

Men Get Depression is a helpful DVD for depressed men and their caregivers. It is a sixty-minute documentary released by PBS in May 2008.

Suicide Hotlines

Most communities have suicide hotlines that can be reached by calling 911. A national hotline can be reached from anywhere in the country: 800-273-TALK.

Online Resources

Here are a few of the major resources available on the World Wide Web. You can also find answers to virtually any question about depression by Googling. There are many support groups available for caregivers as well. Networking with other caregivers online can be a source of support.

www.mengetdepression.com is a helpful site that describes the PBS movie *Men Get Depression* and has links to helpful websites.

www.nimh.nih.gov. A resource from the National Institute of Mental Health (NIMH) on nearly any mental health topic.

www.depressedanon.com. Depressed Anonymous, a 12-step self-help program for depressed individuals.

www.reutershealth.com. Information on drugs and herbal treatments.

www.mayoclinic.com. Information on disease and treatment from the renowned Mayo Clinic.

www.health.harvard.edu. Health information from Harvard Medical School.

www.menningerclinic.com. Mental health information from the Menninger Clinic.

www.webmd.com. Health information.

www.wellspouse.org. Information on support groups by state.

subscriptions@inspire.com can help caregivers find support.

www.dougbey.com is the website for my books. You can contact me here if you have questions or comments. I will do my best to respond.

Index

Index

Index

Index

About the Author

Douglas Bey, Jr., M.D. grew up in Normal, Illinois attending the laboratory schools at Illinois State University where his father was a mathematics professor. He graduated from Cornell College in Mount Vernon Iowa, University of Illinois College of Medicine in Chicago, Illinois Masonic Hospital for a rotating internship, and the Menninger School of Psychiatry in Topeka, Kansas. He served a year at Fort Knox and then a year as the 1st Infantry psychiatrist in Vietnam before beginning his private practice of psychiatry in Normal.

Photo © 2009 Robert E. Handley, Photographer

Dr. Bey is board certified in psychiatry with special qualifications in geriatric psychiatry. He served as a board examiner for the American Board of Psychiatry and Neurology for many years and is a Distinguished Life Fellow of the American Psychiatric Association. He is past president of the McLean County Board of Health, the McLean County Medical Society, and the medical staff of a local hospital.

About the Author

His wife Deborah is a nurse who works with him in his part time private practice. He has four children, a godson, and five grandchildren. Once a week he consults at Sharon Healthcare in Peoria. He likes to say his practice is limited to nice people.

Dr. Bey's previous books are *Wizard 6* and *Loving an Adult Child of an Alcoholic* (co-authored with his wife Deborah.)